The Gospel of John

Question by Question

The Gospel of John

Question by Question

Judith Schubert, RSM

Paulist Press
New York/Mahwah, NJ

In grateful memory of my loving parents,
Jeanette and Michael John,
who have touched countless lives
as shining images of God's gracious mercy and hospitality

The scripture quotations contained herein are from the *New Revised Standard Version: Catholic Edition* Copyright © 1989 and 1993 by the Division of Christian Education of the National Council of the Churches of Christ in the United States of America. Used by permission. All rights reserved.

Cover and book design by Lynn Else

Library of Congress Cataloging-in-Publication Data

Schubert, Judith.
    The Gospel of John : question by question / Judith Schubert.
        p. cm.
    Includes bibliographical references (p.   ).
    ISBN-13: 978-0-8091-4549-2 (alk. paper)
    1. Bible. N.T. John—Study and teaching. 2. Bible. N.T. John—Criticism, interpretation, etc. I. Title.
    BS2616.S38 2008
    226.5′0071—dc22

                                                                    2008012886

Published by Paulist Press
997 Macarthur Boulevard
Mahwah, New Jersey 07430

www.paulistpress.com

Printed and bound in the
United States of America

Contents

Contents

Contents

Contents

Contents

Acknowledgments

I thank the Sisters of Mercy and Georgian Court University who supported a semester sabbatical at the beginning of this research. They provided me with a time to reflect, research, and begin this project. I also thank family, friends, colleagues, students, and adult study groups who have both encouraged me and participated in providing material for the topic. Special thanks to Andrea Rittenhouse, a former graduate assistant, who has assisted in the work from a summer research grant provided by the University. Final thanks to Chris Franke, a dear friend and colleague, whose encouragement brought me to this point.

General Introduction

Welcome to the world of gospel study, where all the news becomes "Good News"! The Gospel of John offers an exciting venture into the discovery of the person of Jesus as well as his relationship to both God and the Johannine community. Most importantly, it invites you to "come and see," to savor scripture with its queries and mysteries in relation to God and to the world. The study will challenge you to stretch your mind and heart as you ponder the biblical text, question its meaning, and listen to its many messages.

The Gospel of John probably has become more recognizable to Christians than any other gospel. For example, the world-famous John 3:16, "For God so loved the world that he gave his only Son, so that everyone who believes in him may not perish but may have eternal life," continues to be telecasted as it flies high on banners during football, basketball, hockey, soccer, and baseball games. It even appears on bumper stickers, tee shirts, billboards as well as on the backs of marathon runners. In addition, other Johannine texts such as Jesus' washing of the feet of the disciples in John 13 or the Samaritan woman at the well in John 4 have become well known in present day Christian circles. In essence, the Gospel of John inspires all Christian traditions of belief.

As you enter the study of each new chapter, you will be met by many fascinating characters, enriching dialogues, and narratives that often do not appear in earlier gospels. The Johannine stories capture a very different Jesus from the one who appears in Mark, Matthew, and Luke. From the very first words of the Gospel, Jesus has been called the "Word," who has existed with the Father before the creation of the world and remains united with him. This Jesus centers on his own person rather than on the "kingdom of heaven/God," an emphasis found in the other gospels. Among other titles in the Fourth Gospel, people call Jesus "rabbi," "son of God," "the Messiah" (Christ), "Holy One of God," and so on.

Moreover, the Johannine Jesus calls the audience to belief in him, which translates into action for others. In the Fourth Gospel the importance of community remains essential. Jesus' frequently used vocabulary of "come and see," "love," "belief," and "joy" offers you somewhat of a "how to" manual of discourse and example for community living. So, as you begin your study, remember to listen carefully to the text as it speaks to you. When in doubt, go back to the text, so that you can hear and savor its message.

Purpose of the Book

The book will be useful for adult study groups, undergraduate introduction courses, and individual use. It allows participants to study the Gospel of John at their own comfortable pace. Many other publications on the topic also offer comments on every chapter of the Gospel or offer topical explanations of the Gospel's subject matter.

This particular book occasionally combines these two practices in that it provides brief commentary on passages that need explanation, and periodically provides background on a topic relative to the Gospel. The book is divided into twenty chapters. Each chapter includes an Introduction of pertinent information that will be helpful before reading the biblical text.

One of the main features of the book surfaces in the *Questions* that appear in each chapter. Such questions aim to assist you to ponder the meaning and message of specific biblical verses. These *Questions* are also meant to help you to clarify both the text and context of the biblical passage as well as to engage in discussion with others. Therefore, you are encouraged to try to answer the question with personal comments and written notes before checking the *Answers* that appear in the second section of the book. In this way you will have the opportunity to tackle the question yourself.

Since this format may be unfamiliar because of its different plan from other books on the Fourth Gospel, give yourself time to adjust so that you will learn to appreciate the advantages of searching the scriptures and savoring the results. This approach aims to teach you how to discover the biblical message beneath the printed words. It also teaches you to trust your own inquiry into the text at hand. Always remember to go back to the text for answers. Read and reread it so that you will develop sensitivity to the inspired word.

After the *Questions,* you will find a *Conclusion,* which will summarize the chapter and advance you to the next chapter. With the framework of the book in mind, I will now present a brief introduction to the culture of first-century Palestine, the meaning of gospel, as well as an overview of the Gospel of John in its context, its differences and similarities with the other three gospels within the New Testament. I shall address the Fourth Gospel itself with an introduction, brief historical background, purpose of the Gospel, arrangement of the Gospel, literary features, authorship, place of writing, and conclusion. Finally, I shall close with instructions for groups who will use the book and a set of questions to discuss either with others or individually.

Culture of First-Century Palestine

The traditions and writings of the gospels in the New Testament come from an ancient world of agriculture and trade. While today the world knows this geographic region as Israel, these first-century writings represent products of an ancient Eastern society from Asia called Palestine, where the mind-set of community dominates all thoughts and action. The community, which consisted of an inner and extended family, the village, and the society at large, operated within a context of honor and shame. Therefore, every action of an individual reflected on the community. It either brought honor or shame to the community; consequently, every person had to act within the norms of that group so as not to dishonor it. When a person brought shame upon the community, punishment would follow in order to restore honor to the family, village, and society. When we become acquainted with ancient societal traditions, we begin to recognize why people reacted the way they did. Therefore, some of the

words, actions, and events of the gospels become more understandable.

Meaning of the Word Gospel

In Roman times, the notion of *gospel* referred to the announcement of good news. Therefore, the Gospel of John, which appears
within the New Testament as the Fourth Gospel, aims to announce
the "good news" about Jesus, the Christ. Thus, a gospel does
not function as a biography of Jesus in the modern understanding of the term. Unlike modern biographies, it does not propose
to record all the facts of Jesus' life, nor is it a record of all Jesus'
sayings.

More recent studies like those of Charles Talbert (*Reading
John*, 62–65), however, suggests that in some ways the form of a
"gospel" has similarities to that of the ancient biography in its
focus on a famous individual with faithful followers. At times the
document becomes a foundation of that community, which
incorporates its own unique tradition into the ancient biography.
While it may follow such tradition, it does not function in the literary form of a modern biography. Rather, as you have just read,
the Fourth Gospel utilizes the ancient literary form of "gospel,"
that is, "good news." Consequently, the ancient author focuses
on the "good news" about Jesus rather than on history or facts
about Jesus. This discussion about the form of "gospel" remains
ongoing.

Some Similarities in the Synoptic Gospels

The first three gospels (Mark, Matthew, and Luke) follow a
similar story pattern in their portrayal of Jesus. This remains one
of the many ways in which they contrast with the Gospel of John.
While only Matthew and Luke include the conception, birth, and
childhood reflections about Jesus, all three gospels follow a pattern whereby the adult Jesus:

1. Has been baptized
2. Spends forty days in the Judean desert preparing for new ministry in his life
3. Calls his first disciples in Galilee
4. Begins his ministry in Galilee
5. Preaches often in parables
6. Performs many miracles in Galilee
7. Takes his last journey to Jerusalem
8. Suffers an excruciating passion

Since the authors of the first three gospels shared many stories with parallel chronology, scholars concluded that these ancient writers shared at least one common written source. An examination of the gospel material makes it clear that at least two of the gospels have common sources and that one of the gospels (Mark) functions as one of the sources. In this context a source can be defined as written material that provides others with content for their own writing. In other words, the evangelists have used other written materials for the basis of their stories within the gospels. Therefore, such likenesses and parallel placement of stories within these three gospels have lead scholars in the past to identify Mark, Matthew, and Luke as the Synoptic Gospels because of their common view. The term *synoptic* comes from *synopsis,* which means summary.

However, the importance of their relationship to one another must be balanced with the uniqueness of each book. Today most scholars would advocate that each gospel speaks for itself and that we need to learn the singular message that it addresses for each specific community to whom it was intended. For example, each gospel within the New Testament presents a different profile of Jesus. Such emphasis can be described as a christological portrait. Among other titles, the Gospel of Mark emphasizes Jesus as a Suffering Messiah, while the Gospel of Matthew features Jesus as Teacher. On the other hand, the Gospel of Luke accentuates Jesus as a Prophet, and, after the resurrection the Prophet like Moses. Despite their differences, all three gospels envision Jesus as one who fulfills the longings of Israel and promotes the kingdom (reign) of God/heaven.

Differences and Similarities between John and the Synoptic Gospels

The Fourth Gospel differs from the other gospels in many ways. Accounts of different stories surface as one of the most obvious distinctions. For example, from the very outset the Gospel of John does not follow the same chronology as the earlier gospels. Instead of beginning with the human Jesus, it opens with a deep christological hymn about Jesus as the "Word" of God, who helped him to create from the beginning of the world. Contrary to the Synoptic Gospels, then, Jesus' work begins in the heavens, and then, for a time, he descends to earth, only to return to heaven.

To clarify the movement of Jesus in the Gospel, remember your classes in mathematics. At one point, you learned about the parabola, which can be described as a curve, like that of the path of an object when thrown into the air. It first rises and then falls back to earth. The movement of Jesus within the Fourth Gospel can be described as that of an inverted parabola. He begins in the heavens, comes down to earth for a time, and then reverts back to heaven. This movement of Jesus has no parallel in the earlier gospels.

Moreover, the Fourth Gospel contains:

1. No birth story
2. No indication about Jesus' baptism by John
3. No forty days in the desert to prepare for ministry
4. No exorcisms
5. No frequent parables like those in the Synoptics
6. No predictions of the fall of Jerusalem
7. No institutionalization of the Eucharist at the Last Supper

Unlike the first three gospels, John emphasizes the person of Jesus and his equal union with the Father rather than frequent mention of the kingdom of God. Therefore, Jesus often speaks about himself, whereas in the other gospels, he rarely does so. These select examples demonstrate the uniqueness of stories and their placement within the Fourth Gospel.

In addition to diverse content, the Fourth Gospel exhibits unique literary differences. Unlike the shorter miracle stories and parables in the Synoptics, the Fourth Gospel utilizes long discourses and narratives to convey its message. In the Fourth Gospel Jesus often dialogues with the character in the story. At other times he speaks in lengthy monologues. Assuredly, the earthly Jesus would not have spoken in such long exalted monologues or used such mysterious language to speak about God. These discourses represent the work of the author of the Gospel, who intended to demonstrate Jesus' self-revelation to others. The setting of these stories takes place frequently in Jerusalem, unlike the other gospels that follow the pattern of Jesus' public ministry mainly in Galilee.

While the Fourth Gospel contrasts in many ways to the other three gospels, it also exhibits a few similarities. The clearest parallels include:

1. The appearance of John the Baptist at the inauguration of Jesus' ministry
2. The passion, death, and resurrection stories at the conclusion of the Gospel

Despite a similar structure of stories at the outset and finale of the other gospels, many scholars now maintain that the evangelist did not necessarily know these other gospels and most likely had a separate source for his material. Yet, the debate about sources for the Gospel of John continues to this day.

Introduction to the Gospel of John

According to the early Christian historian, Eusebius (*Ecclesiastical History*, 6.14.7.), as far back as the second century CE, Clement of Alexandria envisioned the Gospel of John as a spiritual work. This inaugurated the tradition of many to view the Fourth Gospel solely in light of its spirituality. In doing so, many treasures of the work remained untapped. Today, however, scholars move far beyond such boundaries to discover the world associated with the text. With multiple methods of study, they take into account the social, environmental, and historical aspects of the stories within the Fourth Gospel. By doing so, scholars discover that the evangelist educates the reader to the various aspects of the life, worship, and customs within first-century Palestine.

For example, referrals to Jewish festivals such as the Passover (Pesach) in John 6, Feast of Tabernacles (Sukkoth) in John 7:8, Feast of Dedication (Hanukkah) in John 10:22 demonstrate a knowledge of the liturgical life of the Jewish communities in Palestine before the fall of Jerusalem in 70 CE. Along the same line, Jewish religious customs about the rites of purification (2:6) and actions that fulfill texts from the Hebrew Bible (19:28, 36) indicate important rituals and thoughts of the people.

Precise details about Jerusalem, such as the pool of Bethzatha (also called Bethesda or Bethsaida) in 5:1–47, the pool of Siloam (9:7), and Solomon's Portico (10:22–23) suggests a strong familiarity with the city. In John 4 the evangelist's references to Jacob's well and the Samaritans, as well as their beliefs and their worship on Mount Gerizim, enable the reader to appreciate the existence of the Samaritan community and the tension between Jews and Samaritans. Such examples demonstrate an accurate knowledge of Judaic life prior to the fall of Jerusalem in 70 CE. Furthermore, some narratives help the reader to envision the customs and challenges of life in an occupied nation.

Brief Historical Background

To understand the purpose of the Fourth Gospel, some historical events in Palestine need be understood. For the sake of inclusion and respect for all faiths, modern scholars use the abbreviation CE to designate the "common era," that is, the year that the Romans changed the calendar. CE equates with the abbreviation AD (anno Domini, in the year of the Lord). Similarly, BCE (before the common era), equates with BC (before Christ). These new identifications eliminate any bias and offer an inclusiveness in the identification of dates for all religions.

Between 66 and 70 CE some Jews from Galilee began a revolt against Roman occupation. As a retaliation for four long years of rebellion, the Romans finally destroyed the Jerusalem Temple and much of the city in 70 CE. The remnant Jewish community and their leaders were forced to leave. The absence of the Temple left them no place to offer sacrifices. Consequently, the priests went without work because their primary function to offer the sacrifice became nonexistent.

Out of necessity the Jewish leaders had to reestablish religious communal practices, which came to center on the words of the rabbis and the liturgy of the synagogue and home rather than on the practices and festivals that took place in the former Jerusalem Temple. The destruction of Jerusalem also left the leaders with a determination to strengthen Judaism by making it more normative. Therefore, varied religious Jewish practices and beliefs that existed prior to 70 CE became less tolerated by religious authorities.

In this reestablishment of Judaism, Jews who followed Jesus found themselves at odds with the new Jewish orthodoxy by the mid 80s. Tension ensued both in religious circles and within Jewish families. Stories in the Gospel reflect such strain between some Jewish leaders and Jesus' Jewish disciples. The pressure culminated in the Jewish Christians' exclusion from the synagogues (John 9:34; 12:42; 16:2). This exclusion affected their lives in every way including events of family, village, society, and so on.

The results of such strain appear throughout John in phrases such as *the Jews*. This term surfaces around seventy times and most often describes certain Jewish leaders, especially from Jerusalem, who oppose Jesus. It does not function as a generic anti-Jewish comment. Remember, Jesus was a Jew. His mother and most disciples were Jewish. Therefore, the evangelist would not employ the term in a general way. When you come to the phrase in the Gospel, you will read it in context and begin to understand how the author uses it in the story.

Purpose of the Gospel of John

The above strained religious history seriously influenced the Gospel of John. Within the book intense controversies surface, such as a growing strain with particular Jewish leaders of Jerusalem, followers of John the Baptist, christological misunderstandings, and so on. To address this reality Raymond Brown (*The Community of the Beloved Disciple*, 59–91) distinguishes six groups within the Gospel that function outside John's community: (1) "the world," the people who choose darkness rather than light; (2) the "Jews," certain leaders, who persecuted and/or excommunicated those Jews who followed Jesus; (3) the followers of John the Baptist, those who proclaimed that God chose John, not Jesus, as the one to follow; (4) the crypto-Christians, Christian Jews who attended synagogue but did not have the courage to admit publicly their faith in Jesus, lest they be excommunicated from the synagogue; (5) Jewish Christians, those followers of Jesus who either left the synagogue voluntarily or forcibly, but who lacked faith for one reason or another; (6) the Christians of apostolic churches, those who were followers of Peter and the other apostles, but did fully grasp the teachings of Jesus, especially in regard to the function of the Paraclete. Brown proposes that the Gospel distinguishes this last group from the Johannine community by the contrasting figures of the Beloved Disciple (BD) and Peter. The Beloved Disciple appears in six passages, in five of which the evangelist contrasts him with Peter (13:23–26; 18:15–16; 20:2–10; 21:7; 21:20–23). Each time the author favors the Beloved Disciple over Peter. While some scholars do not necessarily agree with all six categories, Brown has provided the readers with a solid explanation of different types of characters within the Gospel.

In contrast to all these "outside" groups, the Johannine community reflects those who believe in the person of Jesus. They represent those who follow Jesus, despite the costs to themselves. Throughout the Gospel the characters that listen and respond to Jesus openly and with courage exemplify this community.

Despite the presence of many polemical passages and outside groups within the work, the Gospel did not function as a defense. Although many texts speak of controversy, they were not intended as messages to outside groups. The evangelist could not have expected the enemies of Jesus to read the Gospel. Therefore, the Gospel did not exist primarily to address issues of conflict. Additionally, the Gospel does not provide evidence that it was intended as a missionary tool for conversion of others.

First and foremost the Gospel functioned as a source of strength for the believing community, who remained under attack and deeply experienced the religious changes that took effect in their lives. They seemed to be dealing with issues such as excommunication from the synagogue (9:34; 12:42; 16:2), dietary regulations and social status (4:9), religious traditional authority (4:12), among other topics. Therefore, the Gospel served as "good news" in their tense situation.

To encourage them, the evangelist employs various narratives and discourses to demonstrate God's deep love for and faithfulness to them through the person of Jesus. Through these stories the community has the opportunity to come to learn and acknowledge that the person of Jesus is enough in their lives. In the Gospel Jesus calls them to believe in him above all else. John 20:31 clearly describes the essential purpose of the gospel with these words: "These are written so that you may come to believe that Jesus is the Messiah, the Son of God, and that through believing you may have life in his name."

In essence, then, the Gospel was written at the end of the first century CE to strengthen Jewish, Samaritan, and Gentile Christians in their faith. As an important Christian document it echoes both the teachings of Jesus as well as situation of the Johannine community for whom the Gospel was originally written.

Arrangement of John's Gospel

Traditionally, the Gospel has been divided into two main sections, the Book of Signs (1:19—12:50) and the Book of Glory (13:1—20:31). The Book of Signs describes some of the miracles that Jesus performed throughout Galilee and Judea. In this Gospel, the word *sign* replaces the word *miracle*. The Book of Glory follows with the events of Jesus' last days in Jerusalem. It begins with the last supper that Jesus had with his disciples and ends with Jesus' resurrection and visitation to them. Most of the stories deal with Jesus' disciples or some Jewish authorities in Jerusalem.

However, both sections contain important material that does not fall under these two categories. For example, the first twelve chapters of the Gospel include much more than signs. This section also contains the call of the disciples, various dialogues that Jesus had with others, long discourses between Jesus and various figures, narratives about the tension between Jesus and some Jewish leaders from Jerusalem, as well as important "I am" sayings of Jesus. Moreover, the second half of the Gospel also includes extensive instructions to the disciples, as well as Jesus' arrest, interrogations, and death. Therefore, I suggest that you, the reader, envision the Gospel of John as one long narrative whose stories often continue themes that connect one chapter with the next. In addition, I ask you to be aware of the continual conflicts within the world of late first-century Jewish Christianity that lie beneath the words of the text. Reading the Gospel within the context of its historical, literary, and sociological framework will continue to enhance your understanding of the Gospel.

In addition, the Gospel of John includes a Prologue (1:1–18) that precedes the narrative and an Epilogue (21:1–25) that follows the first ending of the Gospel. The Prologue functions as an introduction to some major beliefs of the Johannine community, which may have existed before the writing of the Gospel. The Epilogue serves to redefine the role of Peter (church) and the Beloved Disciple (Johannine community) and their relationship to one another.

Literary Features of John's Gospel

The Fourth Gospel consists of many dramatic stories and conversations that demonstrate the literary skill of the evangelist. Throughout the Gospel this author sets the stage carefully with literary techniques so that the audience will develop an interest in the message of the particular narrative. Good storytelling employs various literary styles. To illustrate the evangelist's skill in this area, I shall present examples from the marvelous story of the woman at the well in John 4.

The evangelist relates the encounter of the Samaritan woman with Jesus within the literary format of the discourse. According to C. H. Dodd (*Historical Tradition*, 315–34), the discourse often includes: (1) a serious declaration by Jesus (4:10), (2) an objection or question to Jesus by another individual(s) due to a lack of understanding of his statement (4:11), (3) a response that comes in the form of a discourse by Jesus to clarify the person's misconception. In general, the discourse contains more questions and answers or it may continue as a long monologue. Moreover, it includes either/both dialogues and monologues to convey its message.

To intensify the interest of the reader, the author employs words with double meanings. This feature allows the topic to deepen and expand. For example, in the dialogue between the woman of Samaria and Jesus in John 4, the topics appear to be water and thirst when Jesus asks for a drink from the well. However, the terms have deeper meanings of the divine gift of life that awaits the woman as illustrated by Jesus' declaration that "those who drink of the water that I will give them will never be thirsty" (4:14).

The evangelist employs the technique of misunderstanding so that the dialogue can continue within the story. When the person does not grasp the meaning of Jesus' metaphor, Jesus uses this opportune moment to continue his message. For instance, the Samaritan woman misunderstands Jesus' comment in 4:10 about giving "living water," with her reply in verse 11, "Sir, you have no bucket, and the well is deep. Where do you get that living water?" This question allows Jesus to extend his remarks and thereby deepen the theological message of the conversation.

The technique of the "rule of two" also surfaces in the story. Dramatists often use this feature to focus on certain main characters and to develop the conversation in the scene. Try to imagine the story being acted upon a stage, where two main figures hold the attention of an audience. While other characters come in and out of the scene and the two characters can change, John often presents two main figures on center stage so that their discourse will develop. For example, in 4:5 the disciples, who accompany Jesus to the village of Sychar, leave him at Jacob's well so that they can buy food (4:8). At this moment both Jesus and the woman have an opportunity to dialogue together. Later, when the disciples return to the well, the woman leaves to speak to her neighbors in the village (4:28). Once again, this moment allows Jesus to speak alone with another party, namely, his disciples.

Clearly, the use of concentric thinking permeates the dialogue between the woman at the well and Jesus. In one sense this feature represents the thinking of people who live in Asia and Africa. We, who live in Western society, follow the ancient Greek logic way of linear or straight-line thought. We tend to seek "the bottom line" in a thought process and often look for "just the facts." If you had geometry, the study of "proof" will refresh your memory of such thinking

On the other hand, the Eastern mind does not ponder an issue syllogistically, that is, a thought process that comes to a conclusion based on two prior statements. Rather, the thought process of the East takes a topic at one level and revisits it at more profound new levels. While this process may seem simply repetitive to the Western mind, the concentric way of thought actually delves deeper into the topic each time it revisits the issue at hand.

In the story of the woman at the well in John 4, the topics of water and thirst reflect such thinking. At first the request for water seems to be a physical one (4:7). Soon, however, the term shifts to a spiritual level (4:10–12). Finally, water describes eternal life (4:13–14). A similar development occurs in the story with the concept of thirst. At the outset of the encounter with the woman, Jesus appears thirsty (4:7), but, as the dialogue progresses, the real thirst comes from the woman, who responds openly to Jesus in the dialogue so that it can move from her desire to quench her physical thirst (4:15) to her deeper thirst for openness to the divine (4:19, 25).

Irony surfaces as another literary characteristic employed by the author. Some scholars propose that the question of 4:12 exemplifies irony. Here the Samaritan woman asks Jesus "Are you greater than our ancestor Jacob, who gave us this well...?" These scholars suggest that she does not think so. Yet, Jesus far surpasses Jacob. Hence the verse shows the use of irony. While in agreement with John's use of irony in other questions throughout the Gospel (John 7:42; 11:50; 18:38; 19:2–3), I suggest that in 4:12 the question does not exemplify the use of irony, but rather is proposed as a true question by the woman.

The evangelist employs the literary characteristic of inclusion to unify the stories within John 4. At the beginning of the chapter (4:3) he mentions Jesus' itinerary and cites it again at the conclusion (4:54). Such repetition ties together the sections within the chapter before the author proceeds to the next chapter.

These examples from the story of the woman at the well in Samaria illustrate a few of the literary techniques employed by the evangelist throughout the Gospel. Therefore, the reader needs to be aware of them in order to recognize the development and purpose of a particular Johannine story.

Authorship and Date

We, who live in twenty-first-century first-world countries, maintain very high standards for correct authorship of a scholarly work. For instance, if a writer uses the work of another author without proper credit to that person's work, the act is called plagiarism. Such an act of stealing another's work results in serious consequences for the offender. During the ancient centuries of biblical writing, correct authorship was not a priority. Ancient tradition placed more emphasis on the authority of the writing rather than the actual writer. Most books of the Bible were written anonymously and we cannot trace their origins to one person, despite the traditions that surround their authorship.

The Gospel of John counts as no exception. The Fourth Gospel does not name an author. While John 21:20, 24 indicates that the "disciple whom Jesus loved...is testifying to these things and has written them," the author's name remains anonymous. While no name appears in these texts, tradition began to associate the Beloved Disciple with John the Evangelist, who also seems to become one with John the son of Zebedee, a disciple of Jesus.

Historically, no discussion of authorship for the Fourth Gospel becomes evident until around 180 CE when Irenaeus proclaims the disciple John of Ephesus as the author of the Gospel. He states that "John, the disciple of the Lord, who had also leaned on his breast, did himself publish a gospel during his residence at Ephesus in Asia" (*Against Heresies*, 3:1.1.). This notion continued with early third-century church leaders, such as Clement of

Alexandria, who also distinguished this "spiritual" Gospel from the other gospels, which he held presented historical facts.

Today, however, due to lack of evidence most scholars conclude that the author of John's Gospel remains anonymous, like those of the other three gospels in the canon. They would also conclude that the writer, like the other authors of the first three gospels, would not have been an eyewitness or a disciple of Jesus. To distinguish the Gospel from others, we continue to name the author as John.

This Gospel emerges as the latest text of the four gospels within the New Testament, probably written toward the end of the first century. The late dating itself suggests that the original disciples of Jesus would have already died by this time. Scholars suggest such a late dating based on the realization that this Johannine community seems to have been well established, on the continued conflict between Jesus and "the Jews," which escalates well after the destruction of Jerusalem in 70 CE, and on the fact that the Fourth Gospel was not mentioned until the second century CE.

Place of Writing

From the writings of Irenaeus (*Against Heresies*, 3:1.1) eighteen centuries ago, tradition held that the evangelist composed the gospel in Ephesus, Asia Minor, which is known today as Turkey. Contributing to this theory is the ancient opinion that the Book of Revelation, the Gospel of John, as well as the three letters of John, were all composed by the same person, namely, John. In this tradition, John was supposed to have begun his writings while on the island of Patmos, before he moved to Ephesus. The use of Greek philosophical vocabulary also suggests that Hellenistic Ephesus might be the place of authorship.

Today mainstream scholars agree that the Gospel and Revelation were written by two different authors. Yet, some still hold Ephesus as the most plausible place of composition because, according to Revelation 2:9; 3:9, hostility existed between groups of Jewish Christians and the synagogue in important cities of Asia

Minor, such as this one. To further the argument R. Brown (*An Introduction to the Gospel of John,* 205) suggests that Paul's meeting some followers of John the Baptist and baptizing them in Ephesus (Acts 19:1–7) demonstrates another polemic between the disciples of John and those of Jesus. Both points parallel similar tension in the Gospel of John.

After a more recent discovery of the Qumran scrolls near the Dead Sea, some scholars maintain that John's Gospel may have its roots in Palestine. For example, it employs similar Hellenistic vocabulary as that found in the scrolls from Qumran, such as *Lógos* (the "Word"), light/darkness, truth/error, spirit/flesh, and so on. Both communities rely on spiritual illumination from their leader. For such reasons some scholars consider the Gospel to have its beginnings in Palestine or nearby Antioch in Syria.

In contrast, others suggest that the frequent travels of Jesus between Jerusalem and Galilee suggest the author's lack of familiarity with the geographical distances between cities/villages in Palestine. At this point no one has offered clear evidence as to the place of origin for the Gospel. The discussion remains open until further documentation emerges.

Introduction to the Fourth Gospel— Questions

1. What does *Johannine* mean?
2. Why do so many Christians perceive the Gospel as a biography?
3. Why was the Gospel written?
4. Why is a miracle called a "sign" in John?
5. Why does the Fourth Gospel contain no birth story, baptism by John, and no forty days in the desert?
6. What does the frequent use of the term *the Jews* mean within the Fourth Gospel?
7. Who is the Paraclete in the Gospel? What is the Paraclete's function?
8. Who is the Beloved Disciple in the Fourth Gospel?

Introduction to the Fourth Gospel— Conclusion

Unlike the Synoptics, the Gospel of John presents a very high Christology. In other words, the author's portrait of Jesus the Christ accents the divinity of Jesus rather than his struggle and growth as a human being. From the very first words of the Fourth Gospel, Jesus comes into the world as the revealed Word of God, who has already existed with God the Father before the creation of the world.

Ultimately, when we read the Gospel of John we enter into an entirely new realm of narratives, which read quite differently from the other gospels. With its mysterious language, stories, dialogues, and monologues about and by Jesus, the Fourth Gospel appears unique in the presentation of the divine person of Jesus rather than focusing on the future kingdom of God/heaven. In every sense the readers will observe how the stories center on the necessity to believe in the person of Jesus.

"How to Use"— Instructions for Using the Book with Groups

The book will be valuable for classroom use in college courses on the Gospel of John as well as adult study groups on the Gospel. In the case of adult study groups, the role of the group leader remains vital. This leader needs to gather people together, to set boundaries of time and location, to invite every person to share his/her own thoughts on the discussion at hand. To help the group leader, some suggestions can be made:

1. Limit the number in a group so that people will feel free to speak at any given time. A limit to the number of participants per group also makes easier the arrangement of meeting place, refreshments, a peaceful setting, and so on.
2. Prepare the reading for the evening and stay with the assigned text for that particular meeting. As you can see from the book, different chapters require diverse amounts of time to study the text properly. Moreover, some chapters will require a slower pace of study because of the intensity of the message. Plan ahead for such needed time.
3. Answers at the end of the book need to be examined after the group has had the chance to address them on their own and with the group. Once again, invite all to speak on the question, even if a person's reply surfaces as another question rather than a response. In this way, both the involvement and ownership of the group will be shared by all.
4. The leader must always keep in mind that, at first, the material of the book may confuse people who have never studied the Bible before. Most often, uninformed readers view the gospels literally rather than as literature with vari-

ous literary genres, such as parables (fiction), miracle stories (called signs in John), discourses, monologues, and so
on. Therefore, the group must read and discuss the introduction to the book so as to prepare them to understand
the biblical text.

5. The leader needs to allow time for the group to ponder the
answers, reread the actual text of the Gospel as well as
introductions and conclusions of each chapter so as to
allow the group to discover new and deeper meanings to
the biblical text. Modern critical analysis takes time to read,
digest, and make sense to the person. It remains essential
that the group always do a close reading of the biblical text,
which will mean reading the primary text over and over
again.

As for English translations, I have quoted from the New
Revised Standard Version (NRSV). In a group it makes sense to
have one solid English translation that will be used by all members so that no one gets caught up in the use of one English word
rather than another. I suggest the New Revised Standard Version
of the Bible because it adheres closely to the Greek text of the
Gospel of John. Roman Catholics may wish to use the New
American Bible (NAB).

CHAPTER 1
John 1

The first chapter of the Fourth Gospel contains two major sections: the Prologue and the call of the first disciples. These two sections differ in presentation. For the purpose of clarity, we shall study these sections one at a time.

John 1:1–18 The Prologue— Introduction

As you begin to read the opening verses of the Gospel of John, you will notice immediately how different they read from the other gospels. While the opening chapters of the gospels of Matthew and Luke concentrate on the earthly beginnings of Jesus with familiar references to his birth, this poetic prelude, which became known as a Prologue, does not. Rather, it presents Jesus as the Word, who has been with God before the creation of the world. Its meaning and placement in chapter 1 raises many questions.

Most likely, the Prologue existed as a hymn of a Christian community prior to the writing of the Fourth Gospel. It presents some sophisticated ideas about Jesus' preexistence before creation, as well as his roles in creation and redemption. Moreover, the author of the Gospel adds verses 6–8 and 15, which present the figure of John the Baptist. Structurally, the ancient hymn can be divided into five sections:

1. 1:1–5   The Word (Greek *Lógos*) brings light into a darkened world.
2. 1:6–8, 15   This insertion into the hymn, which introduces John the Baptist solely as a witness to

23

		Jesus, plainly presents Jesus' superiority over John.
3.	1:9–13	The rejection of Jesus by the world contrasts with the acceptance of Jesus by the community.
4.	1:14	This verse presents the highpoint of Jesus' coming into the world.
5.	1:16–18	These verses reflect the superiority of the divine Jesus over the human Moses.

John 1:1–18 The Prologue—Questions

9. What is the purpose of the Prologue (1:1–18)? Why is it placed at the very beginning of the Fourth Gospel?
10. Why is Jesus described as the "Word" *(Lógos)* in 1:1?
11. Verses 2 to 5 seem to use themes of the first creation story in the Book of Genesis. Why is the creation theme being emphasized?
12. Why is John the Baptist inserted into the hymn? Why was he presented in such a humble manner?

John 1:1–18 The Prologue—Conclusion

As you began to read the Prologue, you may notice the opening phrase, "In the beginning," in John 1:1 echoes the creation story in Genesis 1:1. Both stories talk about the past, which no one has witnessed. Both passages identify a time that belongs to God, not human beings. Creation has always been and still remains a function of the Divine, who forms the world with its beauty and life from "the beginning" even to this present day. Both the Prologue and the Creation hymn in Genesis describe God as Creator, as one who cares for all creation and brings light into each life.

Like God's creative actions in Genesis 1, Jesus as Revealer brings life and light to the world. The two themes permeate many stories throughout the Fourth Gospel, where the Johannine Jesus identifies himself as light and life (8:12; 9:5; 11:25; 14:6). Life and light go hand in hand. When we are "enlightened" by the Revealer (Jesus), we have life. The granting of life is revelation and it remains truly a gift!

The theme of Jesus as the "Light" remains tied to the theme of life. In the Hebrew Bible (Old Testament), the prophet Isaiah announces that "the people who walked in darkness have seen a great light; those who lived in a land of deep darkness—on them light has shined" (Isa 9:2). In the Book of Isaiah, the prophet describes the light that Israel receives as a messianic event, that is, as a saving moment in history for the people. Here, when Jesus as Light enters into the historical world, it did not recognize him. More specifically, "the world," which also signifies his own people, "did not accept him." Rejection by God's people surfaces as a common theme in the prophetic and wisdom literature of the Hebrew Bible (Old Testament). The remnant that *does* accept Jesus becomes "children of God."

The center of the original poem (1:9–14) presents the incarnation. Simply put, incarnation means the embodiment of Jesus in fully human form. The clause, "the Word became flesh," indicates that Jesus became a human person. Therefore, the complete humanness of Jesus cannot be denied. The act of incarnation brings Jesus' human existence into reality with all the attributes of being human, such as the need to learn and grow, as well as human weakness or frailty. It remains incomprehensible that a divine being would take on the weakness of human form. When you really put some thought into the matter, it remains miraculous that the Word, who ranks equal to God, became a human being. The hymn's strong proclamation counteracts those who denied Jesus' humanness and proclaimed that he was totally spirit. In the letters of John (1 John 4:2 and 2 John 1:7), the author attempts to correct a misunderstanding about Jesus' nature being only divine. After a time this heresy within Christianity became known as Docetism.

In addition to Jesus becoming "flesh," the Prologue declares that he "lived among us" ("pitched a tent among us"). This action ties him solidly to the human world and its history because Jesus came to live on earth among others, as we also live among the earthly community. The Johannine audience knows the theme of dwelling/pitching a tent. It appears in the Hebrew Bible as an expression of divine presence among people, especially in their nomadic movement from Egypt to the Promised Land in the Book of Exodus (25:8; 29:45). Later, when the Israelites became settled in the land, the prophets employed the same theme to describe God's continued presence in the Jerusalem Temple (Zech 2:10; Ezek 43:7). The stationary Temple in Jerusalem replaced God's dwelling in the former portable tabernacle after the Israelites wandered through the desert and became settled in the land of Canaan (present-day Israel). Now, as the divine Jesus "dwells/pitches a tent," his presence offers hope and companionship to those who choose it. If they so choose, they will be changed forever because of these immeasurable gifts.

In this Prologue, Jesus not only speaks the word of God, he is the Word of God Incarnate, that is, the Word that became flesh. Jesus functions as the revelation of God, which means that God becomes known to others in life through Jesus. Jesus, who holds the special status as son "close to the Father's heart," remains the key person who reveals God to all those who listen. Thus, Jesus stands above all earthly and heavenly beings, always alongside God the Father. Therefore, the divinity of Jesus cannot be mistaken.

Throughout the hymn, we come to understand that the Word of God has become personified in Jesus. God chose Jesus as the one to whom we go for light and life, for creation and redemption. All of us owe our existence to him. Without Jesus (Word), the world remains in darkness. The Prologue helps us to appreciate the precious gift of creation, from all the beauty of nature to the very act of life itself. As followers of Jesus, we, too, are called to create in a manner that brings light to others rather than darkness, that brings life to others rather than death, that brings love to others rather than hate.

John 1:19–51—Introduction

After the Prologue, the narrative section of the chapter begins with John the Baptist, who has already been introduced in

1:6–8, 15. Now, he witnesses to Jesus himself and calls him the Lamb of God. The narrative occurs within a five-day period. The first two days relate both the story and the comments of John the Baptist. The testimony of John emphasizes the superiority of Jesus over John.

The third to the fifth days describe the call of some of the disciples of Jesus. The stories take place first in the region of Judea and then in Galilee. In this narrative the first disciples of Jesus respond with great enthusiasm after being in Jesus' presence. Chapter 1 sets the stage for others, who will also follow Jesus as the revealed Word of God.

For reading purposes this section may be divided as follows:

1. Testimony of John the Baptist (1:19–36)
2. Initial call and response of Jesus' first disciples (1:37–51)

John 1:19–51—Questions

13. Why did the religious leaders ask John if he were the awaited Messiah, Elijah, or the prophet? What did they mean?
14. When John the Baptist calls Jesus the "Lamb of God" in 1:29, 36, what does he mean?
15. In John 1:46 what is all the fuss about Jesus coming from Nazareth?
16. For the contemporaries of Jesus, what is the problem about Jesus' birth?
17. What does the title "Son of God" mean in John's Gospel?

John 1:19–51—Conclusion

Testimony of John the Baptist (1:19–36)

John 1:19–36 highlights the comments and actions of John, who witnesses to Jesus. When some religious leaders were sent from Jerusalem to question John about his identity, he stated firmly that he was *not* the Messiah, or Elijah, who was thought to return at the time of the Messiah, or the prophet (like Moses). John's strong negative response, "I am not," clearly contrasts to the very positive proclamations of Jesus, who announces later in the Gospel, "I AM" (the bread of life, the light of the world, the way, the truth and the life, and so on).

When John identifies himself as a "the voice of one crying out in the wilderness" (1:23, a reference to Isaiah 40:3), he decreases further his own importance. When we cry out in wilderness, who can hear us? To enhance the importance of Jesus, he comments later that "I myself have seen and have testified that this is the Son of God" (1:34). Moreover, two times John identifies Jesus as "Lamb of God." One of those times he adds "who takes away the sins of the world." As we all know, God is the One who removes sin. Here, John the Baptist describes Jesus as divine. In all his statements, then, John fulfills his role solely as witness to the coming of Jesus.

In addition to his remarks, John's actions also point to the importance of Jesus. For example, when the leaders question why John baptizes, he responds that, while he baptizes with water, one greater than he will come, whose sandals he is not worthy to tie. In wealthy households a servant would have performed this debasing chore. John's remark indicates that, compared to Jesus, he would not even deserve to be considered a servant. Thus, John paves the way for the One much more important than he.

What is the point of the author here? The Gospel writer intends to demonstrate that John's role comes nowhere near that of Jesus. In the Fourth Gospel no narrative describes John baptizing Jesus as in Mark 1:9 or Matthew 3:13, nor is he described as a relative of Jesus as in Luke 1:36. Rather, the author replaces John's function as baptizer and relative of Jesus. In this Gospel John's sole function is that of a witness to the person of Jesus. The significance of John decreases, while the importance of Jesus increases. John, therefore, testifies to the superiority of Jesus. Like a scene in a drama, John now leaves the stage and Jesus moves to center stage.

Call of the First Disciples (1:37–51)

After John identified Jesus, two of John's disciples left him to follow Jesus. This first step initiates their call (vocation). The word *vocation* comes from the Latin verb *vŏcare*, which means to call. Each one of us has been called by God to become our best selves. It becomes our responsibility to discover our call in life.

When Jesus acknowledges the disciples' search with the question, "What are you looking for?" he initiates the next step in their call (vocation). The disciples respond by addressing him as Rabbi, and inquire as to where he stays. The Hebrew term *rabbi* translates as teacher. The Fourth Gospel reserves the title for Jesus as one employed by his disciples, except for 3:26, where John the Baptist's disciples honor him with that name. In the first century, rabbis such as the famous Gamaliel from the school of Hillel had disciples and a place where they could meet and stay. Therefore, this question relates to their commitment to follow Jesus.

Jesus answered the inquiry by inviting them to "come and see." The phrase, "come and see," appears occasionally in the Fourth Gospel as a theological call to discipleship by Jesus himself (1:39), by one disciple to another (1:46), or by a disciple to a group of people (4:29). In this context the phrase functions clearly as a profound invitation to follow the path of the divine. As an invitation, the gentle words do not force but encourage others to follow their hearts. In this way Jesus offers a taste of another way of life, one that leads to real Life.

As it turns out, the two disciples not only accepted Jesus' invitation, but Andrew, one of the two, spoke with Simon, his brother, to tell him that "we have found the Messiah." The Hebrew title *Messiah* translates into Greek as "the Christ." The word means "the anointed one." As you may have noticed, Andrew's description of Jesus represents one of the many titles used for Jesus in 1:19–51. Other titles include "Lamb of God," "Son of God," "Rabbi," "King of Israel" and "Son of Man."

After Jesus met Simon, he changed his latest friend's name to Cephas, an Aramaic word that in Greek translates *Petra* ("Rock"). Throughout the Bible, a change of names often signals a new way of life for that person. Today, Christian naming at both baptism and confirmation also represents a new way of life for the person involved.

The narrative continues with the call of Philip. When Jesus saw him, he offered a more direct invitation with the call "Follow me." Philip responded immediately to the divine summons and joined Jesus. Soon after, Philip found Nathaniel and told him about Jesus the Messiah, the son of Joseph from Nazareth. The phrase "son of Joseph" does not contradict the virginal conception. Rather, it provides credibility to Jesus as acceptable in society because he was legally Joseph's son. Philip's comment also counteracts later slanderous remarks by Jesus' opponents, who declare "we are not illegitimate children" (8:41), a suggestion that Jesus had such a birth.

Nathaniel replied in words that echoed the sentiments of others in first-century Palestine when he questioned rhetorically, "Can anything good come out of Nazareth?" This pretentious rhetoric illustrates the prejudice against Jesus' place of origin. It parallels today's "other side of the tracks" remarks. The comments of Nathaniel echo the people's utter distaste of a messianic figure from Nazareth, a place nowhere near Jerusalem or even identified in the Hebrew Bible.

At the same time, however, Nathaniel goes willingly to meet Jesus and speak with him. His very words and actions demonstrate his openness and honesty. Soon after a meeting and verbal exchange with Jesus, Philip exclaims, "Rabbi, you are the Son of God! You are the King of Israel!" Now, Philip has joined the others in God's call to follow Jesus.

CHAPTER 2
John 2

John 2—Introduction

The second chapter of John presents two main stories of great contrast: a joyous celebration of a wedding and an angry display of physical force. The person of Jesus appears center stage in both accounts. The conclusion of John 2 also highlights the people's response to Jesus as he attends the Jewish feast of Passover in Jerusalem.

The change of water into wine at the wedding in Cana represents the first sign in the ministry of Jesus. Like some other signs, the miracle contains four parts: (a) introduction (2:1–2), (b) the exchange (2:3–5), (c) the sign/miracle (2:6–9), (d) the response to the sign (2:7–12). As you have read in the Introduction, the old traditional division of the Book of Signs appears in John 1—12, while the Book of Glory reflects John 13—20. The first scene set in Cana takes on great importance because it inaugurates the other signs and it anticipates the extravagance of the coming of Jesus into the world.

The cleansing of the Temple (2:13–25) marks the next major event within the chapter. It takes place on the feast of Passover, one of the major feasts in Judaism. In the time of the Temple, Passover was considered a pilgrim festival, when devout Jews would travel to Jerusalem to worship and celebrate. For this reason, Jesus and the disciples traveled up to Jerusalem from Cana. This story discloses a very different Jesus. In this scene he appears to become violent after he encounters the money changers at the Temple in Jerusalem.

Both stories in this chapter divulge different sides of Jesus. When reading such accounts, be sure to consider the actions of Jesus in light of the situation of the story and the people whom he addresses within it.

For reading purposes the chapter may be divided as follows:

1. Wedding feast at Cana in Galilee (2:1–12)
2. Cleansing of the Temple (2:13–25)

John 2—Questions

18. Why was the wedding set in Cana?
19. Along with the disciples, Mary appears as a guest at the wedding. Is she an integral part of the story?
20. Why isn't Mary named and instead called "mother of Jesus"?
21. In 2:4 Jesus addresses his mother as "woman." Wasn't it very rude to speak to her that way?
22. What does Jesus mean by "my hour" in his answer to Mary in 2:4?
23. Why is the changing of water into wine so excessive? Throughout the gospels other miracles are often performed for serious reasons, such as being healed, being brought back to life. What makes this sign so important and why was so much wine produced?
24. What is the Passover festival in 2:13, 23?
25. Aren't we supposed to be patient and forgiving toward people? If that is so, why does Jesus become so incensed at the money changers and seem to lose his temper?
26. Why does he drive them out of the Temple in 2:13–22?

John 2—Conclusion

Wedding Feast at Cana in Galilee (2:1–12)

The Cana narrative connects with the call of the disciples in John 1 and concludes that story in John 2:11. As a literary piece, the wedding at Cana represents a two-level story. The initial tale consists of a straightforward account of a miracle (2:1–3, 6–10).

At a later time, the dialogue between Jesus and his mother (2:4–5) was added. This addition marks an intrusion into the original miracle story and causes many questions.

As we read the account of the wedding, we come to see that that the story does not focus on the sign (miracle) itself, nor on the need of the bridal couple, nor on Mary, nor on the disciples. Rather, the entire story centers on Jesus. When Jesus changes water into wine, he becomes a savior to the families in need. The narrative, therefore, emphasizes the importance of Jesus, and the only proper response to the miracle comes from Mary and the disciples, who believe in him.

Like many of the stories in the Synoptic Gospels, the Cana narrative takes place at a meal. From all accounts, Jesus often spoke important words or performed vital actions at a meal. Why? We all have experienced the importance of sharing a meal with others. It offers the perfect opportunity to relax with family and friends, to share personal opinions, to ask important questions, to listen to others, and to appreciate them. More importantly, a meal with a prominent event attached brings even more opportunities for the larger community, which includes family, friends, neighbors, and so on. Therefore, the wedding at Cana proved to be the perfect setting for this inaugural sign.

The event has both human and divine implications. On the human level the ancient Jewish wedding feast celebrates not only the individual bride and groom, but, more significantly, the honor of the two families as well. They are the ones who demonstrate to the village and synagogue the good news about their son and daughter with a prepared traditional ceremony followed by an extensive feast of food and wine. In first-century Palestine the marriage of a virgin bride would begin on a Wednesday and last seven days, while the marriage of a widow would last three days (Judg 14:12; Tob 11:18).

To pay for the expensive celebration, the family would use their financial resources, as well as gifts from friends and family. This joyous event would be well planned and would bring great honor to both families within the society. If the food or drink did not last the length of the celebration, the families would suffer dishonor. People would wonder whether these two families had monetary resources or even if they had very many friends. Whatever the reason, the families would be shamed in the community and would lose their place in society. Therefore, as insignificant as the need of a miracle may appear to the modern reader, it certainly represented a serious issue for the families involved, especially for the young married couple.

In the story the act of Jesus changing 180 gallons of water into the finest wine appears quite extravagant, especially after the guests have enjoyed the festivity already for some time (2:10). On the human level, it assures the honor of the families in two ways: the abundance of the wine guarantees that no shortage will occur, and the top quality of the wine demonstrates to the village that the families have financial means and/or an abundance of friends who support the marriage.

As you may have guessed, the most significant value of this first sign emerges on the divine level. In the Hebrew Bible Isaiah the prophet (54:4–8; 62:4–5) utilizes the wedding feast to anticipate messianic days. The replacement of choice wine in abundance from water also signals messianic days in other prophets (Amos 9:13–14; Hos 14:7). In any case, the miracle fosters a time to rejoice. All that the prophets have anticipated and promised has been fulfilled in Jesus. Thus, the writer of John's Gospel made a forceful point when he chose to place the wedding story at the beginning of the Gospel. This first sign marks the arrival of the time of God. The wedding feast of Cana functions as a magnificent anticipation of divine celebration. This sign reminds the reader that the joy and happiness of messianic times has arrived. Jesus, the Christ (which means Messiah), has come to earth to be among us. This reality, indeed, calls for a celebration like no other!

When you read 2:1–12, you may notice that verses 4 and 5 interrupt the flow of the story. Without these two verses, the text flows as a straight miracle story. When the dialogue in 2:4–5 between Jesus and his mother becomes part of the account, it disturbs the smoothness of the tale. Moreover, the conversation between mother and son sounds a bit strange.

When Mary had told Jesus that the guests have no wine in 2:3, she demonstrates her immense sensitivity as both a beloved mother, whose son has become her protector, and as a dear friend to those about to be shamed. At this point in the feast, empty wine jugs would result in dishonor to both families as well as diminish their social status within the community. Therefore, Mary's courageous compassion prompted her to take action and go to Jesus for a solution. As we read the biblical texts, we come to see that, in effect, Mary changed the mind of her divine son.

On a human level, the mother of Jesus must know in her heart that, whatever Jesus does, he will come to the aid of the young couple and their two families in order to save them from shame. The surprise in the story appears in the reply that Jesus gives her. On the divine level, it makes more sense to understand Jesus' peculiar response to his mother when he calls her "woman." Jesus' answer to Mary does not have to do with disrespect, for the title "woman" functions as a title of honor in the gospels. Rather, his address of "woman," instead of "mother," informs the readers that Jesus belongs totally with God the Father as he ministers to others. In this jubilant scene, both Mary (2:5) and the disciples (2:11) respond in belief. Most importantly, remember that this first sign inaugurates a new reign, that of God, through his Son, Jesus.

Cleansing of the Temple (2:13–25)

The next scene, the cleansing of the Temple, marks one of the few episodes that appears in all four gospels. In the Synoptic Gospels, however, it appears at the end of Jesus' ministry shortly before the passion narratives (Mark 11:15; Matt 21:12ff.; Luke 19:45ff.). Unlike those gospels, the author of the Fourth Gospel places the cleansing of the Temple at the outset of Jesus' ministry instead of at the end of it. When the author places the scene here in the Gospel, he provides for the replacement theme that runs throughout the Fourth Gospel. In this case, Jesus stands as the replacement for sacred structures of Israel's past. Here, for instance, the person of Jesus replaces the Temple for worship.

In the history of Israel, periodic worship in the Temple replaced worship of God. Time and time again the prophets of the Hebrew Bible warned the people to return their hearts to God

(Jer 7:1–15; 26:4–6; Hos 6:6–8). Most often the prophets intended their message especially for the religious leaders of Jerusalem. At these times the leaders practiced religion, not faith. In other words, they performed all the outward religious practices but they did not allow their hearts to be changed.

In first-century Palestine, the Temple in Jerusalem remained the religious center of Judaism. In addition, it also became an economic and political focal point of life among the Jews. Consequently, when Jesus took a whip of cords and turned over the tables of the sellers and money changers, his actions impacted all three levels, namely, the religious, economic, and political. Through this radical action, Jesus rejects what became central in the cult of the Temple. In one sense, his harsh actions signaled a call to repentance from the present corrupt Temple practices and a call to acknowledge the replacement of the Jerusalem Temple with the person of Jesus.

As the images of the wedding feast at Cana and the abundance of wine illustrate the coming of the Messiah, so, too, do the forceful actions of Jesus in the Temple. Now, Jesus replaces the dishonored Jewish Temple with the honorable sacred space of himself. Unlike the Cana feast, where Mary and the disciples believed in Jesus, the words and deeds of Jesus in the Temple scene caused some of the Jewish authorities to resent him.

CHAPTER 3
John 3

John 3—Introduction

The third chapter of John's Gospel presents two main episodes: Jesus' dialogue with Nicodemus the Pharisee and John the Baptist's final testimony to Jesus. The initial scene (3:1–21) introduces the first discourse within the Gospel. Like other discourses within the Gospel, the writer introduces some fine literary skills to keep the conversation lively. For example, he employs the "rule of two," which provides the reader with two main characters to hold his/her attention. The writer employs a dialogue form at the outset of the discussion, and changes it later to a monologue by Jesus. In addition, the technique of double-meaning words or misunderstanding help to further the point of the discourse. Overall, such literary techniques provide a lively discourse that moves along to the point at hand.

Jesus speaks with a religious leader and teacher of the Jews. In effect, Nicodemus represents two types: some leaders of official Judaism and those people who have become impressed with Jesus but are not yet ready to take the risk to follow him. He may be like Jewish leaders at the end of the first century who would have liked to believe in Jesus, but who lacked the courage to make a final decision. While Jesus speaks about divine realities, Nicodemus struggles with such realities only on a human level.

The next main section (3:22–36) appears with no real introduction or transition. It also returns John the Baptist to the narrative. This story marks the last time that John appears in the Fourth Gospel. In John 3 both men, namely, Nicodemus and John the Baptist, have close ties with Judaism. In both sections the men claim that Jesus comes from a divine source.

For reading purposes the chapter may be divided as follows:

1. Jesus' encounter with Nicodemus at night (3:1–21)
2. Final testimony of John the Baptist (3:22–36)

John 3—Questions

27. As the chapter begins, some titles do not appear completely clear. For example, what is a Pharisee (3:1), what is a rabbi (3:2)?
28. Why did Nicodemus come to Jesus at night?
29. Why does Jesus introduce statements with "Very truly/ Amen, amen"?
30. Does "born again" as used by some Christians today have anything to do with Jesus' conversation with Nicodemus in 3:3?
31. In 3:5 how are we born of the Holy Spirit?
32. Who is included in "our testimony" in 3:11?
33. Why is the title "Son of Man" used in 3:13? What does it mean?
34. In 3:14 what is meant by "the serpent in the wilderness"?
35. Why is John 3:16 so popular today? As I watched national sports' games on TV, I saw the reference several times on banners.
36. Isn't 3:18 awfully exclusionary? How can we explain the fact of other religions and denominations in light of this verse?

John 3—Conclusion

Jesus' Encounter with Nicodemus at Night (3:1–21)

The dialogue in John 3 takes place between two teachers: Nicodemus, whom Jesus describes as "a teacher of Israel" (3:10), and Jesus, whom Nicodemus addresses as "rabbi" (3:2), which means "teacher." I mention this point because, in most instances, usually two teachers in dialogue have some common understanding. In this episode, however, Nicodemus does not display any insight at all from his lengthy conversation with Jesus.

In general, the Johannine discourse proposes to transpose the discussion to a higher level by making the answer to each question go deeper into the topic at hand. However, in this case it does not function as it could because Nicodemus misinterprets Jesus' answers to his frequent questions. Thus, he appears trapped in his own inability to hear Jesus. After a time, even Jesus seems frustrated with Nicodemus as he remarks, "Are you a teacher of Israel, and yet you do not understand these things?" (3:10).

At the very outset of the discourse, one of the significant points that the writer makes refers to the time of Nicodemus' meeting with Jesus. Nicodemus comes to see him "at night" (3:2). While the evening activity could reflect the custom of rabbis to study the scripture at night, it does not make sense in this scenario. Most likely, the decisive movement of Nicodemus portrays his fear of disapproval from his fellow Jewish leaders. If he comes at night, no one can identify him.

Despite his own anxiety, Nicodemus was drawn to Jesus. In the true tradition of Jewish study, he went to meet, discuss, and ask questions of Jesus. Jesus brings encouragement to Nicodemus by meeting him on his own terms, that is, at night. While Nicodemus arrives in darkness, Jesus brings him light by offering him enlightenment into the realities of God. The meeting commences with a dialogue about being born again, from above, a second time, of water and the Spirit (3:3, 4, 5, 6, 7). The response of Jesus moves the text from the darkness of night to the light of heaven and the Spirit.

The subject of birth emerges as the main topic of the discourse. It has always been an important issue in society. Most often, a person's social status in the world depends on both geography and genealogy. An individual's place in life has been closely allied with honor. Birth designates such honor. For example, if a child has been born to privilege, most likely he/she would be honored all during life. Certain privileges, status, and way of liv-

39

ing would already be determined by birthright. On the other hand, if the child came from peasantry and poverty, he/she would probably remain unprotected and vulnerable all during life. No special esteem, power from ownership or prestige would be given to such a person. The one factor that could change a person's rank in life would be to be physically born again into another status.

In this discourse Jesus moves the discussion on birth to a monologue on the theology of the incarnation. This theology first appeared in the *Lógos* hymn in John 1:9–14. As you recall from chapter 1, it describes Jesus as having been above with God and coming down upon the earth among his people ("lived among us," that is, "pitched his tent among us" in 1:14) in order to draw them up to God. In this discussion about being born again, Jesus explains that, since God comes from above, the one and only entrance to God is to be born from above. He uses examples such as the "Son of Man" who came down from heaven and must be lifted up, just as Moses lifted up the serpent in the wilderness. To be "lifted up" (3:14) here refers to Jesus' death (lifted up on a cross), resurrection, and ascension. Jesus links all that is above (heaven) with all that is below (earth). When Jesus has been "lifted up," the Spirit (3:8) will be given to those who remain below.

In order to recognize Jesus as being from above and one with God the Father, a person must believe, that is, have faith in Jesus. Faith comes from above because it is a gift from God. Therefore, one who believes in Jesus and acts upon such faith has already been born from above. Jesus' words were misunderstood because Nicodemus still thought on the human level ("of the flesh"), and had not yet opened himself fully to Jesus ("of the spirit").

Final Testimony of John the Baptist (3:22–36)

The next section arrives abruptly after a quick transition phrase, "After this" (Greek *metà taûta*). In the Fourth Gospel these two words appear frequently when the writer wants to change the subject matter or geographic location. The writer moves Jesus from Jerusalem to the Judean countryside, where John the Baptist again enters the scene. Interestingly, the subject matter connects with the previous episode, where Jesus spoke to Nicodemus about birth. Here the topic highlights purification rites performed by John, other Jews, and Jesus himself. In this introduction the writer establishes that both Jesus and John baptized. As you may know, baptism has often been described as a new birth. In this way, the narrative is united with the previous discourse about birth as it mentions new birth (baptism).

John the Baptist's final testimony within the Gospel creates the heart of the story. When some of John's disciples question their leader about the activity of Jesus, they dispute the authority and power of Jesus. From this we realize that tension existed in the first century between the followers of Jesus and the followers of John. Probably it lasted well into the time of the Fourth Gospel.

The complaints of John's disciples provide him with the opportunity to present his final and powerful testimony about Jesus. When the disciples request John's opinion about Jesus, he does not defend himself or the importance of his own work. Rather, John defers to the importance of Jesus with a clear response. He identifies Jesus with two strong biblical images that were familiar to the people at that time. To accentuate the importance of Jesus, John uses the titles "bridegroom" and "Messiah" to refer to him. In the Hebrew Bible the prophets used the symbol of the bride to identify Israel and that of the bridegroom to portray God (Hos 2:19; Isa 54:6). Here John bestows the title on Jesus and, in effect, identifies him as divine. As in the ancient marriage ceremony, the bridegroom (Jesus) has come upon earth to claim his bride (Israel).

The other title of "Messiah" also has strong and familiar traditions among his fellow Jews. For centuries the people have awaited the coming of the Messiah. For John to suggest that Jesus represents the long-awaited One certainly shifts authority and power away from himself and over to Jesus. To make his intentions ever clearer, John remarks to his disciples, "He must increase, but I must decrease" (3:30). From such lucid remarks,

41

John has made his role and that of Jesus known to the disciples: John acts as a witness to the importance of Jesus.

John continues in his role of witness when he alludes to himself as the one who is of "the earth" (3:31) and describes Jesus as being the "one who comes from heaven" (3:31). Notice in these verses the similar images found in the previous story of Nicodemus. In that discussion about rebirth, Jesus repeatedly emphasized to Nicodemus the importance of heavenly/divine thought, which comes from God, rather than an earthly/human one, which comes from our limited selves.

CHAPTER 4
John 4

John 4—Introduction

The fourth chapter of John's Gospel closely connects with the preceding chapter in three ways: First, the introductory verses (4:1–3) take up a common topic of baptism when they speak about Jesus; second, it parallels John 3 when it portrays Jesus as greater than John; third, it contrasts the unbelief of a well-educated leader of Judaism with the deepened faith of a disregarded woman of Samaria.

In this chapter of the Gospel, the writer introduces beliefs of the Samaritans. The group lived in the region of Samaria and represented a married mixture of the remnants of the old Northern Kingdom of Israel and foreigners, who were sent to Samaria as POWs by the Assyrians hundreds of years earlier (2 Kgs 17:23–41; Neh 13; Josephus, *Antiquities,* 11. 297–347). Due to this assimilation by marriage, the religion of the Samaritans differed from Judaism in some respects. For example, Jews brought sacrifices for worship to the Jerusalem Temple, while Samaritans worshipped on Mount Gerizim; Jews believed in all the biblical prophets, while Samaritans believed only in Moses as prophet. For such reasons, Jews looked down upon the Samaritans as impure, both in practice and religious belief. Subsequently, hostility between the two groups deepened over the centuries. Today, a small community of Samaritans still lives in that region.

In John 4 the author introduces a woman into the narrative. While she could easily seem suspect at first, the audience learns a great deal about what it means to be a true disciple of Jesus because of this woman. In many ways she, who remains nameless, contrasts with the preceding figure of Nicodemus. The story of

43

the woman at the well contains many lessons on the value of openness, honesty, truth, and humility.

The chapter concludes in Cana, the same spot as the wedding feast in John 2. From a distance Jesus healed the son of a royal official, who had been ill. Thus, Jesus performed the first two signs in John's Gospel while in the village of Cana. This sign introduces the first of the three healing miracles (signs) found in the Fourth Gospel. The other two signs appear in John 5 and 9.

For reading purposes the chapter may be divided as follows:

1. Jesus' encounter with the unnamed woman of Samaria (4:1–42)
2. Second sign at Cana: healing of the royal official's son (4:43–54)

John 4—Questions

37. In 4:1–42 why isn't the Samaritan woman at the well named, considering Jesus' long, intimate conversation with her?
38. How could John record the lively conversation between Jesus and the woman without anyone having been there to hear?
39. How could she possibly have had five husbands, since people didn't live very long in those days?
40. What was the mountain of Gerizim? Where is it?
41. What is the point of Jesus' announcement that he is the Messiah in this story in relation to his "hushing up" that fact in stories in other gospels?
42. What is living water?
43. Why does Jesus seem to trust the woman of Samaria more than the other persons in the preceding chapters of the Gospel?
44. In 4:27 why were the disciples shocked about Jesus' conversation with the woman?
45. The phrase "come and see" in 4:29 has been used before in the Gospel. Is there a connection?

46. In 4:42 why do the villagers speak unkindly toward the woman? Isn't she the reason they were able to meet Jesus at all?
47. Why was Jesus in Samaria? Didn't the Jews avoid Samaria?
48. In 4:53b why did the whole household believe when the father believed? That would never happen now.

John 4—Conclusion

Jesus' Conversation with the Woman of Samaria (4:1–42)

The daring discourse of the Samaritan woman at the well offers the reader Johannine artistic skill at its best. At the same time, the story describes many unusual circumstances for a first-century drama. First, due to the intense heat, noontime is the least likely time to come to a well to draw water in a desert country. Second, a woman stays at the well when a strange man comes to it. Third, a man speaks to an unknown woman. In some parts of the East, even to this day, a man does not speak to a woman stranger, especially in public. Fourth, and more surprisingly, a male Jew speaks with a female non-Jew. In ancient cultures, the laws of purity dominated. Any man who would have contact with a woman during her menstrual cycle would become unclean. Consequently, men avoided contact with women.

In this powerful drama the two main characters, namely, Jesus and the woman of Samaria, have a lively exchange. Up until recent times, anyone who researched this story would have found a very different slant on the woman. Often she was referred to as "the sinful woman" in articles and books, as well as in Sunday sermons/homilies. She was looked upon as a great sinner because of her many husbands. We were told that the powerful Jesus brought her needed forgiveness. In the various writings and sermons, the woman remained the object, not the subject of the discussion. Writers and preachers alike neglected to credit her with any redemptive qualities. Now, however, biblical scholarship has become far more sensitive to stories about women. Scholars have grown in their ability to overcome gender prejudices of the past and to study a narrative with new, inclusive eyes. Any serious student of the Bible must also study the text in this way.

In this remarkable meeting, Jesus and woman cross over all kinds of societal boundaries, such as gender, social, religious, ethnic, and geographical lines. In the ancient world and in much of the world even to this day, men and women must obey the societal norm for space. Men are permitted in the public sphere, while women must remain in the private. Women may go to a public space, such as a market, only to do the required chore. Then, they must return to the private sphere. Never do they speak with strangers of the opposite sex.

The story, however, describes a very different picture. In their conservation and their actions, both the woman and Jesus redefine the limits of public and private space that separate men and women (Malina and Rohrbaugh, *Social Science Commentary on the Gospel of John*, 99ff.). Jesus inaugurates the move by his request for water, which would include a shared drinking cup. By doing so, he risks contamination as noted in the ritual laws of purity. When the woman speaks to an unknown Jewish man, she also exceeds the boundaries of man/woman contact.

This story parallels and contrasts with the previous discourse between Jesus and Nicodemus. For example, both discussions utilize similar literary techniques such as those I have discussed previously in the introduction of the book. For example, the dialogue includes such techniques as question/answer, misunderstanding, and the rule of two prominent characters to advance the conversation and deepen it. However, while Nicodemus does not deepen his belief in Jesus as a result of the conversation, the Samaritan woman does. Moreover, Nicodemus comes to Jesus in the dead of night, which in this case represents ignorance and misunderstanding. In contrast, the Samaritan woman responds to Jesus at high noon, which signifies enlightenment and a positive response.

In the story the evangelist never mentions why the woman draws water at noon, a time when no other woman would be at the well because of the intense heat as well as the necessity for other household chores. The only hint of any personal issues arises with the question of the woman's marital status in 4:16. Could this be a cause of tension within the Samaritan community where she lived? If so, her presence at the well at noon, when she would have peace and quiet, makes sense. Whatever happened between the woman and the village, the narrative implies that the community had shunned her in some way. In three ways the name-less woman exemplifies one of the marginalized in the world: The ancient society disdains her gender, Judaism spurns her religion, and the village scorns her person. Yet, to the reader's astonishment, the woman overcomes all these negative reactions to her and remains quite positive. Her deepening faith and selfless actions continue in the face of adversity.

Within the dialogue, a range of topics appears. While Jesus' request for a drink of water (4:7) and his suggestion, "Go, call your husband," (4:16) has been unfulfilled, the woman engages in active dialogue with him. In the conversation, topics move from still water from the well to a "spring of water gushing up to eternal life" (4:14), from her personal marital status to her profound proclamation of Jesus as prophet (4:19). Note that when the woman professes Jesus to be a "prophet," she does not mean just any prophet. As you many recall from the introductory notes, the Samaritans did not believe in all biblical prophets. They held that only Moses could be honored as a true prophet. Therefore, when the woman identified Jesus as prophet, she implied parallelism with the great prophet Moses, the most important biblical figure in the Hebrew Bible for both Jews and Samaritans.

The dialogue continues in its theological topics. It climaxes at the moment when the woman declares that she awaits the arrival of the Messiah and Jesus claims to her surprise that "I am he" (4:26). When we read the dialogue between the woman and Jesus, we notice the deepening level of their conversation and confidence toward each other. Unlike the previous chapter, when Nicodemus could not break through his resistance to Jesus' words, the woman of Samaria does. As a result of her unreserved trust, she has the ability to hear and dialogue with Jesus about the important issues of life. The courageous woman of Samaria has captured the trust of Jesus. Since the woman responds to Jesus and opens her heart to his insightful wisdom, Jesus can reveal himself to her.

His ever-deepening trust of her becomes evident as he showers her with verbal gifts of self-revelation, which culminates in his Messiah proclamation. When Jesus admits openly to the woman that he is the Messiah, he chooses her as the first person in the Fourth Gospel to whom he reveals himself. As you may have guessed, it remains quite ironic that Jesus, will all his divine qualities and endless options, chooses this unnamed and despised woman of another religion to share his true self. Thus, he exhibits his trust and respect for her person.

Moreover, when the topic of her past marriages and shared living arrangements surface, Jesus never judges or condemns her actions. Rather, he continues the dialogue because of the openness and truthfulness of the woman. In effect, Jesus treats the woman as a respected confidant.

The woman's conversation with Jesus concludes with the return of the disciples (4:27). The writer comments that they "were astonished" that Jesus spoke with this woman. After all, she was a Samaritan, a people who were at odds with the Jews. Furthermore, the person remained both a stranger and a woman! Despite their many questions and potential accusatory comments, the disciples said nothing to Jesus about their wonderment. Their uneasiness about questioning Jesus (4:27) contrasts sharply with the brave inquiries of the woman. Fear blocks growth in individuals, in community, and in society. Decisions made through fear rarely benefit anyone. On the other hand, this story demonstrates that courage, openness, and truth lead to God. The woman's fortitude with Jesus brought countless blessings to her and to the others.

In one other way, the actions of the woman contrast with those of the other disciples. After the woman leaves the scene to go to the village, Jesus speaks to the others in a parable-like fashion. He states, "I sent you to reap that for which you did not labor. Others have labored, and you have entered into their labor" (4:38). Aside from Jesus, the woman appears as the only other one who has labored because she returned to tell her neighbors in the village about Jesus. At this instance, Jesus encourages his other disciples to appreciate the self-sacrificing labors of this nameless woman.

To appreciate the selfless kindness of the woman, the conclusion of the story has her return to the village to announce the good news about Jesus. In effect, the nameless woman of Samaria exemplifies the epitome of a model disciple. She dialogues with Jesus, opens her heart to him, presents no self-defense or self-justification when presented facts about her life, risks ridicule so that others benefit from Jesus, and brings others to Jesus through her words and actions. The writer of the Gospel fosters the valuable role of the woman leader when he states, "Many Samaritans from that city believed in him [Jesus] because of the woman's testimony" (4:39).

Healing of the Royal Official's Son (4:43–54)

After a brief and somewhat awkward introduction (4:43–45), the next story begins with Jesus' return to Cana, the site of the wedding feast in John 2. This account describes the second sign in the Gospel, namely, the cure of a royal official's son. While the son lay sick in Capernaum, Jesus heals him from afar in Cana.

We cannot help but recall the first sign performed also in Cana because the writer refers to it twice (4:46, 54). Such emphasis indicates some similarities between the formats of the two Cana miracles: Jesus returns to Galilee; a person requests something from him; momentarily, Jesus seems to distance himself from the request; the one who requests persists gently; Jesus performs the miracle. Moreover, the writer's emphasis on Cana helps to distinguish the two stories in John 4 from one another. It also anticipates a show of belief from the royal official, recalling the belief of the disciples after the performance of the first sign in John 2. Therefore, the inclusive mention of Cana serves many purposes.

Some scholars suggest a link between this sign in Cana and the miracle stories of the centurion (Matt 8:5–13) or the servant (Luke 7:1–10) found in these other two gospels. Whatever the case, a royal official would be of high status in the town. People would show him great respect because of his social position. Normally, no high-level figure would make an important request of someone below his rank, such as a carpenter from Nazareth. Therefore, this story immediately reveals the humility and openness of the official.

Even after Jesus replied with a harsh retort, "Unless you see signs and wonders you will not believe" (4:48), the official did not back down. Rather, he continued to request help for his son. When Jesus answered, "Go, your son will live" (4:50), the faith of the royal official went from a belief in the power of Jesus to a belief in the person of Jesus. At that moment, the royal official saw no sign, no healing of his beloved son. Rather, he left Jesus to return to his home because he now believed in the words of Jesus alone. This deepening of faith leads to the conversion of the entire man's household (4:53). The second sign of Jesus healed not only the son, but also deepened the beliefs of the family.

We do not know what religious tradition the man held. If he were Gentile, this second sign indicates the spread of Christianity to them, just as the first episode in John 4, the encounter of Jesus with the woman, infers the spread of Christianity to the Samaritans. In addition, both stories testify to the reality of the importance of belief in the person of Jesus.

CHAPTER 5
John 5

John 5—Introduction

John 5 introduces the conflict between Jesus and the Judean and Galilean religious leaders that will continue in the next five chapters. Some of the conflict comes in the form of threats to kill Jesus. The actions of Jesus surface amid various Jewish feasts. In John's Gospel Jesus replaces these important Jewish feasts with himself. His famous "I am" sayings will reveal the replacements.

The chapter commences with the words "after this" in 5:1 and closes with same words "after this" in 6:1. These same words form an inclusion, which represents a literary technique to open and close a section. Thus, John 5 appears as a comprehensive unit that begins with a miracle story (sign) and ends in a very important lengthy discourse. This format appears in other chapters in John, where the miracle itself does not seem to be center stage. Rather, it serves as a catalyst for the important discourse that will follow. Throughout 5:19–47 Jesus remains the only one who speaks.

This chapter leads the way for the many difficult moments that Jesus faced over his performance of miracles on the Sabbath (for example, 7:22, 23; 9:14, 16). For strict Judean leaders, to heal on that particular day of rest means to dishonor the third commandment and all that it encompassed. Any type of work on the weekly Sabbath day has been forbidden for hundreds of years before the time of Jesus. Both the Law and the prophets spoke out against it (Exod 20:8–11; Deut 5:12–15; Jer 17:21; Neh 13:19; and so on).

In addition, the discourse opens with a comparison between Jesus and God the Father (5:19–30). In this section Jesus clarifies his relationship to the Father and the two acts that belong to

51

them alone, specifically, the bestowal of life and judgment. Both his actions and words cause a growing rift between himself and certain religious leaders of Judaism.

For reading purposes the chapter may be divided as follows:

1. Third sign (Jerusalem): cure of the paralytic on the Sabbath (5:1–18)
2. Jesus' relationship with God (5:19–47)

John 5—Questions

49. What festival is mentioned in 5:1?
50. What does the "stirred up" water mean in 5:7?
51. Why does John have to mention that the miracle took place on the Sabbath?
52. In 5:14 why does Jesus connect sin with sickness?
53. John seems quite clear about why Jesus was killed and who he is in 5:16–47. Why don't the disciples seem to get it?
54. Why did the officials think that by calling God his Father, Jesus made himself equal to God?
55. Does 5:22–23 seem conceited? Is that Jesus speaking?
56. What does the "Son of Man" mean in 5:27?
57. In 5:24–29 Jesus speaks in terms of the present moment and then in terms of the future. Is he talking about the *parousía* or the *eschaton*? What do these terms mean and what is the difference between the two?
58. What did Moses write about Jesus (5:46)?

John 5—Conclusion

Cure of the Paralytic in Jerusalem (5:1–18)

In format the chapter can be divided into three sections: the introduction; the miracle, which itself can be separated further into three parts (the issue, the miracle itself, and response to the miracle); and the extended dialogue. The setting in this scene takes place at the pool of Bethzatha, which represented a place of great healing for the ancients. Therefore, the healing of the paralyzed man took place at a very appropriate site.

In the twentieth century, archeologists did not find the five porticoes that originally comprised the edifice, but they did uncover two connected pools near the present day Church of St. Anne in Jerusalem, which lies inside the walled city. In the first century, this area was situated outside the walls near the northeast corner of the Temple. In the second century, the emperor Hadrian used this location for the cult of Asklepios, the healing god.

The author presents many parallels between the healing story here in John 5 and the healing of the blind man in John 9. Both stories have the following similarities:

1. They occur during a Jewish religious feast.
2. Jesus heals both people on the Sabbath.
3. They become cured after they follow Jesus' commands.
4. The two narratives describe how some Jewish leaders condemn the actions of Jesus because he healed on the Sabbath.
5. Both stories state that these leaders judge Jesus and that he, in turn, judges them.

On the other hand, the personality of the paralyzed man in John 5 does not develop within the narrative, whereas the story of the man born blind in John 9 describes a development of his believing attitude toward Jesus.

Jesus' Relationship with God (5:19–47)

The miracle itself remains brief and clear, as in other signs within the Gospel. The tension arises after the completion of Jesus' merciful cure of the infirm man, when the issue of working on the Sabbath arises. At first, some religious leaders complained about Sabbath law being broken only by the cured man because he carried his mat (bed), which was prohibited on the Sabbath (see Exod 20:10; Neh 13:19; Jer 17:21–22). After the man

explained that Jesus had cured him, these officials "started persecuting Jesus, because he was doing such things on the sabbath"
(5:16). Therefore, the text clearly states that Sabbath violation
caused a major rift between Jesus and these religious officials.

To counteract their persecution, Jesus clarifies his relationship
to God the Father in order to justify his behavior on the Sabbath.
When he equates himself to God in 5:17 with the words, "My
father is still working, and I also am working," these officials were
furious and considered him a blasphemer. They became angered
enough to want to kill him. Jesus knew what their reactions
would be because he knew how obstinate bystanders like them
would judge the situation. Yet, despite their growing resentment,
not only does he make this bold statement, but he continues to
expound his theme of equality with God the Father in 5:19–30.

The discourse commences in 5:19. It climaxes with the argument about the violation of the Sabbath, which resulted from the
preceding cure. It also further details Jesus' unanticipated claim
to divinity in 5:17. In the discourse, Jesus insists on his joint work
with the Father. The phrase "very truly" in 5:19 and 5:25 acts as
an attention grabber to make the listeners aware of very important forthcoming statements. After both phrases, Jesus announces
that both the Father and he have the power to "give life" and to
"judge." In Judaism as well as Christianity, these acts have always
been the prerogative of God. Therefore, the Sabbath cannot
interrupt the actions of the Divine.

In 5:21 the introductory phrase, "just as...so also" equates the
divine functions of the Father with those of his Son, Jesus. The
power to give life prepares the reader for the raising of Lazarus in
John 11 and Jesus' own resurrection in John 20. Moreover, the
giving of life signifies a new era, the era of God.

In 5:24–27, Jesus announces the arrival of divine life to all who
believe in him. Clearly, Jesus indicates that this divine life begins
in the present moment with statements such as "anyone who
hears my word and believes in him who sent me HAS eternal
life,... DOES not come under judgment,... HAS passed from
death to life,... the hour...is NOW here" (I inserted the capital-
ization to emphasize the message). Here Jesus talks about resurrection and eternal life in the present moment, which indicates

that this life begins here and now. He speaks of the need to believe him right now because how people believe and behave in the present determines their future in divine life.

These verses contrast with those in 5:28–29, where Jesus speaks of judgment in terms of the future. Here Jesus addresses those who have already died and "will hear his voice and will come out." Those who have lived their lives already doing good, being compassionate and forgiving toward others, will merit "the resurrection of life." They will continue in a loving *life* because they have given life and love to others. At the same time, those who have lived in selfishness, self-absorption, and uncaring ways will achieve the "resurrection of condemnation" because they have brought pain, dissension and death to others. In a very real sense, then, this discourse refutes any type of predestination. Jesus indicates that we are the ones who choose either *life* or *death* in the future by the very way in which we lead our lives in the present. Such everyday living determines our future in the next life.

The above discussion does not rule out the possibility of personal and/or communal change in our lives. As humans we all sin. In biblical terms, the Greek term to sin, namely, *harmartano*, means "to miss the mark." Throughout life we "miss the mark" in various ways: resentment, unkindness, nonaction, refusal to forgive, coldness toward others, and so on. In all such instances, we have the ability to change our ways and our attitude *if* we open our hearts to God and ask for help. As living, developing human beings, we need to change in order to grow in every aspect of our lives. Growth cannot happen without change. Therefore, as we grow and mature in our attitudes and actions, we choose *life* because we have changed. Our growth brings life to others. If, on the other hand, we refuse to change, to listen to others, to reach out to them, we have already chosen *death*. In this case, our stagnation causes death to others.

In the second part of the discourse (5:31–49) Jesus discusses his relationship with his Father. He points out that he must do good works like those of his Father, who has sent him. The tension over the miracle being performed on the Sabbath in this Gospel differs from those being done in the Synoptic Gospels. For example, when Jesus performs miracles in the Gospel of Mark

(2:27), it states that the Sabbath was instituted for humankind and not for God. While the outcome may be the same, namely, the gratitude of the one healed, as well as the wrath of some Judean leaders, the reason remains different. In the Fourth Gospel the evangelist centers on the actions of Jesus being the reflection of God. He, like his Father, performs good works and gives life to others anytime, even on the Sabbath.

However, these leaders refuse to listen. So, Jesus points out three witnesses that verify the truth he speaks: John the Baptist, who testified about Jesus; his own good works, such as the cure of the paralytic; and God the Father, who sent him to perform such good works. These leaders do not accept Jesus because they do not believe in Jesus or want to come to him for *life*. Therefore, they refuse to accept the witness of John the Baptist about Jesus. They also do not accept Jesus' selfless actions or profound words, even though they have been educated to do so. Their loveless reactions to Jesus reflect their resentment toward him. They choose death and become enraged rather than choose life and become enriched.

Despite their lack of faith, Jesus refuses to judge them. He tells them that Moses will judge their unbelief, since they placed their hope in him. Finally, in 5:46 Jesus states, "If you believed Moses, you would believe me, for he wrote about me." By this Jesus implies that these leaders do not believe the Torah (first five books of the Bible, traditionally composed by Moses), which represents a very serious accusation against them. Such words would surely enrage the already close-minded leaders. Moreover, the introduction of Moses leads the way for the bread of life motif in John 6.

CHAPTER 6
John 6

John 6—Introduction

John 6 presents a series of manifestations of Jesus to others: in the feeding of the five thousand, in the disciples' journey to the other side of the sea, and in his self-revelation as the "bread of life." While the sign (miracle) and discourse took place in Jerusalem in the previous chapter, John 6 opens with Jesus on the hills and then on the shores of the Sea of Galilee (Sea of Tiberias) far from the city. The shore towns of Capernaum and Tiberias are mentioned in these stories. The sign of the multiplication of the loaves and fishes takes place sometime near the next Jewish Passover the following spring. The Gospel does not explain the absence of the intervening months between John 5 and 6.

Once again this chapter opens with the phrase, "after this." The theme of Jesus as the origin of life permeates the whole chapter. It functions as a replacement theme. Jesus replaces the feast of Passover as well as provides both momentary and everlasting nourishment in the form of bread, and then wine.

The origin-of-life theme surfaces in two basic questions that arise during the chapter. The first, in 6:5, is when Jesus asks Philip, "Where are we to buy bread for these people to eat?" While the query sounds like a true question, it serves a rhetorical purpose. Jesus knows how to feed the people in body as well as spirit. Later in the chapter, he will proclaim in many and varied ways that he is the "bread of life" (6:35, 41, 48, 51, 55, 58). At the end of the chapter, in 6:68, Peter asks a second related question to the origin-of-life theme: "Lord, to whom can we go [that is, for the bread of life]?"

In one sense both questions form a literary inclusion because they appear at the beginning and end of the chapter so as to keep intact the theme of the origin of life. In both the two miracles and in the extended conversation, Jesus surfaces as the one who gives life to all who believe in him.

For reading purposes the chapter may be divided as follows:

1. Fourth sign: the feeding of the people along the Sea of Galilee (6:1–14)
2. Jesus walks on the sea and leads his disciples to safety (6:15–21)
3. Bread of life discourse and "I am" sayings of Jesus (6:22–71)

John 6—Questions

59. Is the Sea of Galilee far from Jerusalem (6:1)?
60. In 6:9 why does the story say that the young boy had "barley loaves"? I thought that the loaves were supposed to be wheat, especially if this is a reference to the Eucharist.
61. In 6:14 what is does mean when the people say, "This is indeed the prophet who is to come into the world"?
62. In 6:17 does the statement, "It was now dark," have any significance?
63. Please explain the meaning of *epiphany*.
64. What does it mean in 6:15 that Jesus withdrew "to the mountain" after the crowd tried to make him king?
65. Do the named towns of Capernaum (6:17, 24) and Tiberias (6:23) have any significance?
66. Why does John 6 contrast Jesus with Moses? Why is Moses so important for the discussion?
67. What is the importance and meaning of the "I am" sayings about Jesus, for example, "I am the bread of life"?
68. Is 6:51—7:1 the reason that Christians have sometimes been thought of as cannibals?

John 6—Conclusion

Sign of Bread and Fish (6:1–14)

Unlike some other chapters, John 6 begins with two signs (miracles) instead of one and then moves on to a long discourse of Jesus. This feeding of the five thousand represents the only miracle story that appears in all four gospels. Of course, minor differences among the stories occur. For example, the author introduces Andrew and Philip into the narrative. This Gospel alone mentions the young boy with the barley loaves who came to Jesus' aid as the crowd grew hungrier. Thus, this first sign in 6:1–15 presents Jesus as the giver of life because he gives bread to those in need of physical sustenance. The point that the crowds come to listen to Jesus instead of "going up" to Jerusalem at this time of Passover suggests that the person of Jesus replaces the feast of Passover.

The occasion of Passover and the motif of bread to feed the hungry recall another story in the Hebrew Bible. In the Book of Exodus Moses interceded with God to feed the escaped Israelites, who fled from the Pharaoh in Egypt. God provided them with manna and quail from heaven. The Israelites ate it as nourishment while they traveled in the desert after the first Passover and their flight from Egypt. Now, in 6:1–15, Jesus provides the hungry with bread and fish. In this way, Jesus replaces Moses as the giver of life. In addition, Jesus "withdrew again to the mountain," as Moses went up Mount Sinai.

As for the miracle itself, Jesus himself recognizes the need of the people to eat and tests Philip in 6:5 with the question, "Where are we to buy bread for these people to eat?" The sacred irony jumps out of the text. The One who will soon declare that he is "the bread of life" now asks where to get bread. We all recognize that without bread (food) we die. Bread gives us sustenance, growth, and life. Therefore, the sign of the multiplication of the bread and fish leads to a deeper reality about not *where* but *who* is the origin of life. The answer lies in the lengthy discourse about Jesus, the bread of life.

Within the miracle the inadequate supply of five barley loaves and two fish (6:9) turned into abundant leftovers of twelve baskets of food (6:13). With God an abundance of generosity signals a divine calling card. Moreover, the language of Jesus' action in 6:11 recalls the actions of the eucharistic meal. While the institution of the Eucharist does not appear in the Gospel of John, the following words suggest the formula adopted by the early Christian community for the Eucharist: "Then Jesus took the loaves, and when he had given thanks, he distributed them to those who were seated." The verb form "had given thanks" comes from the anglicized Greek term *eucharist,* which means "thanksgiving." The eucharistic formula used here anticipates the washing of the feet at the Last Supper in John 13 in that Jesus will offer the disciples a "how to" live out the Eucharist in their lives. In the later chapter, the author replaces the verbal formula of the Eucharist meal with an action of great humility for the community. Together, they describe both the sacredness of the meal and the outcome of true participation in the Eucharist.

Jesus Leads His Disciples to Safety (6:15–21)

The scene of the disciples being led by Jesus to safety as they crossed over the sea (6:16-21) reminds the reader again of the conglomerate group of Hebrews and others who escaped from Egypt and crossed over the Reed Sea on their way to freedom. In the Book of Exodus, God brought them to safety under the guidance of Moses, while here in the Gospel Jesus, God's own Son, brought the disciples to safety himself. In parallel stories in the Synoptics (Mark 1:32–34; Matt 8:16–17; Luke 4:40–41), the scene serves as a nature miracle, where Jesus rebukes the sea and the disciples marvel in awe of his strength over it. Here, however, the account differs. The writer focuses not on the power of Jesus but on his words of self-revelation. Now, let us turn to more details of the story itself.

After the feeding miracle, Jesus removed himself from the crowd because they wanted to make him king. The text mentions

that "he withdrew again to the mountain by himself" (6:15).
This reference to "the mountain" in 6:15 forms an inclusion with
the beginning of the narrative in 6:3, where it has been first
reported that Jesus "went up to the mountain." As you may
recall, an inclusion represents a literary device that holds a story
together by having the same phrase/words at the beginning and
end of the piece. Thus, an inclusion ties the story together and
ends the account of the multiplication of the loaves and fish.

After the event the people proclaim Jesus as Mosaic prophet
and try to force him to be king so as to meet their physical needs.
Their words and actions demonstrate their misunderstanding of
Jesus' mission. Such misunderstanding leads to unbelief in and
rejection of the real Jesus. This response of the people leads Jesus
to flee by himself to the mountain. As for the disciples, they also
left the spot and by evening went by boat to Capernaum, where
they encountered a severe storm at sea. Suddenly, they saw Jesus
walking on the sea toward them and "were terrified" (6:19).

Remember that they had just rowed three or four miles out
into the center of the sea. Night has fallen, they are exhausted
from rowing, a storm arises, and then they see Jesus "walking on
the sea." Naturally, they become "terrified." When we add the
ancient beliefs about monsters under the sea into the equation, it
becomes really understandable that they would be "terrified" in
every sense of the word.

Immediately, Jesus eases their fear with the climatic statement
of the entire episode. In 6:20 he proclaims tenderly to them "It
is I; do not be afraid." Literally, the Greek term *egō eimi,* which
means "I am," has been employed. The proclamation will be seen
later in this chapter, as well as throughout the Gospel. The
announcement recalls the answer to Moses' question in Exodus
3:14, when he asked God his name. The divine reply to Moses
was "I am who I am." You may remember that Jesus gave this
reply to the Samaritan woman's question about the arrival of the
Messiah in 4:26, when he said that "I am he." Here, however, the
statement does not answer a question. Rather, Jesus' announcement proclaims to the disciples that, as the Son of God, he is
divine and that his divinity overcame the sea and all that lies
beneath it. Consequently, fear has been conquered with hope. As

in the case of the feeding of the crowds in the preceding narrative, Jesus comes to the rescue of others.

Bread of Life Discourse and "I AM" Sayings of Jesus (6:22–71)

John 6:22–24 introduces the next large discourse section with an explanation of what happened to the crowds who were with Jesus and had miraculously been fed the day before. The text narrates that they went by boat to Capernaum to find Jesus. When they found him, they greeted him as "rabbi." The Hebrew term means "teacher" and shows respect to the person addressed. Jesus warns them not to seek him solely because of the miracle of food the day before. Such food perishes. In the Greco-Roman world of first-century Palestine, the majority of people lived in poverty. They barely made enough to clothe and feed themselves and their families. Therefore, the possibility of receiving daily sustenance from Jesus made them most anxious to stay with him. In their minds, a continuance of his barley bread and fish would make future life possible for them because they could cease worrying about the purchase of daily food.

In this scene Jesus recognizes their hopes for physical relief, but offers them a deeper level of growth. He calls them to "the food that endures for eternal life" (6:27). He tries to encourage them to a deeper level of commitment to him rather than just to his gifts of food. Jesus invites them to a lasting and more meaningful commitment. He encourages them to believe in him.

Belief describes a complete openness of the heart and a loyal devotion to "the other." The concept of belief in Jesus permeates the Fourth Gospel. "To believe in" occurs countless times throughout the chapters to indicate or to encourage a person's wholehearted commitment to the person of Jesus. This invitation "to believe in" Jesus initiates a long solemn discourse about the person of Jesus. It exemplifies one of several such discussions in chapters to follow. In their own way, these discussions emphasize Jesus as the revealer of God, as the one sent by God and the one who invites others to follow.

From here on in the discourse, Jesus reveals his role as the bread of life, as the one who comes down from heaven, as the one sent by the Father, and as the one who gives eternal life. Yet, despite Jesus' summons to seek heavenly food that gives life to the world, the crowd does not comprehend his words and asks for another sign like the manna in the time of Moses that their ancestors received daily in the desert. Interestingly, the references to these specific stories in Exodus exemplify the chosen reading at the time of Passover. Here, then, the feast of Passover, which in the other gospels occurs at the celebration of the Last Supper, connects with Jesus as food for eternal life. Jesus supersedes and replaces the Jewish Passover.

Once again the author parallels Moses and Jesus over this issue of bread. After Jesus reminds them that God sent the manna, not Moses, he refers to the true bread, which "comes down from heaven and gives life to the world" (6:33). While bread serves as a temporary reprieve from hunger, the bread of life (Eucharist) affects the recipients forever. As one sent by God the Father, Jesus emerges as the one who nourishes anyone in need.

When they asked for this bread, Jesus responds with a powerful proclamation, "I am the bread of life" (6:35). He repeats this disclosure again in 6:48 as he alludes to the Exodus story of manna in the wilderness. Moreover, he reveals this divine reality in other ways throughout the discourse, such as, "I am the living bread" (6:51), and, "whoever/ the one who eats this bread will live forever" (6:51, 58). Yet, they still do not comprehend. Finally, Jesus describes the bread as his flesh (6:51, 53–57) and the drink as his blood (6:54). This difficult announcement, which refers to the participation in the Eucharist, serves as a proclamation of relationship and intimacy between Jesus and the believers. Yet, from such a declaration, many people questioned, complained, were offended, and often made negative decisions about their relationship with Jesus.

In John 6, then, people seem to exhibit all sorts of emotion. At first many seem to want to follow him. While to follow Jesus signifies a step in the right direction, the motives of the people do not necessarily lead to belief in Jesus. In 6:2 a large crowd followed Jesus because of the signs he performed. After the sign of the multiplication of the loaves and fish, the people want Jesus to meet their earthly needs (6:14–15) by forcing him to be king. After Jesus' proclamation about being the "bread of life," they still do not acknowledge his person. Rather, they want their needs met and ask to be given "this bread always" (6:34). Ultimately, when Jesus proclaimed the bread as his flesh and the drink as his blood and announced that they must partake of these for true life, the leaders, the crowd, and many of his disciples did not accept his teachings and left him. While he offered them the food of eternal life, they refused his gift.

By the end of the discourse the life-filled actions and words of Jesus have proven to bring loss of true life to the unbelievers. Many left Jesus. One disciple stayed in physical presence, but had hardened his heart and would soon betray him. The evangelist states that Jesus talked to the inner group of the Twelve after so many left him. This moment marks the first time in John's Gospel that Jesus speaks alone with his inner group about their personal responses to his words. When he asks them about their intentions to stay or leave, Peter replies rhetorically in the name of the others, "Lord, to whom can we go? You have the words of eternal life" (6:68). Furthermore, Peter states, "We have come to believe and know that you are the Holy One of God" (6:69). With this profound reply, Peter capsulizes some themes of John 6, such as the acknowledgement that Jesus is the chosen one and he gives the words of eternal life.

CHAPTER 7
John 7 and 8

John 7—8 The Feast of Tabernacles (Sukkoth) and Discourses

John 7 and 8 form one unit of thought, with the exception of the story about the woman caught in adultery (7:53—8:11). For that reason we shall study first the passages that form a unit and then move to the adultery narrative, even though the narrative comes logistically in between the two connecting blocks of material.

The controversy with some religious authorities from Jerusalem in John 5 continues in John 7 and 8. This controversy takes place during and relates to the feast of Tabernacles/Booths (Sukkoth). The scene continues in Galilee from John 6 until Jesus travels as a pilgrim to Jerusalem for that feast. John 7 connects with John 8, where the feast continues. Both chapters contain themes that reflect the observance of Tabernacles/Booths (Sukkoth) in the feast's use of water and light. The topic of water appears in 7:37–38, whereas the topic of light surfaces in 8:12. As a result, chapters 7 and 8 will be presented as a whole, using three major divisions:

1. John 7, which introduces the feast of Tabernacles (Sukkoth)
2. John 8:12–59, in which the feast of Tabernacles continues
3. John 7:53—8:11, the woman caught in adultery

John 7—Introduction

Overall, John 7 divides into three sections: the opening scene (7:1–13); midway through the feast of Tabernacles (7:14–36); the last day of the feast (7:37–52). Within these sections many themes appear, such as the appearance of Jesus' brothers, the tensions between Jesus and those who did not believe in him, the contrast again between Moses and Jesus, the Sabbath issue of performing miracles on that day, the issue of Messiah again, the question of the origins of Jesus, and a failed attempt to arrest him.

John 7—Questions

69. In 7:1 why were the Jews looking for an opportunity to kill Jesus?
70. Please explain the Jewish feast of Tabernacles/Booths (Sukkoth).
71. In 7:3, 5, 10 what does *his brothers* mean? Did Jesus have brothers or does the term mean something else here?
72. What does it mean in 7:5 that "not even his brothers believed in him"?
73. The word *complain(ing)* comes up in 7:12, as it did in 6:41. Does it have the same meaning in ancient times as it does today?
74. Why were some people who believed in Jesus afraid to support him, as 7:13 states?
75. Does the phrase *going/went up* to Jerusalem have any meaning? Often it seems that Jesus goes south to get to this city.
76. What was the Jewish expectation of the prophet, as in 7:40?
77. What did the crowd mean when it exclaimed that Jesus was the Messiah in 7:41?

John 7—Conclusion

Feast of Tabernacles (7:1–52)

John 7 demonstrates the growing disbelief in Jesus from some religious leaders of Judea as well as his own relatives. As a result, much dissatisfaction appears in these various groups of people. Similar to the tension in John 5 and 6, "grumbling" causes division within the Judaic community. Throughout the chapter, such division appears not only evident, but it seems to increase. As a result, Jesus' words of rebuttal and accusation become stronger.

Like John 5 and 6, the chapter opens with the phrase, "after this" *(metà taûta)*, as a typical transition into another narrative of the Gospel. At the beginning of the chapter Jesus is still in Galilee, where he had been in John 6. Once more, the writer announces that some Judeans wanted to kill him. Therefore, the division among the people concerning Jesus becomes more apparent with each specific instance. For example, 7:5 states that "his brothers did not believe in him." Moreover, the tension against Jesus increased outside his family as well. When he did not appear at the feast with other Galileans, some religious leaders of Jerusalem questioned his whereabouts and many in the crowds "murmured" against him. Some questioned his academic background and authority to teach, while others criticized him as a seeker of his "own glory" (7:18). Some blurted out to Jesus' face, "You have a demon!" (7:20). Other religious leaders went even further and tried unsuccessfully to have him arrested (7:32).

Comments and actions like these caused a division among the people. While some still believed in Jesus, they did not acknowledge it on account of their fear. Fear remains one of the most crippling of all diseases. Fear blocks our ability to listen attentively, to think clearly, to decide wisely, and to grow maturely. If we live our lives in fear, we remain enslaved. Decisions made in fear impede growth because they do not tolerate new possibilities. Lives lived in fear cause our inner life to die slowly. Fear hinders hope, and without hope in our lives we have already died within ourselves. Therefore, characters like Nicodemus in John 3, who came in darkness to meet with Jesus, as well as some of the believers in the crowd, who were afraid to support Jesus, could not grow at that moment of their lives. Their fear crippled their abilities to make the right choices for themselves, and thus they lost out on the grace-filled moments that were given to them.

One final proclamation of Jesus caused more consternation among the people. On the last day of the feast, Jesus announced to the crowds: "Let anyone who is thirsty come to me" (7:37). During the feast the symbolic act of carrying water from the pool of Siloam to the Temple each day symbolizes the people's prayer for early rain during the upcoming rainy season. The procession of water also commemorates the flow of water from the rock, which occurred while the followers of Moses wandered in the desert (Exod 17:1–7).

With his powerful proclamation in 7:37, Jesus replaces the feast of Tabernacles with himself. Consequently, the listeners questioned Jesus' authority and origins. This discussion created further division among the people. On one side people backed Jesus momentarily with the exclamation, "This is really the prophet," or "This is the Messiah" (7:40–41). These people collided verbally with those who questioned the origin of the Messiah's birthplace with the belief that "the Messiah does not come from Galilee.... The Messiah is descended from David and comes from Bethlehem" (7:41–42).

Even when the debate thrived among the leaders, defense of Jesus could not override the stubbornness of his objectors. In 7:50–52 Nicodemus, the Jewish leader of John 3, spoke up. The evangelist mentions that he held membership in the Sanhedrin. In the first century CE the Sanhedrin served as the supreme religious council among the Jews. It was centered in Jerusalem and was composed of three leadership groups, who acted as a judicial court for the people. The Sanhedrin became the link to the Roman governor, who occupied the land. It also preserved order among the Jewish population.

Despite his entreaty, Nicodemus could not persuade colleagues from the Sanhedrin to give Jesus a hearing. Many saw Jesus as the opposition and refused to view him in any other way. John 7 concludes with the resentment against Jesus at an all-time high.

John 8:12–59—Introduction

Despite the fact that the narrative about the adulterous woman appears at the beginning of John 8, most scholars view it as a later insert, thus disrupting the flow of the story. For this reason, it will be studied after the continued discourse during the feast of Tabernacles, which comprises 8:12–59. In John 8:12 and following, Jesus continues to dialogue with the crowds in Jerusalem during the feast. As in John 7, he employs an image from the Tabernacle feast itself in his conversation. Among the topics of his address, he speaks of light, judgment, departure, self-identity, Abraham, freedom, and truth.

John 8:12–59—Questions

78. Why is the issue of Jesus' testimony such an important one in 8:13–14, 17–18?
79. Why does Jesus teach in the Treasury of the Temple in 8:20?
80. What does it mean in 8:48 when some Jews accuse Jesus of being a "Samaritan" and having a "demon"?

John 8:12–59—Conclusion

This section opens with a profound pronouncement of Jesus to his audience in Jerusalem. Through his remarkable revelation, "I am the light of the world" (8:12), Jesus again replaces a theme of light from the feast of Tabernacles (Sukkoth) with himself. In 7:37, he utilized the theme of water from the feast to invite all the people to come to him for their needs of thirst. Likewise, here in 8:12 Jesus uses the feast's theme of light to announce that he remains the true Light. Furthermore, this "I am the light" saying prepares the reader for John 9, the story of the man born blind.

As you remember in John 7, the theme of light surfaced. At the time of Jesus, large golden torches were lit in an outer court of the Temple during the feast. Jesus now declares that he replaces that theme of light. Moreover, this "I am" *(egō eimi)* saying reminds the Jerusalem audience of Moses' first encounter with God in the desert when he asked God his name. Therefore, most likely they would recognize Jesus' reference to himself as divine.

The powerful "I am the light of the world" declaration does not stand alone. With the same breath, Jesus continues his proclamation with the powerful words, "Whoever follows me will never walk in darkness but will have the light of life" (8:12). Here Jesus accomplishes several things.

First, he invites others to follow him. In the time of Jesus, persons of great authority, for example, a well-known rabbi or a miracle worker, often had disciples who followed him. Here, like an authoritative person in the ancient world with disciples, then, Jesus opens discipleship to all who believe in him. His solemn words about light resemble passages in the Hebrew Bible, such as those in the creation story in Genesis 1:14, where God enlightened a darkened world with the words, "Let there be light." Today, we realize the important value of light in our world. For instance, after two weeks of dark bad weather, people can't wait to see and feel the sun. Further, we know the difference between the realities of being enlightened on a topic or being ignorant of it. Light plays an essential role in every aspect of our being. It brings all levels of life to us.

Second, Jesus contrasts light with darkness. In the Book of Wisdom 7:26, the author professes Wisdom to be a "reflection of eternal light." In this sense, God's image is one of light, while evil remains that of darkness. Throughout the Hebrew Bible, light and darkness were contrasted (Gen 1:3–5, 18). Light reflected God's goodness, while darkness represented the absence of God. Often light symbolized salvation (Ps 27:1, 56:13; Isa 9:2, and so on). In the first century CE, the writings of the Essenes, a Jewish splinter community who lived in Qumran on the shore of the Dead Sea, often contrasted light with darkness in their preaching and writings.

Third, Jesus uses the verb *to walk*. In contemporary society, we may have heard about the old Indian saying that prohibits any judgment of another's behavior or actions until we have "walked" in their moccasins for a few miles. In other words, we must be able to put ourselves in the shoes of another by envisioning ourselves in their circumstances before we evaluate their behavior. Here in the text, Jesus associates the verb *walk* with following him, within the phrase, "never walk in darkness." This phrase declares that, if we follow Jesus as the "light," we shall never walk in darkness. Instead, we shall walk in the way of God by actions that reflect enlightenment, such as openness toward others, refusal to judge others, and so on.

In the Judaic tradition, the verb *to walk* (Hebrew *halak*) has been used sometimes with darkness to signify evil as a contrast to light, which described the way of God (Isa 9:2; Eccl 2:14, and so on). Therefore, the mention of *walk* in 8:12 strengthens Jesus' argument about his being the eternal divine light for Israel. Moreover, when Jesus connects "light" with "life," he reflects the ancient belief that the two elements go hand in hand. When he proclaimed himself as the "light of the world," he also implied that he brings "life" to all people, if they so choose. Yet, Jesus' remarks initiate another controversy. This one arises over Jesus' self-testimony about his relation to God the Father, as well as to his disciples. The Pharisees refute his words and attempt to dishonor him.

As the conversation continues, we notice that it follows the same pattern as other discourses in previous chapters. When Jesus speaks, people do not understand and then Jesus explains the misunderstanding. This literary format in the conversation provides the opportunity for the speech to continue. For example, in 8:31–59, Jesus claims to the Judeans who continue to believe in him that "you will know the truth, and the truth will make you free" (8:32). This announcement about truth and freedom is misunderstood by the listeners. Subsequently, Jesus tries to clear up their misunderstanding with more explanation.

In contrast to superficial belief in him, which does not last, Jesus calls the audience to deeper belief, one that will bring them to truth and freedom. When he employs the terms *truth* or the *word,* he describes the divine message that he reveals. Likewise, when Jesus speaks of freedom, he means freedom from sin, rather than political or other types of freedom. His invitation leads to a discussion about Abraham.

In rebuttal to Jesus' invitation, the listeners state emphatically that, as descendants of Abraham, they have not been enslaved, but live in freedom. By their response, it becomes quite clear that they misunderstand Jesus' deeper meaning of freedom from sin because they refer to political freedom. Furthermore, they declare that "Abraham is our father" (8:39). Shortly thereafter, while in continued debate with Jesus, they change their lineage to say that "we have one father, God himself" (8:41).

The argument about lineage continues to deepen the insults from both parties. Jesus refutes their claim to divine ancestry as he reminds them, "If God were your Father, you would love me, for I came from God....He sent me" (8:42). Yet, they do not love Jesus. On the contrary, they become angrier. Therefore, they do not honor God's revealer or possess freedom.

Jesus continues to remind them that they are not free because "you are trying to kill me...you cannot accept my word...you are not from God...you dishonor me" (8:40, 43, 47, 49). The verbal attacks become stronger and culminate with Jesus' heated remark, "You are from your father, the devil" (8:44). Such remarks about ancestry cause verbal sparks to fly because their heritage has been undermined. To have the devil as a father would indicate great dishonor and shame. With his potent assertion, Jesus generates more opposition.

The reaction of the audience proves to be quite resentful and they counteract with destructive remarks. In the heat of the rebuttal they describe Jesus as "a Samaritan" who has "a demon" (8:48). These two titles reflect their undeniable growing disdain of Jesus. As you recall from the discussion in John 4, a Samaritan had a very low and scornful status in first-century Judaism. A Samaritan was regarded as unclean, unfaithful, and, in sum, a half-bred heretic. Furthermore, the audience's reference to Jesus as being possessed indicated that he retained evil within himself. Both comments prove to be extremely destructive in regards to Jesus' honor as a person.

Unlike people in Western societies, those in the East consider honor as paramount for their survival. When a group insults another's reputation, it causes destruction to that person's worth in society. Here, when many witnesses scorn Jesus, his entire honor in the eyes of others is at stake. They completely dishonor Jesus.

In reply Jesus assures them that he seeks not his own honor but that of his Father, God. Above Abraham and the prophets, Jesus reveals truth and offers freedom to others from the beginning because "before Abraham was, I am" (8:58). In reaction to the entire scene, his adversaries discontinue the verbal attack and begin a physical one. The crowd attempts to kill Jesus by stoning. This attack demonstrates their escalated anger and sense of verbal defeat. To resort to extreme physical violence reflects an inability both to continue the dialogue successfully as well as absorb the profound words of Jesus.

John 7:53—8:11—Introduction

The story of the woman caught in adultery has been placed here in this study for five reasons:

1. Due to differences in the text, most scholars agree that the story does not come from any Johannine material or source.
2. They consider the passage an addition or insertion into the text because it does not appear in early Greek manuscripts of the Gospel of John.
3. Its placement in 7:53—8:11 interrupts the discourses about the feast of Tabernacles, and therefore, it was decided to place it here, after the study of the discourses about the feast.
4. Despite its origin, the story represents an important one about the mistreatment of women in first-century Judaism.
5. This narrative connects in subject matter with the attempted stoning of Jesus in 8:59.

The text does work into Jesus' stay in Jerusalem. The passage appears as a remarkable story about an adulterous woman. The religious leaders in this passage intend to dishonor Jesus and the decision that he makes. Instead, the reverse occurs. In the end, Jesus challenges those opposed to him with one unforgettable statement. Throughout the narrative the tension between the male accusers and Jesus grows stronger as the story reaches a climax and a conclusion.

John 7:53—8:11—Questions

81. In John 3 we learned the meaning of the term *Pharisee*. What then, is a *scribe*, as mentioned in the phrase, *scribes and Pharisees* in 8:3?
82. In John 7:53—8:11 why wasn't the man also taken in adultery?
83. Why were the scribes and Pharisees the ones that caught the woman? Did they patrol?
84. What did Jesus write in the dirt or was the writing aimless?
85. How did Jesus addressing the crowd as an individual stop the mob action?
86. Is this a story about adultery or sin in general?
87. Does it seem to you as though sexual misconduct is judged more harshly than other sins, even today? Why?

John 7:53—8:11—Conclusion

Despite the fact that the narrative sounds more like stories from the other three gospels, rather than John, the lesson from the account of the woman caught in adultery remains very important. The story appears to be about the question of punishment for an adulterous woman. However, the real intent of religious authorities in this passage runs deeper. While they use the situation of the woman as an excuse, they take this opportune moment to confront Jesus in his stance on the Mosaic Law. If Jesus follows the Law of Moses, the woman will die; if he forgives her, Jesus will have broken the Law of Moses (see Lev 20:10; Deut 22:22). As always, Jesus rises above their malicious intent. Even though this small group of leaders plans to dishonor Jesus, as well as murder the woman, Jesus transcends their evil intent with a challenge of forgiveness and mercy. After he poses a challenging question to them, they eventually walk away in shame.

The opening scene in the early morning describes Jesus moving from the mount of Olives to the Temple. To do this, he would walk down the hill of the mount, through the Kidron valley and up to the Temple Mount. The writer indicates that while Jesus taught the people, some scribes and Pharisees brought an adulterous woman before him. In 8:3 the verb *caught* indicates that the men actually seized her while in the midst of a sexual act with someone other than her husband. The text never states whether this act was voluntary on her part, which remains a vital piece of information. Moreover, the text presents no reason why the religious leaders failed to bring the guilty man for judgment. Therefore, a suggestion from some scholars that the man may have run away or been unidentified seems to pale when we realize that this strong action verb *caught* leaves no doubt that the judgmental group trapped both parties in the act of intercourse or rape.

In the Hebrew Bible, the laws of Leviticus 20:10 and Deuteronomy 22:22–24 both assign punishment for the man as well as the woman. Clearly, the group does not observe the laws of Torah in this case. The fact that they never accuse the guilty man of anything, not even mentioning his role in the encounter, demonstrates a clear bias against women. This androcentric group, which intends to punish the woman severely, represents a patriarchal society that dishonors women.

Try to imagine the brutal mishandling of this petrified half-dressed woman by a self-righteous group of angry protestors who have the power to end her life. In ancient Palestine and even in many societies today, women have few, if any, religious or legal rights of their own. Rather, they live under the authority of their father until, after an arranged marriage; they leave his house to live under the authority of their husband.

The men who had caught the woman in the act of adultery threw her right in the middle of the crowd, where they demand punishment for her grave sexual sin. The honor code has been broken. Once again, the seriousness of this offense lies in the dishonor that has been brought to the family name and to the males in the family, especially the husband and the father. When one person in the family commits an offense, all members are shamed. Furthermore, sexual sin on the part of a woman brought grave dishonor to both family and community.

The tension between Jesus and the accusing group ensues as the dialogue continues. After they stood her shamefully before

75

Jesus and the crowds, those in the group confronted him with a reminder that "in the law Moses commanded us to stone such women," followed by the question, "Now, what do you say?" (8:5). Their accusatory statement characterizes an incomplete assessment of the legislation in Torah. The evangelist identifies the purpose of their question as one of trickery (8:6). Yet, Jesus rises above their expectations. At this point of the narrative, the woman no longer functions as the center of the story. She stays marginalized. Rather, the movement between Jesus and the scribes and Pharisees becomes paramount. As he responds by actions, rather than words, Jesus bends down to scribble on the ground. According to Bauer and Arndt (*Greek-English Lexicon of the New Testament and Other Early Christian Literature*), the verb "wrote/drew" in 8:6 has the connotation of merely to "draw" or to "write accusations." Whether or not Jesus wrote down other infringements of the Torah, the Jewish leaders pressed him to answer their question of 8:5.

In response, Jesus straightens up. The posture would give Jesus eye-to-eye contact with the accusers. He finally replies to their question with forceful words: "Let anyone among you who is without sin be the first to throw a stone at her" (8:7b). In this powerful response, Jesus upholds the Law of Moses about adultery, which the religious leaders stated in 8:5. Yet, he adds another important dimension that caught the accusers completely off guard. His reflective answer causes the accusers to do some immediate self-evaluation about their own lives of fidelity. If they remain so eager to judge another, even to the extent of taking life away from the woman, then they must be sinless in their own lives.

The former anxious executioners now become very silent. Once again they have been beaten verbally by Jesus. For this instant, however, Jesus' strong reply does not absolutely protect the woman from death. While we do not know explicitly if Jesus intended to assure the woman's safety, the narrator states that again he bends down and begins to write on the ground. With this moment of thoughtful reflection, Jesus may have tried to provide these angry leaders with a chance to look into their own lives rather than to judge quickly another's life. Moreover, he gave them an opportune moment to recognize their blatant prejudice against women in the interpretation of the Mosaic Law. Whatever Jesus wrote, the nonverbal action was very effective. One by one the accusers turned and walked away. By their actions, the religious leaders demonstrate two important points, namely, that they, too, have sinned against the Law and that they either have the courage to acknowledge it within their own lives or have been shamed into doing so.

Again the scene shifts to focus on the woman, her behavior, and the response of Jesus. After an interval of time, Jesus looks up to see the condemned woman alone in front of him. The two figures form a pictorial scene of hope. The woman, who has been publicly shamed and brutalized with mistreatment, stands before Jesus without any accusers. In 8:10, Jesus address of "woman" represents a title of respect, as in the case of the Samaritan woman in John 4:21. Jesus asks the woman, "Where are they? Has no one condemned you?" For the very first time in the entire narrative, the woman speaks as she replies, "No one, sir." All the accusers who brought her to Jesus have melted away.

The final conversation between Jesus and the woman displays a divine mercy that outweighs any observance of religious law ("Neither do I condemn you. Go your way, and from now on do not sin again"). Jesus' departing conversation with the woman shines out to the world about the importance of divine compassion, which must always temper justice. At the same time, the instructions to both the religious leaders (8:7) and to the woman (8:11) demonstrate that Jesus shows no partiality in this story. Both the men and the woman have been called to reflect on their own past ways, to change them and to start new lives of goodness.

CHAPTER 8
John 9

John 9—Introduction

The narrative of a man blind from birth takes place in Jerusalem. Contextually, this story connects with preceding chapters. For example, it may remind you of the story in John 5:1–9, where Jesus cured a man with paralysis. Like the story in John 5, this sign occurred during a Jewish festival on the Sabbath and at a pool in Jerusalem.

Furthermore, the story also forms a link with the feast of Tabernacles (Sukkoth) in John 7 and 8, where Jesus proclaims, "I am the light of the world. Whoever follows me will never walk in darkness but will have the light of life" (8:12). As you may recall, this fall feast used a large golden candelabrum that shined brightly within the courts of the Temple. When Jesus makes his announcement in 8:12, he replaces the theme of light within the feast of Sukkoth and becomes the eternal "Light of the world." Here in John 9 he demonstrates his revealing words from the preceding chapter with both the cure of the man born blind as well as words of encouragement to the man.

One major question encompasses the entire chapter, namely, "Who is really blind?" While the question never appears in the text, it permeates all seven scenes of the story. As you ponder the introduction and sign (miracle), conversations between the man and the neighbors, Jesus and the man, the man and the religious authorities, the parents and the authorities, you will come to recognize those who represent the "blind" and those who represent the "sighted" or enlightened people in the eyes of God. As you read the story, imagine that the episode takes place on a stage, where characters appear and disappear. Usually, two main characters or groups take center stage at one time. Within such staging, the author develops the theme of Jesus as the Light of the world in a magnificent interwoven story that demonstrates the results of generosity, belief, courage, fear, and ignorance.

For reading purposes the chapter may be divided as follows:

1. The cure of the blind man (9:1–7)
2. Discussion with the neighbors (9:8–12)
3. The cured man's encounter with the Pharisees (9:13–17)
4. The Pharisees' questioning of the parents of the blind man (9:18–23)
5. The cured man's second encounter with the Pharisees (9:24–34)
6. Jesus' meeting with the man and the Pharisees (9:35–41)

John 9—Questions

88. In 9:2 why do the disciples equate blindness with sin?
89. In 9:4 what do the day and the night images mean?
90. Why does Jesus use mud made from saliva in 9:6?
91. Is the pool of Siloam still there today? Is it visible to a visitor?
92. Why do the Pharisees blame Jesus for doing something so kind on the Sabbath?
93. In 9:20 why didn't the parents of the blind man help him out in front of the Jewish authorities?
94. In 9:34 the religious authorities are so angry. What does "and they drove him out" mean?
95. What does Jesus mean in 9:35 by the use of "Son of Man"?
96. Was the blind beggar the first to affirm that Jesus was the Son of man?
97. Why were the Pharisees so literal about blindness in 9:40?

John 9—Conclusion

The Cure of the Man Born Blind (9:1–7)

After a reading and reflecting on this the multilayered story, it becomes clearer that the author carefully knits all pieces of the narrative together with exquisite literary skill. Throughout the entire episode, the question about those who have sight and those who remain blind takes center stage. In addition, the Sabbath question continues to surface as a foil against belief in Jesus.

The scene opens at the pool of Siloam, which lies at the southeast corner of the walled Jerusalem at the juncture of three valleys, namely, the Hinnom, Central (Cheese Makers), and Kidron valleys. Like other pools in Jerusalem, many residents believed in its curative powers. Unlike the health-care system of today, Malina and Rohrbaugh (*Social-Science Commentary on the Gospel of John*, 175) maintain that the physicians in the ancient world never touched a sick person; rather, they philosophized on the symptoms or descriptions of pain from the illness. Therefore, in many cities and villages, the everyday common people granted the revered folk healer authority to heal the sick. The signs performed in John 5 and 9 reflect such actions.

The Discourse and Interrogation that Follow the Cure (9:8–41)

Jesus encounters a man blind from birth as he walks near the Siloam pool, while still in Jerusalem from the feast of Sukkoth. As you may have noticed up to this point in the Gospel, when Jesus performs a miracle, it appears to happen quickly and without any fanfare. As already mentioned, the author uses a sign (miracle) in order to promote a discourse, which usually follows it. The same scenario applies to the cure of the blind man. In two short verses (9:6–7), the man receives the ability to see. After Jesus made spittle with his saliva and commanded him, "Go, wash in the pool of Siloam," the man returned with sight. To wash in the pool of

Siloam would add to the healing process. The use of saliva on an external part of the body, such as a cut, has long been seen as curative. In addition, according to Mediterranean tradition, saliva wards off evil, known as the evil eye. Furthermore, the issue of doing work on the Sabbath again surfaces as a major contention in this sign. The comment in 9:14, "Now it was a sabbath day when Jesus made the mud," alerts the audience to the seriousness of the prohibition against work on the Sabbath.

After an unsuccessful interrogation of both the cured man as well as his parents, the authorities interrogated the healed man for a second time. They initiated the inquiry with the command, "Give glory to God!" (9:24). The summons reflects an oath formula used in the Hebrew Bible before a testimony or admission of guilt. Examples of the oath formula appear in passages such as Joshua 7:19 and Jeremiah 13:16. Their intimidation is an unsuccessful attempt to shame him into choosing Moses over Jesus. The second part of their statement in 9:24 becomes a unanimous comment about Jesus, namely, "We know that this man is a sinner." Now, the officials no longer simply question the man born blind, they harass him.

By now, however, the sighted man has become stronger in his belief in Jesus. This leads him to be more courageous and bold in his replies. Unlike his parents, who replied in fear, he chooses to challenge the very leaders who attempt to intimidate him. As they ask him to repeat the events of his healing, he replies, "I have told you already, and you would not listen" (9:27). His comment on their refusal to hear further demonstrates their hardness of heart. Then the man adds some humorous sarcasm with the rhetorical question, "Do you also want to become his disciples?" Enraged, the authorities defend their position as disciples of Moses. Their weak reply leads the man to add further humorous replies with a final declaration, "If this man were not from God, he could do nothing" (9:33). In great anger, the authorities excommunicate him.

Soon after the incident, Jesus seeks out the sighted man and offers him a new life, life in Christ. When Jesus initiates the discussion in 9:35–38 with the question, "Do you believe...?" the man asks for help to deepen his faith and finally replies, "Lord, I believe." Thus, the man, who was blind from birth, gains much more than physical sight. Since he opened his eyes, he has become truly "enlightened" in the ways of God. His belief in Jesus grew with each encounter, beginning with the neighbors, who initially brought him to the Jewish authorities, who came to resent and condemn him. The worse the situation became for the sighted man, the deeper became his faith in Jesus. His final act of belief, "he worshiped him," which describes a liturgical act reserved for God, reflects the depth of the man's belief in Jesus. Thus, this man, who had been born blind, became sight-filled in every way. He may have known little but learned much. The physical miracle of sight led to a total enlightenment, an opening of his heart to God.

Unlike the faith-filled man, the Pharisees continued to proclaim their innocence. When they heard Jesus make a final comment to the man, they asked him a rhetorical question, "Surely we are not blind, are we?" (9:40). The authoritative and self-serving remark of these religious leaders clearly illustrates that they have failed to grow at all in the presence of Jesus, who is the Light. These men, who were sighted and supposedly enlightened by intense formal education in religious matters, threw themselves into darkness and blindness. While they first appeared to be somewhat open-minded to the explanations of how the blind man became sighted (9:16–17), they became more blinded and resentful of the truth that they encountered. At first they were doubtful of the miracle, but, by the second interrogation of the man, they became hardened in their blind thoughts. They refused to learn and grow. Finally, they descended into resentfulness both of the formerly blind man and of Jesus.

Jesus responds to the question of these arrogant close-minded leaders with the reply, "If you were blind, you would not have sin. But now that you say, 'We see,' your sin remains" (9:41). In so many ways, the leaders were offered the opportunity to "see" more of the gifts of God, but they refused. Therefore, these leaders, who were sighted from birth, became blind because of Jesus. They would not accept the gift of God in their lives. Yet, because they still defended their position as sight-filled leaders, Jesus could not touch their hearts. Consequently, their sin remained. The verb *to remain* (Greek *menō*) forms a key concept in John.

While in 9:41 the verb denotes continued infidelity on the part of these Pharisees, in later chapters Jesus will employ the same Greek verb to signify his sustained fidelity to the disciples.

This magnificent story offers hope to those who believe. Clearly, it represents the triumph of light over darkness. Moreover, as the author has illustrated in other narratives, belief in Jesus remains the key to all that is life. To follow Jesus necessitates a vision and openness to the reality of what is possible in God's creative world. Finally, the theme of stubbornness of some Pharisees against Jesus in John 9 connects with their continued obstinacy in John 10 and subsequent chapters.

CHAPTER 9
John 10

John 10—Introduction

You may notice that John 10 seems to continue the discussion of John 9 between Jesus and some Pharisees without a break. Nowhere does the author indicate any change of location or occasion. In John 9 the topic centers on blindness while here in John 10 Jesus introduces a new pastoral topic about sheep. Both stories address the refusal of some Pharisees to listen to the invitational words of Jesus.

The chapter offers a variety of topics as well as a movement in time and place. The overall themes in 10:1–18 offer messages in the literary forms of parable and discourse. The narrative also concentrates on the person of Jesus as both shepherd (10:11, 14) and gate for the sheep (10:7, 9) with powerful *"egō eimi"* ("I am") sayings. Other texts refer to the celebration of the feast of Dedication (Hanukkah), the increased tension between Jesus and some of "the Jews" (10:1, 31ff.), and, for safety reasons, Jesus' departure from Jerusalem to the Jordan where John had baptized earlier.

As you consider this chapter, remember that the movement from the fall feast of Tabernacles (John 7, 8) to the winter feast of Dedication (John 10) will eventually progress to the upcoming spring feast of Passover in John 13—20. This calendar sequence leads to Jesus' moment of "glory," that is, his death, resurrection, and ascension.

For reading purposes the chapter may be divided as follows:

1. Jesus' portrayal of the good shepherd (10:1–18)
2. Divided views about Jesus at the feast of Dedication (Hanukkah) (10:19–42)

John 10—Questions

98. The gate would seem to be the easiest way to enter the sheepfold. Why would anyone want to climb in by another way?

99. If Jesus is the "shepherd of the sheep" who is the "gatekeeper"?

100. Is it correct that the gatekeeper for the sheepfold in 10:3 is *not* the shepherd?

101. In 10:6 what doesn't the audience understand in Jesus' remarks about the sheep or the image of sheep?

102. In 10:7 how can a person be a gate?

103. Shepherds earn a living by raising sheep to be slaughtered and eaten. How can that be considered good?

104. In 10:16 who are the other sheep that do not belong to the fold?

105. In 10:17 what does it mean to say that Jesus lays down his life "in order to take it up again"?

106. In 10:22 what is the festival of the Dedication?

107. Why doesn't Jesus just answer questions directly, for example, in 10:24, 25? It certainly would have made studying the Bible easier.

108. If Jesus were walking in the Portico of Solomon, where did the crowd get the stones to throw in 10:31? The Portico sounds like a porch on a building.

109. Does 10:35 mean we are all "gods"?

John 10—Conclusion

The Good Shepherd (10:1–18)

John 10 commences with a dramatic statement of honor, when he employs the phrase, "Very truly, I tell you." Some of the older translations stay closer to the original Greek with the phrase, "Amen, Amen, I say to you." I mention this point because the double use of "Amen" points to emphasis and acts as a preface to an important announcement, elucidated in 10:1–6. As a matter of fact, 10:6 uses the Greek term, *paroimian,* which means "similitude," to indicate that the enclosed narrative verses present parable-like stories somewhat similar to those found in the Synoptic Gospels.

The first parable (10:1–3a) centers on the gatekeeper of the sheep as well as the gate itself. It offers the only proper way to enter the sheepfold, namely, by way of the gate. Other ways are not honorable. As Jesus indicates clearly, the one who climbs over the fence/wall does not have admirable intentions. He even goes so far as to call that person "a thief and a bandit." Such derogatory labels refer to those who simply steal ("a thief") all the way to antisocietal members of civilization who live on the fringe and steal land, kidnap people, or attempt to overthrow governments ("a bandit").

The second parable (10:3b–6) identifies the close relationship between shepherd and sheep. In ancient Palestine, a shepherd knew his sheep and often called them by name. Moreover, instead of walking behind the sheep, he led them. They followed because they knew the sound of his voice. Anyone who has been raised or lived on a farm with sheep knows that these timid animals do follow the one who takes care of them. The sheep do not appear to be afraid of this person because they recognize by sound and sight their familiar leader, who cares for their needs. On the other hand, when sheep encounter a complete stranger, they flee, especially if that person's voice sounds strong or frightful to them. Jesus' audience would be all too familiar with the ways of sheep and the importance of a truly good shepherd. However, 10:6 states that the audience did not understand the meaning of this particular figure of speech (parable) as a way to share his thoughts. Therefore, Jesus continues to explain his meaning in the verses that follow, as he often had to do in the Synoptic Gospels when he used a parable to make a point.

Besides a misunderstanding of the parable, Malina and Rohrbaugh (*Social-Science Commentary on the Gospel of John,* 179) offer additional suggestions for the audience's inability to understand Jesus. They remind us that during the first century CE the older biblical traditions of the rustic metaphor of the "good shepherd" do not apply to the current perception of a shepherd. Jewish society in Palestine considered the profession of hired shepherd a dishonorable one and placed them with other despised groups such as sailors, ass or camel drivers, and butchers. They were seen as thieves because they disregarded the grazing property of others as well as abandoned the owner's sheep in time of trouble. Moreover, their absence from the home at night made it impossible to protect their own women and children. In short, a shepherd could not be trusted. Perhaps such notions do provide an added cause for the audience's inability to comprehend these parables of Jesus.

The next section (10:7–18) explains more clearly the two preceding parables because up this point the audience appears to be puzzled. Here Jesus proclaims more strongly the pastoral themes of the gate and shepherd. In this section he declares himself to both a "gate" and a "good shepherd" using the powerful *egō eimi* ("I am") sayings. He reminds his audience of the importance of his words of honor by a repetition of the phrase, "Very truly, I tell you."

In 10:7–10 the identification of Jesus as "the gate" appears only in this Gospel. This image centers on the right way to come close to the sheep. It serves to extend the metaphor of Jesus as the "good shepherd" in the sense that he not only leads the flock but also becomes a way for their entrance into new life. Once again Jesus reminds us about "thieves" and "bandits." When he adds the comment that they come to "kill and destroy" the lives of the sheep, he goes a step further in condemnation of them. Why? When you remember the tension that has escalated between certain Jewish leaders and Jesus since the feast of Tabernacles in John 7 and 8 and the refusal of some of the Pharisees to be "sighted" (enlightened) by Jesus' words in John 9, his comments become clear. When these leaders refuse to even listen to the "Word" of God, namely, Jesus, they become deaf and blind to God's will. Now, not only do they prevent themselves from growth in life, they "kill and destroy" growth for the Jewish communities whom they are sent to serve. On the other hand, Jesus as "the gate" provides life and freedom to all who desire it. He offers them life by granting entrance into the sheepfold to authentic leaders who will provide for the sheep. He grants freedom as "the gate" by allowing the sheep to pass through it to the free range of pastureland, which brings life and light to the sheep.

In 10:11–13 the identification of Jesus as "the good shepherd" appears as an important *egō eimi* ("I am") saying. The author attaches to both proclamations explanations about the true shepherd and a hired hand. Here he employs another very detailed parable to explain the differences between the two parties. On the one hand, the "good shepherd" protects the sheep at all times, even to the point of death. The point of dying for the sheep extends the biblical concept of the "good shepherd" theme. This highly noble gesture appears nowhere else in the Bible. As you have probably guessed, it reflects what will take place later within this Gospel, namely, that the shepherd cared so much for his sheep that he laid down his own life. Take note that Jesus does not lose his life in John's Gospel. Rather, with his own power he decides to surrender it to the authorities. Moreover, the "good shepherd" knows his sheep completely. In this way he becomes a model for others.

On the other hand, the second theme concerning the hired hand contrasts sharply with the "good shepherd." Jesus speaks about the attack of a wolf, the scattering of sheep, the snatching of other sheep, and the contrasting responses to such an attack. Whereas in times of danger the selfless shepherd would protect his sheep to the point of death, the hired hand would run away from them. He would neglect all his responsibilities for the sheep because he does not love them. This description parallels the way some leaders of the Jews have neglected their people.

In 10:14-18, after Jesus repeats, "I am the good shepherd," he closely associates himself both with God the Father and his flock. To further a unity with others outside of Judaism, Jesus announces in 10:16, "I have other sheep that do not belong to this fold. I must bring them also, and they will listen to my voice. So there will be one flock, one shepherd." As you have already read in the introduction of the book, the tension between Jews and Jewish Christians had sharpened and led to the latter's expulsion from the synagogues. At the same time, other non-Jews such as Samaritans and Gentiles had become part of the Johannine communities. Therefore, Jesus' courageous announcement continued to bring hope to those who listened to him. Jesus further announces that his proclamations have been anchored in his loving relationship with his Father. This cherished relationship flows onto his sheep, whom he protects and loves.

Divided Views about Jesus at the Feast of Dedication (Hanukkah) (10:19–42)

The reaction of some Jews (10:19–21) brought an expected division among them, just as it had in John 7—8. Pure truth has always been hard to hear. In some sense, then, the author implies that a change of heart may still be a possibility. In any case, these verses serve as a transitional segment that leads to the remaining part of the chapter.

The entire final section (10:22–40) centers around the winter feast of Dedication (Hanukkah). In the Mideast, the feast occurs in the dead of winter. The narrative states that Jesus walked within the grounds of the Temple along the Portico of Solomon. Brown (*The Gospel of John*, vol. 1, 405) suggests that this porch would be the only place among all other porticoes, whose closed side would allow protection from the strong desert winds of the East.

At this spot some Jews "gathered around" him. As the strain between Jesus and some leaders increased, the description of Jesus surrounded by the opposition adds tension to the story. In 10:24, they present the first of their two questions: "How long will you keep us in suspense? If you are the Messiah, tell us plainly." In this chapter Jesus used figurative language such as the "the gate" and "the good shepherd" to present himself. In answer to their question, he continues to respond to them by the mention of his previous good works rather than answer their question directly. Nowhere in the Gospel does Jesus answer his opponents in a direct manner, since many would not believe him anyway. As Jesus continues to speak metaphorically as a true shepherd, the questioners seem to become deaf to his words. They refuse to understand Jesus because they do not believe in him. On the other hand, his own sheep know him, hear his voice, and comprehend his message. They both see (John 9) and listen (John 10). As a result, they will "never perish" (10:28). The unity between the Father and Son underlines the unity that Jesus has addressed throughout this chapter between the "good shepherd" and his sheep. Later during the Last Supper narrative (17:11), Jesus prays to his Father that "they may be one, as we are one." Unity has always been a vital element of community. Within the Johannine community, belief in Jesus constitutes such unity.

As Jesus again spoke of his relationship with the Father, those who questioned him became incensed. When he clearly proclaimed, "The Father and I are one," in 10:30, they could no longer contain their anger because they heard only words of blasphemy rather than words of life. In 10:31 the author describes their uncontrollable anger with the comment, "The Jews took up stones again to stone him." Recall that in John 8:59 on the last day of the fall feast of Tabernacles/Booths (Sukkoth), some leaders tried before to stone Jesus after he described his relationship with the Father.

In response to their fury, Jesus asks them to see the works that he does, works that reflect the goodness of God. They reply that the works did not form the basis of their anger, but his description of himself as divine did. Therefore, they accuse Jesus of blasphemy "because you, though only a human being, are making yourself God" (10:33). Disunity among these leaders due to their refusal to see the works of Jesus or listen to his inviting words formed the basis of the present situation. Jesus responds to their accusation with two arguments: The first, in 10:34–36, comes from the Hebrew Bible where others have also been called gods; the second, in 10:37–38, expresses an appeal to the accusers to recall the good works of Jesus. After Jesus continues to respond about his oneness with the Father, these leaders try to arrest him, but he escapes once again.

The chapter concludes with a description of Jesus' flight to safety across the Jordan, where John had baptized previously. Unlike certain hardened leaders in Jerusalem, the author points out that, here, many people believed in Jesus. As a final point, John 10 prefaces John 11 and the events of the week of Jesus' passion, death, and resurrection with the various phrases and themes that have been used throughout the chapter. For example, the phrases "laying down his life" (10:11, 15) and "taking it up again" (10:17) demonstrate the authority of Jesus over all life. Moreover, the attempted arrest and stoning of Jesus in this chapter represent themes that lead the reader into subsequent chapters of John that deal with Jesus' death and resurrection.

CHAPTER 10
John 11

John 11—Introduction

John 11:1–44 serves as the climax of Jesus' ministry. In this chapter Jesus performs his final sign, namely, the restoration of life to the dead Lazarus. This most profound sign in the Gospel truly reveals Jesus as "resurrection and life." The narrative also places Jesus in Jerusalem for his last days before the crucifixion.

While the first sign in John 2 was performed in a rural setting amid the joyous celebration of a wedding, this final sign appears on the outskirts of the city of Jerusalem within the somber atmosphere of a funeral. As Jesus returns earthly life to the dead Lazarus, the official decision to take Jesus' life will be made by religious leaders in Jerusalem (11:45–53). Therefore, this last sign confirms the decisions and events that lead to his murder. As Jesus gives life to a person, others bring death to him.

While some of the other signs throughout the Gospel briefly describe a particular miracle and then proceed quickly to the discourse that interprets the sign, John 11 follows a different pattern. Here the evangelist presents three conversations that precede the miracle: (a) Jesus with Thomas and other disciples (11:7–16a); (b) Jesus with Martha (11:17–27); (c) Jesus with Mary (11:28–34). The conversations explore the significance of the sign before it even takes place. Within these dialogues Martha's initiative, openness, and spiritual insights cannot be missed. Her insightful conversation with Jesus represents the most important of the three exchanges in the story.

For reading purposes the chapter may be divided as follows:

1. Introduction about the illness of Lazarus (11:1–6)
2. The discussion and decision of Jesus to go to Jerusalem (Bethany) (11:7–19)
3. The important dialogue between Jesus and Martha (11:20–27)
4. The meeting between Jesus and Mary, the other sister of Lazarus and Martha (11:28–33)
5. The actual raising of Lazarus by Jesus (11:34–44)
6. The reaction of some Jewish leaders to this gift of life (11:45–54)

John 11—Questions

110. In John 11 what do you make of raising Lazarus from the dead, or, indeed, of any of the miracles/signs?
111. Aren't there more stories about this family of Mary, Martha, and Lazarus in other gospels?
112. What do you make of Martha and Mary's message in 11:3 and Jesus action in 11:6?
113. In 11:6 what does it say about Jesus if he let two days go by before going to his friends' home when they were in such distress?
114. In 11:16 why did Thomas suggest dying with Lazarus?
115. In 11:25 what does "I am the resurrection and the life" really mean?
116. Was Martha mad at Jesus? I do not blame her if she were.
117. Why did Jesus weep at Lazarus' tomb if he knew he could/would bring his friend back to life?
118. Why did the Jewish leaders find Jesus' ability to raise the dead so threatening? Why didn't they at least try to take personal advantage of the talent?

John 11—Conclusion

Dialogue with Martha and Mary and Raising of Lazarus (11:1–44)

The first scene in this chapter (11:1–6) sets the stage for all that will follow. The opening verse introduces the reader to Mary, Martha, and Lazarus, who appear for the first time as characters in the Gospel. The specific mention of their names suggests that Jesus cared deeply about each one of them.

These three siblings live in the village of Bethany, which is situated on the southeastern slopes of the Mount of Olives, about two miles from Jerusalem. When the author connects Mary with the anointing of Jesus, an action that will not occur until John 12:3–8, he seems to presume that the Johannine communities are already familiar with the family from Bethany.

Furthermore, the author continues to take for granted the deep friendship between this family and Jesus. In 11:3 the sisters send this message to Jesus: "Lord, he whom you love is ill." With this description, some commentators suggest that perhaps Lazarus surfaces now as the unnamed disciple whom Jesus loved, which we shall discuss in later chapters (John 13—21). I do not agree. Here in 11:3, the Greek term for "whom you love" is *hn phileis*, which indicates a brotherly/sisterly type of love. However, in all but one of the passages that refer to the Beloved Disciple, the verb *agapaō* has been used in the texts. This verb for love signifies the highest form of love, that of unconditional love.

John 11:7–10 describes both Jesus' choice to honor the request of his friends by a return to Judea and the reaction of the disciples to his resolution. They do not want him to go because of the recent attempts on his life when he was in Jerusalem in John 10. Jesus' response about working during sunlight hours and seeing the light of the world reminds us of John 9:4–5, where, in the story of the man born blind, Jesus tells his disciples that he must perform the works of God "while it is day" because "as long as I am in the world, I am the light of the world."

In 11:11a, the literary phrase "after this" *(metà toûto)* appears. As you may have noticed, this phrase surfaces throughout the Gospel and represents the typical Johannine expression to signal a change of topics. Subsequently, Jesus returns to the topic of Lazarus in 11:11b–15. Jesus informs the disciples that Lazarus has "fallen asleep." While the designation "asleep" may serve as a preface to the awakening of Lazarus later on in this chapter, here the common term serves as a euphemism for death. Today, when someone informs us about the death of another, the phrase "passed away" commonly has been used. Clearly, most people understand the meaning. However, the author employs the technique of misunderstanding on the part of the disciples in order to move the dialogue to greater depth. This moment provides the opportunity for Jesus to clarify that "Lazarus is dead" and that he must go to him. Thomas, who envisions the outcome of this difficult decision in light of the threats against Jesus' life, bravely declares, "Let us also go, that we may die with him" (11:16).

John 11:17–19 provides a transition of place for Jesus and introduces an important dialogue between Jesus and Martha. When the author states in 11:17 that Lazarus has been dead four days, the comment reflects an ancient rabbinic belief that the soul could possibly remain in the body for three days, but no longer. After such time, the person had to be dead because nothing remained of the spirited previous life. The repeated comment about "four days" in 11:39 forms an inclusion that tightens the cohesiveness of the story. In addition, the mention of the many consolers in 11:19 indicates that Lazarus and his sisters were prominent members of the community. The large the support of mourners reflected an honored position in society. The transition also introduces Martha into the scene.

The next section (11:20–27) functions as a vital one within the chapter. Although John 11 centers on Jesus as he restores life to Lazarus, the figure of Martha becomes an integral part of the drama. For example, she, along with her sister, informs Jesus about their brother's critical illness (11:3). A few verses later (11:5) the author names the three siblings, with Martha at the head of the list: "Jesus loved Martha and her sister and Lazarus." While ancient lists begin usually with male names, in 11:5 the appearance of Martha's name before the others suggests both her leadership role and/or closeness to Jesus.

Discipleship plays a key role in the Fourth Gospel, where it is associated with love. When Jesus discovers another person who responds openly to him, he begins to cherish that person and shares his teachings and revelation with that individual. Therefore, the fact that Jesus loved Martha (1:5) indicates her special position as disciple and friend. Later in the Gospel (15:15), Jesus describes the term *friend* in such a way that it become a synonym for disciple.

The practical application of the strong bond of friendship surfaces in Martha's conversation with Jesus about the death of her brother and the significance of life. The exchange between Martha and Jesus contains the most significant dialogue within the entire narrative because of the deep theological realities they come to share. Furthermore, she comforts their mourning neighbors and deepens their faith in Jesus. In effect, her unwavering belief in Jesus marks her as an effective leader, a model disciple, and a true friend to Jesus. The following verses (11:20–27) will highlight these qualities of Martha.

As soon as Martha realized that Jesus had come to Bethany, "she went and met him." Her caring friendship and hospitality lead her directly to Jesus. Nothing keeps her away from him. When they meet, Martha speaks freely about the absence of Jesus before her brother's death. She adds immediately a hope for the future: "But even now I know that God will give you whatever you ask of him" (11:22). Even though Lazarus died and had been entombed in the absence of Jesus, Martha's belief in the person of Jesus cannot be shaken. Her trust in Jesus surpasses her grief and anguish over the death of her brother. Here, her continued fidelity to Jesus illuminates both her words and actions.

In typical Johannine fashion, the conversation deepens as Jesus reassures Martha that "your brother will rise again" (11:23). Martha's reply, "I know that he will rise again in the resurrection on the last day" (11:24), expresses both her belief in the words of Jesus and her hope in a later resurrection. In the first century CE, the Pharisees maintained a confidence in a future resurrection from the dead (Acts 23:8; Josephus, *Jewish War* 2.8.14). In theological terms, this belief is known as future eschatology (*eschatology* refers to the final or end time). Martha's reply, therefore, reflects the belief of the Pharisees about a future eschatology. Her reflective words allow Jesus to converse with her on an even deeper level.

In 11:25 Jesus continues the dialogue with a profound *egō eimi* ("I am") saying: "I am the resurrection and the life" (11:25). What has been a reflection of Pharisaic Jewish theology in 11:24 now leads to a profound self-revelation of Jesus to his trusted friend, Martha, in 11:25. Moreover, this surprising announcement moves the discussion from future to realized eschatology, because the hope of resurrection shifts from a future moment to a present reality in the person of Jesus. He develops his announcement with the additional statement, "Those who believe in me, even though they die, will live, and everyone who lives and believes in me will never die" (11:25b–26). Jesus' self-revelation only to Martha verifies the truth that he considers her as a faithful friend, disciple, and leader.

He continues the rich dialogue with the question, "Do you believe this?" (11:26b). Incorporated back into the conversation, she responds, "Yes, Lord, I believe that you are the Messiah, the Son of God, the one coming into the world" (11:27). This powerful reply reveals a three-part theological testimony that demonstrates her unwavering faith in Jesus. You may notice that it mirrors somewhat the final statement of the first ending of the Gospel in 20:31 that "these things are written so that you may come to believe that Jesus is the Messiah, the Son of God, and that through believing you may have life in his name." Both pronouncements reflect the heart of Jesus' message in the Fourth Gospel, namely, that faith in him leads to true life. By her reply, Martha confirms her belief in the life that Jesus offers her and becomes a model for all other disciples.

The magnitude of Martha's profound proclamation about Jesus being the Messiah (the Christ) in 11:27 offers additional insights. If you take a moment to read Peter's reply to Jesus at Caesarea Philippi in the Gospel of Matthew, you will notice strong similarities. In Matthew 16:16, you will see that Peter answers Jesus' previous question, "Who do people say that the

Son of Man is?" with the acclamation, "You are the Messiah, the Son of the living God." This faith-filled response guides Jesus to commission Peter as a leader in the future apostolic era: "You are Peter, and on this rock I will build my church" (Matt 16:18). If the result of Peter's statement leads to leadership, should not the same role apply to Martha in the Johannine communities? Karris (*Jesus and the Marginalized in John's Gospel,* 87) suggests that Martha's confession *is* the very foundation of the Johannine church. Schneiders ("Women in the Fourth Gospel and the Role of Women in the Contemporary Church," 41) believes that Martha's proclamation remains equally significant to that of Peter in Matthew's Gospel. Both ground the promise of future leadership within their own communities.

The Mary narrative (11:28–37) follows Martha's dialogue with Jesus and precedes the raising of Lazarus from the tomb. It portrays Mary's intense grief and her influence on Jesus and her fellow mourners. While the section does not illustrate any lengthy theological dialogue as does the one that Martha had with Jesus, it clearly illustrates three points: (a) The evangelist demonstrates Mary's love for her dead brother as well as for Jesus; (b) Mary's leadership arises in her influence on the emotions of Jesus as well as others; (c) it brings the role of the "the Jews" into the episode to prepare for the split within the Jewish community about the decision to put Jesus to death.

The section commences in 11:28 when Martha relates to Mary the "good news" that Jesus wishes to see her. Here the interaction between the sisters bridges the two sections about them. When Mary hears Martha's comment, she moves immediately from her private space in the house and goes out to a public space where Jesus waits. This brave movement to meet Jesus echoes her sister's and illustrates her devotion to Jesus. When Mary encounters him, her words (11:32) also echo those of Martha (11:21).

Greeting her friend in the context of her brother's death, Mary begins to weep. These tender tears cause others to weep, including mourners who had followed her from the house. The tears spark in Jesus a similar response: "He was greatly disturbed in spirit and deeply moved" (11:33), "Jesus began to weep" (11:35), and "Jesus, again greatly disturbed" (38a).

As he observed the pain-filled sorrow of the mourners and the heart-wrenching loss of Mary, he was "deeply moved" (11:33). The Greek, *enebrimēsato,* which means "deeply moved," describes Jesus' profound, heartfelt response to the entire scene (11:38a). The Greek verb implies indignation. Some critics maintain that it demonstrates Jesus' anger toward Mary because she publicly challenges him, while others state that it represents his irritation toward the mourners because of their lack of faith. I propose that neither suggestion is adequate. Within the context of the story, "deeply moved" describes Jesus' anger over death itself and its painful blow on family and friends of the deceased.

Following this intense moment, Jesus positions himself at the entrance of the tomb in order to perform the miracle. He is reminded again that Lazarus has been entombed for four days, yet he calls for belief. Before the miracle takes place, Jesus prays, a moment that demonstrates his continued bond with his Father.

In 11:38b–44 he gives three vital commands. The first one regards the removal of the large stone, which covers the entrance to the limestone bedrock tomb. When you envision the scene, picture a huge round rock that functions as a door and has to be rolled back to clear the passageway. The second command appears in 11:43, when Jesus cries out "Lazarus, come out!" In 11:44 Lazarus obeys the call and appears at the entrance of the tomb, bound in the clothes of death. Talbert (*Reading John,* 176) informs us that the ancient Jewish burial consisted of linen wraps, which went from the head to the feet and were tied, with a separate cloth for the face. Finally, Jesus gives the third order, "Unbind him, and let him go." In all three commands, Jesus calls forth life. In the first instance the removal of the stone affords light, air, and life into the deadened tomb. Through the second instruction, Jesus calls Lazarus back to life, back to his grieving family and friends, back to a world of hope. As a result of the third command, Jesus calls Lazarus to a renewed life of freedom, one that has the power to overcome constraints.

In these verses the author presents a physical sign, where a dead man has been brought back to his former life only to die again. Yet, as Schneiders (*Written That You May Believe: Encountering Jesus in the Fourth Gospel,* 183) maintains, the real gift in this entire story lies in the reality that Jesus has promised Martha, as well as all followers, that "I am the resurrection and the life" (11:25). He proclaims deep divine truths as he demonstrated in his other previous signs. For example, in John 6, Jesus gave physical bread to show that "I am the bread of life" and in John 9 Jesus offered physical sight to demonstrate that, "I am the light of the world." In all these instances the miracle leads to a deeper reality of Jesus' union with the community through his gifts of sustenance, light, and everlasting life.

The great irony of the chapter appears in the last section (11:45–55). As Jesus gives life, influential Jewish leaders decide he must die. Here the faith of many Jews has been counterbalanced by cries of condemnation from these leaders. They fear Jesus' influence and power among the people. During a formal meeting of the council (Sanhedrin), the high priest Caiaphas urges the death of Jesus as a sacrifice for the nation (11:50). Once his oracle has been invoked, it cannot be dismissed. In the end the council planned to murder Jesus. As a result, Jesus departed to Ephraim. This town, which only appears in the Fourth Gospel, seems to have been located near the desert of the Jordan valley, around fifteen miles northeast of Jerusalem.

The chapter concludes with the mention of the approaching Jewish festival of Passover (Pesach). You may recall that the last feast mentioned had been that of a winter observance, namely, Dedication (Hanukkah) in John 10:22-42. Therefore, this festival would have occurred about four months later, near the beginning of the spring season. Since Passover (Pesach) was celebrated as a pilgrim feast, many Jews traveled to Jerusalem to observe it. At this point the authorities watched for the arrival of Jesus so that they might arrest him. These concluding verses lead directly into the narrative of John 12, as it mentions Jesus' return to the Jerusalem area prior to this spring feast of Passover (Pesach).

CHAPTER 11
John 12

John 12—Introduction

The final days of Jesus' earthly existence have already been introduced with the announcement of the upcoming feast of Passover (Pesach) in John 11:55–57 as well as with the plot to kill Jesus (11:53). The death of Jesus permeates every scene within the chapter. The placement of the narrative follows the Lazarus' episode and moves Jesus closer to his death and burial in the chapters that follow. John 12 is also connected to John 11 with the figures of Martha, Mary, and Lazarus, who reappear as good friends and faithful disciples of Jesus. To associate these two chapters specifically, the evangelist describes the anointing of Jesus in 11:2 as if it had already taken place. However, it does not occur until 12:1–8.

As you begin to read the chapter, notice Mary, who rises to a dominant role in John 12:1–8 as she anoints Jesus. Without a word spoken, her generous actions contrast sharply with the cold words of Judas, who complains about her extravagant gesture. As a whole this chapter captures the final moments of Jesus' public ministry and each of three scenes provides preparations for his entrance into the last phase of his earthy ministry.

For reading purposes the chapter may be divided as follows:

1. Mary's anointing of Jesus at Bethany (12:1–8)
2. Jesus' entrance into Jerusalem (12:9–19)
3. The discourse with the Greeks and others to preface the upcoming death of Jesus (12:20–50)

John 12—Questions

119. In John 12:1–8 what was the point of naming Mary, the sister of Lazarus, as the one who anointed Jesus' feet, since the anointing stories in the other gospels don't mention her?
120. What is nard? Can you still buy it?
121. Does Jesus really think it was okay to disregard the poor in 12:8?
122. Why did Judas, of all people, complain about the sin of extravagance?
123. Why wasn't Lazarus crucified along with Jesus if the chief priests thought of it in 12:10?
124. Why were palm branches used in 12:13? Weren't they awfully large for carrying around?
125. Do you really think that a voice came from heaven or was it actually thunder as in 12:29?
126. How does "when I am lifted up from the earth" indicate the kind of death Jesus was to die as reported in 12:32, 33?

John 12—Conclusion

The chapter opens with a reference to the feast of Passover. Once again the author connects his narrative with important Jewish feasts. At this opening scene Jesus leaves Ephraim, where he had hidden from those who wanted to arrest him (11:57). He returns to Bethany, despite the grave danger that awaits him. Immediately, the chapter moves to the story about a preparatory action of anointing that will anticipate Jesus' death and burial.

Mary of Bethany Anoints Jesus (12:1–8)

As you read about the reappearance of Jesus in Bethany, you may have noticed that it took place amid a commemorative meal with Jesus and his friends. In the Greco-Roman world, meals were a true sign of friendship and solidarity. Usually, the host would invite people of the same rank within society. These peers celebrated together on special occasions such as holidays and other festal occasions. Therefore, this meal exemplifies the deep bond between Martha, Mary, Lazarus, and Jesus.

Within the meal scene (12:1–8) the evangelist mentions Martha briefly in her leadership capacity as hostess. However, her sister, Mary, rises to the prominent role as she anoints Jesus. In many ways Mary's anointing of Jesus reinterprets similar stories in the other three gospels. The village of Bethany had been the chosen spot of anointing in both Mark and Matthew, as well as in John. John's version joins some of the elements of former narratives. However, the author of John's Gospel remains the only one who identifies Mary of Bethany as the one who performs the significant task.

In 12:3 "a pound of costly perfume" exemplifies her unconditional love and devotion to Jesus, as she uses the entire amount on him. When one friend attends to another friend, who faces a serious critical moment such as arrest and death, money has no meaning. Therefore, the preliminary action of anointing Jesus makes perfect sense to Mary. Her generous gesture anticipates his kingly burial by Nicodemus (19:39). Moreover, in former times anointing was performed on the kings of Israel (1 Samuel 10:1; 16:13) to mark a sacred event of their leadership. The theme of kingship will continue in the next section as Jesus enters Jerusalem amid the cheering crowds and later at the crucifixion, when Pilate identifies him on the cross as the "King of the Jews."

At this moment Judas Iscariot speaks up in bold confrontation. Despite Mary's devoted act, he complains about the extravagant gesture that seems to have been wasted on Jesus. He adds that the sale of this costly perfume could have been used for the poor. Yet, his words do not hold weight in this revered moment because Jesus quickly counters his objections. He reminds Judas that although the poor always remain, "you do not always have me" (12:8).

Within this anointing story in John 12:1–8, then, the figures of Martha, Mary, and Judas illuminate two types of disciples, namely, those who minister faithfully and those who stray. Martha and Mary represent the devoted ones who never deviate from true service. While the scene does not contain any dialogue between Jesus and Martha or Mary, it does emphasize their important roles as disciples. Their honorable behavior counteracts the self-serving comments of Judas.

Jesus' Entrance into Jerusalem (12:9–19)

The author connects this entire episode (12:9–19) of the entry of Jesus into Jerusalem for his final days with comments about the raising of Lazarus. This association, which provides you with motifs of death, resurrection, and joy, anticipates the future days of Jesus' own life. Verses 9–11 introduce the crowds, who came to see Jesus and the raised Lazarus in Bethany. These verses also allow resurfacing of the intent of some leaders in Jerusalem to murder Jesus because of his increased following. Despite their objective, the crowds continue to appear joyous the next day as they anticipate Jesus' arrival into Jerusalem.

In all four gospels Jesus' final entrance into the holy city remains a joyous occasion with the acclamation of the crowds, who proclaim the words of Psalm 118:26. The shouts of "Hosanna!" surface as one of the entrance psalms, which Jewish pilgrims sang as they approached the hills of Jerusalem at festival time. When Jesus sits upon a donkey to enter the city, the Johannine author associates this gesture with an excerpt from the prophet Zechariah. In the Hebrew Bible, the prophet called for the people to rejoice and fear not because "your king comes to you…riding on a donkey" (Zech 9:9). Like Mary's anointing of Jesus, this action also connects with a kingly function, that of riding into the holy city with people acclaiming him along the path.

As you have found throughout the Gospel, often the disciples do not comprehend the words and deeds of Jesus. Verse 16 reiterates their misunderstanding of Jesus until after the resurrection. Still, the crowds continue to acclaim him, which allows some Pharisees to become even more frustrated with the situation. These descriptions of the disciples, crowds, and select legislators lead to the next section, which describes the conclusion of Jesus' ministry.

Conclusion of Jesus' Public Ministry (12:20–50)

The last section of the chapter introduces the arrival of the Greeks (12:20–26). In the previous verse (12:19), when the Pharisees declared that "the world has gone after him," the mention of the Greeks represents such an event. Previously, in 7:35 the author introduced the Greeks as a possibility of Jesus' movement beyond Israel to people outside Judaism. Here the presence of "the Greeks" does signify that Jesus' mission reaches further than Israel. He extends himself to anyone in the world who believes in him, despite cultural or religious affiliation.

When "the Greeks" request to see him, Jesus announces that now the "hour has come for the Son of Man to be glorified" (12:23). While the author has mentioned the future coming of "the hour" on previous occasions (2:4; 7:30; 8:20), this proclamation marks the first time in the Gospel that Jesus declares that the hour has finally arrived. Remember, for John "the hour" does not only signify the death of Jesus, but his resurrection and glorification as well. Therefore, the hour surfaces as the moment of glory.

To address "the hour," Jesus employs a parable about a grain of wheat, which illustrates the necessity of Jesus' death, so that his resurrection and glorification may follow. It also anticipates a future bountiful harvest of believers through these events. In 12:25–26 the two sayings about love/hate and serve/follow echo sayings in the Synoptic Gospels but with its own emphasis and additions of "in this world" and "eternal life." All suffering must be seen in the light of resurrection and glorification. Moreover, the emphasis on service is associated with the person of Jesus and its result, that of being honored by the Father.

Although no formal agony in the garden scene appears in John's Gospel, the words of Jesus in 12:27–28 have some similarities to the Synoptic Gospels in that Jesus intends to do his Father's will. However, in the Fourth Gospel, the scene contrasts with the other gospels in that it occurs amid a public audience and in this Gospel Jesus concentrates on "the hour" and "glorification." As Jesus prays to his Father, a voice from heaven responds. This divine response does not seem to be intended for the comfort of Jesus. Remember that in the Fourth Gospel the Johannine Jesus does not need assurance because his divinity has been emphasized since the beginning verses of the Prologue in John 1:1. Therefore, the voice from heaven aims to assure the crowd of both the status of Jesus as well as God's closeness to his Son. For some it succeeds but others in crowd do not believe. For Jesus, both the coming of the Greeks and the voice from heaven lead to the arrival of "the hour."

In 12:31–36 Jesus speaks of the time of judgment, the overcoming of evil in this world, and his being "lifted up from the earth." With these sayings he describes his death and the effects from it. As Jesus reintroduces the theme of light and encourages his audience to "believe in the light, so that you may become children of the light," you may recall Jesus' announcement in 9:5, when he proclaims, "I am the light of the world." Those who believe in Jesus will be enlightened by him. Subsequently, they have been encouraged to act. After these words, Jesus hides again.

Since the Johannine author often employs the literary technique of repetition to underline important points, the remainder of the chapter continues the themes of light and judgment. It also speaks of the necessity of belief in the person of Jesus, because faith in him translates into faith in his Father. The lack of faith from some Jews as well as the belief of others also reappears.

CHAPTER 12

John 13

John 13—21—Final Days of Jesus

John 13 introduces the traditional Book of Glory (John 13—21), which has an entirely different focus from the preceding chapters. Above other themes, the second half of the Gospel centers on the love of Jesus for his disciples. Many of the chapters exemplify the meaning of such deep, divine love. Moreover, in these chapters Jesus presents a final testament to his disciples before he dies. While the first half of the Gospel (John 1—12) encompassed three years around the ministry of Jesus, the second half takes place within a few days and includes the final meal and conversation, as well as his last days on earth.

John 13—Introduction

The meal, which takes place before the annual feast of Passover, uncovers the depth of Jesus' love for his own as he humbly washes their feet, an act performed by the slaves of the wealthy households. Moreover, in John 13 the "hour," which denotes the moment of "glory," begins to set the scene for the chapters to follow. For Jesus, this time depicts his final days on earth, the time of his arrest, judgment, death, resurrection, and ascension. Finally, the scene in John 13 also offers the reader a glimpse of the evil actions of Judas Iscariot in the midst of divine love without limits.

For reading purposes the chapter may be divided as follows:

1. Jesus washes the feet of the disciples (13:1–11)
2. Discourse that follows the foot washing (13:12–38)

John 13—Questions

127. Why does the Last Supper take place before Passover rather than on Passover as in the other gospels?
128. Why does Jesus speak so long in the Last Supper scene?
129. In John 13:1–20 what happened to the traditional Last Supper? Does the foot washing replace it? What does this mean for our liturgy?
130. Why would Jesus wash the feet of the disciples as an act of love?
131. What does it mean in 13:2 that "the devil had already put it into the heart of Judas son of Simon Iscariot to betray him [Jesus]" and in 13:27 when it states that after Judas ate the bread "Satan entered into him"?
132. What was Peter thinking?
133. In John 13:16 Jesus says that "servants are not greater than their master." In what context does he refer to the disciples as "slaves"?
134. In 13:23 what is the point of not naming the disciple whom Jesus loved?
135. What was the point of indicting Judas with a piece of bread in 13:26? Is this connected with our liturgy when we use bread?
136. What is Jesus saying in 13:31–32?
137. Why was the same idea repeated in 13:34–35 and 15:12–13?

John 13—Conclusion

This chapter begins with a brief rendition of the continuation of Jesus' cyclic life of leaving the earth and returning to the Father, Jesus' continual love for his disciples "until the end," and the acknowledgement that Judas had let evil penetrate his heart. These theological points summarize somewhat both the words and actions that follow in this tender scene of the Last Supper.

Unlike the other gospels, where the Last Supper occurs on the feast of Passover, in the Gospel of John it takes place on the preparation day before the celebration. Moreover, it does not focus on the Eucharist. Rather, in this scene the author already presupposes the importance of the Eucharist, which has been symbolized in John 6. Instead, here Jesus concentrates on the effects that the Eucharist would have in the lives of the disciples, namely, unqualified love for one another. Such love translates to acts of humble service and forgiveness. These qualities generate true Christian community because they reflect the deeds of Jesus.

The foot washing symbolizes such exemplary love. Through action Jesus reminds the disciples of the humble service that they must give one another. Moreover, his symbolic action exemplifies a deeper meaning. As a departing gesture, Jesus reminds his disciples that this humble deed signifies an act of forgiveness. As he washes away the physical dirt, he also washes away any hurtful actions that they performed against him. Moreover, his low physical stance of bending down before them confirms his intent of solidarity among them.

This lowly gesture of foot washing goes beyond anything we hold in the independent American tradition of achieving greatness. In our twenty-first century material philosophy, society speaks in terms of climbing to the top, of doing things for ourselves, of self-made success, of being the best (being #1), of being treated with respect, and so on. This philosophy does not seem to allow for lowly gestures, humiliations, or failure according to the standards of the world. In effect, the words and actions of Jesus remain completely countercultural to the beliefs of today's Western world. In so many ways, the world does not comprehend the ways of the divine and responds like Peter, who at first wanted nothing to do with the humbling actions of Jesus.

In 13:8–10 Peter misunderstands the deeper meaning of the foot washing. Yet, with great compassion and understanding, Jesus does not rebuke Peter but reminds him that in time he will comprehend the meaning of the gesture. While Peter lingers on the first level of meaning, Jesus speaks on the deeper level. In 13:12 he poses a profound question to all the disciples when he asks, "Do you know what I have done to you?"

What has Jesus done to them? He has overturned the rules of the honor status in ancient Palestine because he, the Master, performed an act of a lowly servant. Jesus has shown them by example that the leader within a community needs to serve the others. Such an act would not be acceptable in this society, where anyone in charge must show his authority by holding his power over others, not by bending down to their needs. More importantly, Jesus demonstrates the way to true community is to build up the group through an open attitude of acceptance and forgiveness, as well as to serve others' needs. By his actions and words, then, Jesus showed the disciples that, even in the midst of betrayal among them, the community needs to exhibit compassion, tenderness, and forgiveness.

The brief words of Jesus in 13:18–21 describe the divisive acts of someone in Jesus' beloved community. When he says that "I am not speaking of all of you" (13:18), he points out the loyalty of the others within the group. The statement, "The one who ate my bread has lifted his heel against me," declares that one of the trusted members of the community had dishonored both Jesus and the group. In the ancient world, to display the sole of a foot against another implies a grave insult to that other person. It symbolizes the crushing of the other's head by one's heel. This inflammatory statement describes the shrewd betrayal of the unfaithful disciple, who will dishonor Jesus as well as his fellow disciples by his selfish, calculated actions. In 13:26 the writer identifies the person as Judas, son of Simon Iscariot. Judas' disloyalty to Jesus causes a later unjust arrest that leads to punishment and death.

Jesus knows how fragile people really are and he realizes that the disciples do not yet comprehend the actions of Jesus, as exemplified by Peter a moment earlier in the story. Yet, in the same passage Jesus continues to voice what will happen to those who remain loyal to him. In 13:20 Jesus states that "whoever receives one whom I send receives me; and whoever receives me receives him who sent me." To receive another person means to receive Jesus and, furthermore, to receive Jesus means to receive God. We must never forget that God dwells within each person, so our kindness toward individuals symbolizes our kindness toward Jesus and, therefore, toward God.

The last section, John 13:21–38, begins with the identification of Judas as the disloyal traitor. As always in the Gospel of John, Jesus remains in charge, even in the last days of his life. After he shares bread with Judas, he commands him to go and do what he must. The sharing of the bread has strong roots in the celebration of the Eucharist. It has always been an integral part of the sacred meal. Of all the members of the community, Jesus gives the morsel of bread to the most unworthy one. Despite any ignorance, future denial of Jesus, or even betrayal, Jesus will never cease to love all his disciples.

The statement about Judas that "Satan entered into him" describes the evil action that he was about to do. In 13:30 the author states that when Judas went out, "it was night." Like the story about Nicodemus in John 3, night signifies ignorance, darkness, evil. Judas left the light of Jesus and went into the darkness of evil. He went from the source of love and enlightenment into the pit of betrayal and blindness.

Once Judas left, Jesus proclaims in 13:31, "Now the Son of Man has been glorified, and God has been glorified in him." The connection between the withdrawal of Judas and the announcement of glory provides a link between the two passages. Once evil has left the room, Jesus speaks even more freely about the hour of glory. He now calls his disciples a unique and surprising term of endearment, namely, "little children." Although they function as grown adults, they sometimes behave like little children, who do not understand the words of Jesus. Despite all this, Jesus loves them as he would precious children. To help them grow in wisdom and knowledge, he even gives them the new commandment: "Just as I have loved you, you also should love one another."

This beautiful, yet difficult command calls each of us to love the other person, not as we would like to be loved, but as God would love us. Divine love insists on integrity, compassion, truth, tenderness, and forgiveness. To be called to treat all other persons in this way puts a real responsibility on the disciples of Jesus. No other way remains acceptable. The chapter concludes with Peter's repeated misunderstanding of Jesus' remarks and a warning by Jesus that Peter will be unfaithful to him.

CHAPTER 13
John 14

John 14—17—Farewell Discourse

While John 13 introduced an entirely new section of the Gospel, namely, the twenty-four-hour period of Jesus' Last Supper, arrest, crucifixion, and death, the next four chapters (John 14—17) continue to provide the powerful words of Jesus within that same time period. Since many of the commands and statements do not always seem unified, many scholars maintain that these chapters combine material from other moments in Jesus' life with his departing message to create a collective farewell discourse. This entire unique unit does not resemble any of the speeches of Jesus before the passion in the other three gospels. Since it does sound like the testament of a dying person in ancient literature, it has come be known as Jesus' farewell discourse.

To understand more clearly Jesus' message within these chapters, each chapter will be addressed separately. Remember, however, that although we shall study the chapters in sequence, the words of the farewell discourse do not necessarily follow a chronological order. John 14 arises as the first part of the discourse with John 16:4–33 providing parallels to many of its statements and themes. As we study each chapter on its own, keep in mind that John 14—17 needs to be seen as a collective farewell discourse. The chapters may be viewed in the following light:

1. John 14:1–31—Part I of the farewell discourse
2. John 15:1–26—Part II of the farewell discourse
3. John 16:1–33—Part III of the farewell discourse, which parallels part I
4. John 17:1–26—Prayer of Jesus to his Father

John 14—Introduction

In the preceding chapter the author prepares for Jesus' words of departure as he and Peter dialogue. However, in John 14, Jesus offers his words of encouragement to a wider audience of disciples as he addresses his departure both at the beginning and the end of the narrative. Within the chapter Thomas (14:5), Philip (14:8), and another Judas (14:22) address Jesus about this departure as well as other topics, but they do not seem to grasp his words, not unlike Jesus' adversaries in preceding encounters.

Throughout the chapter Jesus employs many verbal imperatives in his teaching, which emphasizes the importance of his message. His instructions to "believe" appear as the subject matter in the first half of the chapter, while the topic of love appears in 14:15ff.

For reading purposes the chapter may be divided as follows:

1. Jesus will go to the Father (14:1–14)
2. The love commandment (14:15–24)
3. Jesus' bestowal of peace (14:25–31)

John 14—Questions

138. In 14:2 will the "many dwelling places" be filled only with Christians?
139. In 14:3 to what does the statement, "I will come again and take you to myself," refer?
140. Does 14:6 imply that access to God will only come through Jesus?
141. Is it in 14:9b that we get the idea that Jesus is God or does that come from elsewhere?
142. In 14:11 does it mean that belief in Jesus/God should be first on our agenda?
143. In 14:14 Jesus seems to be saying that if we ask him anything he will accomplish it. How is that possible?

144. Why does the author use the term *Advocate,* which sounds so much like a lawyer? Why doesn't the author use *Holy Spirit?*
145. Why does "Rise, let us be on our way" appear at the end of 14:31? It doesn't seem to fit.

John 14—Conclusion

The reality of Jesus' need to leave permeates the discourse in John 14. The scene opens with an encouraging and hope-filled imperative: "Do not let your hearts be troubled" (14:1). The consoling message demonstrates that the Johannine Jesus tries to comfort his friends at the time of his departure from them. The second half of that statement "Believe in God, believe also in me," assures them that faith in him will carry them through these and future critical moments of their lives. The next three verses (14:2–4) provide consolation that the disciples will have dwelling places for them in heaven after Jesus departs. The mention of different dwellings has no important significance in this conversation. Rather, Jesus' dwelling with his Father and the assurance that they also will abide with him is his main point. In addition, Jesus also promises them his own return.

In 14:5, 8 the questions of Thomas and Philip, like Peter in 13:36–38, represent an immediate misunderstanding of the disciples. When Thomas questions Jesus about the way to him, Jesus responds with another important *egō eimi* ("I am") saying: "I am the way, and the truth, and the life" (14:6). These three words—*way, truth, life*—surface as an underlying theme of the discourse. In 10:7, 9 recall that Jesus spoke about being "the gate," whereby people go through him for eternal life. Here a similar analogy arises with Jesus proclaiming that "I am the way." Like other *egō eimi* ("I am") sayings, this announcement identifies a part of who Jesus is. Yet the statement does not end there because "the way" has to direct the followers somewhere. Therefore, the remainder of the proclamation informs us of what Jesus as "the way" does, namely, he leads those who believe to a truth-filled life.

Again Jesus speaks about his union with his Father. He makes it clear that he functions as the way to the Father. At this point Philip asks Jesus to show them the Father. Jesus responds to his confusion with more discussion about his relationship with his Father. Statements such as "no one comes to the Father except through me" (14:6) and "the Father may be glorified in the Son" (14:13) demonstrate the unity of Jesus and his Father. Still, the disciples remain mystified.

The next section (14:15–24) centers on the importance of love. In these verses Jesus associates love with fidelity to God's commandments. This commitment between a person and God's commands reflects the union between the Father and the Son. As a continuance of Jesus' reassuring help at his departure, he explains the results of their love and belief as well as disbelief. Although he must depart, Jesus assures his disciples that he will send "another Advocate" to be with them forever (14:15). The fact that the term *another* appears with *Advocate* indicates that the earthly Jesus has already functioned in this capacity during his time with his disciples. As you already know, an Advocate provides assistance to a defendant within a courtroom setting. In this context, the first Advocate (Jesus) has already provided the way to truth and life. The next Advocate, which has been identified as the "Spirit of truth" in 14:17, will continue personally to guide all disciples to divine life. Since the Advocate belongs to the world of Jesus, those who refuse Jesus will not be gifted with the Advocate because they choose to refuse life.

The concluding remarks of the chapter (14:25–31) continue the theme of departure and allow another mention of the Advocate to surface. This time the Advocate is described in the role of teacher and is called the "Holy Spirit, whom the Father will send in my name" (14:26). The mention of the double-worded title, "Holy Spirit," occurs here in an entirely new way, namely as a teacher. Here, however, it takes on a personal tone. As Jesus has been "sent" by the Father, so too the Advocate will be "sent" by the Father in Jesus' name. Therefore, the Advocate will represent the Son, just as now the Son represents the Father on earth. This Spirit will guide and teach as well as remind the disciples of all that Jesus taught.

The identification of the Advocate becomes clearer in 14:28 when Jesus reminds the disciples: "I am going away, and I am coming to you." This double statement assures the disciples that Jesus will be with them in a new way. In the past they have counted on the physical presence of Jesus. Now, in the future, they will be gifted with the presence of the Spirit of Jesus within them. The Advocate will be a new and personal presence of Jesus, a presence that will abide within them and remind them of all that Jesus taught during his earthly ministry. With Jesus' Spirit guiding and directing them, they will always be united to God.

With this assurance Jesus offers his disciples the peace of God. The world cannot offer such deep peace, even though the Romans tried with *Pax Rōmāna* (Roman peace). The Latin phrase represents an extended period of time (27 BCE–180 CE) wherein the Roman Empire experienced relative peace, with no civil wars or large invasions and a military system that squelched smaller uprisings. Interestingly, as you may recall, both the Jewish revolt (66–70 CE) as well as the fall of Jerusalem (70 CE) occur during the so-called *Pax Rōmāna*. Therefore, the peace of the world never becomes true peace.

Unlike temporary peace, this peace that Jesus leaves the disciples has deep and long-lasting effects. Accordingly, it connects with the role of Advocate, both from the earthly Jesus and from the Spirit of the glorified Jesus. Such peace will bring the disciples the needed strength and enlightenment to battle the evil of this world. However, we need to keep in mind that, within the context of the story, the promise of peace addresses a future moment. For, as Jesus says, "the ruler of the world" (14:30), who represents evil, will soon confront Jesus as well as the disciples.

CHAPTER 14

John 15

John 15—Introduction

The atmosphere of departure is interrupted with the insertion of another timeless parable about the topic of the vine, vine grower, and branches. These are familiar topics to people who grow fruit for wine. The image of the vine has a strong tradition in the Hebrew Bible, where Israel has been portrayed as the vine (Isa 5:1–7; Hos 10:1), but not always in a positive light. In addition, the vine also represents divine wisdom (Sir 24:17). In this parable Jesus, rather than Israel, represents a strong, healthy vine that brings strength and love to its branches.

Subsequently, in 15:12–18 Jesus announces the command of love within the context of community. The opposite of divine love translates as hatred by the world, a topic that appears in 15:18–25. As you read the discussion about love and hate, remember that, in reality, members of the Johannine communities or their parents have already experienced the fall of the Temple in Jerusalem, the growing tension between Christian Jews and other Jews, as well as expulsion from their synagogues. Therefore, the concept of hate and shunning was all too familiar to them.

The chapter concludes with another mention of the Advocate, a theme, as you recall, that appeared in the previous chapter.

For reading purposes the chapter may be divided as follows:

1. 5:1–11   Parable of the vine and branches, with commentary
2. 15:12–17   Jesus' command on love
3. 15:18–25   Remarks about the hatred and rejection of the world

4. 15:26–27   Reappearance of remarks about the
                Advocate

John 15—Questions

146. In 15:6 the description of throwing away and burning branches to describe people who do not abide in Jesus seems awfully cruel. Does it really mean what it says?
147. In 15:10 is it enough to keep Jesus' commandments?
148. Does Jesus mean the Ten Commandments or the loving-one-another command, which follows in 15:12?
149. In 15:13 are we to take laying down our lives for friends literally?
150. In 15:19 don't we actually belong to the world by virtue of being human beings?
151. Does 15:22 mean that those who have not heard the gospel cannot sin?
152. Where do the words of 15:23 leave Jews, Muslims, and so on? Don't they love God too?
153. Is 15:27 why some Christians and 12-step programs use personal testimony as part of their ritual?

John 15—Conclusion

According to John, 15:1–11 occurs at the time of the Last Supper, where Jesus speaks the parable to his friends, not to the crowds. Therefore, the words have a more intimate context of union, love, and belief. The section contains a parable, which Jesus explains to his disciples, as he did in John 10 with the parable of the good shepherd.

Jesus introduces this parable with another important *egō eimi* saying, "I am the true vine." He continues with "my Father is the vinegrower" (15:1). Although the subject of the vine and the branches has a familiar ring both from the Hebrew Bible and from the parables in the other three gospels, in this parable Jesus underlines two separate relationships: one with his Father (15:1) and one with his disciples (15:5), who "are the branches." Moreover, the adjective *true* in "I am the true vine" points to Jesus as the one who represents the will of the Father. This adjective clearly indicates that his disciples have been called to follow him rather than Israel, which symbolized the vine in the past, because now, as Jesus proclaims, "I am the true vine."

Within this parable each of the three components has a different function. The vine grower (God) prunes the good branches so that the vine grows healthier and produces more fruit. At the same time, he cuts down the dead branches because they no longer remain attached to the strength of the vine. The true vine (Jesus) brings life-producing strength to the branches. Accordingly, the branches "remain" strong and attached to the vine so that they can weather all types of temperature, as well as endure winds and storms. Without the vine, the branches wither and die.

The verb *to remain/abide* (Greek *menō*) occurs frequently within the parable (15:4, 5, 6, 7, 9, 10). The repetition of this verb indicates its importance. The verb *remain/abide,* underscores the necessity of the disciples' union with Jesus and the Father. As long as the disciples "remain" closely linked with the healthy vine (Jesus), they shall bear much fruit from the strength of the vine. To further the point, Jesus adds that God will be glorified by the good works of the disciples. The fruits of this union appear in the realm of joy and love.

The next section (15:12–17) announces Jesus' command of love. It also describes his deep love for his disciples when he calls them "friends." Jesus' command to "love one another as I have loved you" encompasses all past commands in the biblical tradition because, if the disciples adhere to this decree, they will maintain the other lesser commands. With one brief summons Jesus has called the disciples to reach far beyond any traditional legislation of the past. If they truly love one another as Jesus loved them, they will forgive all grievances and they will raise their level of daily living to reach beyond the mere observance of external religious laws. With this command, Jesus summons the disciples to think, act, and behave like their inclusive, forgiving, and open-hearted leader does. Self-sacrifice represents an essential element in this command of love, as well a needed element for the growth of community.

In 15:18–25 Jesus reminds the disciples about those outside the community of believers, who will oppose, reject, and hate them. Jesus describes such opposition in terms of "the world." As the Johannine communities have been called to be defined by love, "the world" represents the opposite of love, namely, hate. As you may recall, Jesus described "the world" in his conversation with Nicodemus in John 3:17–21 as those who love the darkness and hate the light. Subsequently, "the world" describes those who choose ignorance, who refuse to open their hearts to however God calls them in life. As a result, such people will bring pain to the Johannine communities by their close-mindedness, hatred, and revenge. Since the disciples do not belong to the world, even though they live within it, Jesus clearly emphasizes that they will be hated by "the world." Jesus tries to warn them that, as his followers, they will also suffer persecution, as he has, because "servants are not greater than their master" (15:20). Those who represent "the world" will simply not accept the mission of the disciples, as shown in their refusal to listen to the divine message of openness and love. In view of the fact that this stubborn stance has been consistent throughout the Fourth Gospel, Jesus comments sadly in 15:25, "They hated me without a cause," in the light of Psalm 35:19. Furthermore, because they have seen the works and heard the words of Jesus, they remain responsible for their choices.

The chapter concludes with another mention of the Advocate, who will be needed to strengthen the disciples in their battles with persecution and other types of evil from "the world." The disciples will be the instruments for the "Spirit of truth," who will continue the message of Jesus' command to "love one another as I have loved you" (15:12).

CHAPTER 15
John 16

John 16—Introduction

Chapter 16 contains themes that you have already studied in the previous two chapters, but with added comments. For example, the topics of persecution, the departure of Jesus, and the role of the Advocate emerge within the discussion. In addition, when Jesus returns to the subject of his departure, he adds an analogy about a woman about to give birth. The chapter concludes with a hope-filled warning to his disciples.

For reading purposes the chapter may be divided as follows:

1. 16:1–4a   Warning about persecution
2. 16:4b–11   Discussion about the departure of Jesus
3. 16:12–15   The guidance of the Advocate
4. 16:16–24   Pain of departure, followed by the return of joy
5. 16:25–33   Warning to the disciples, with words of triumph

John 16—Questions

154. In 16:2 why does Jesus say, "They will put you out of the synagogues"? I thought Christians went to churches?
155. Doesn't 16:2b further the idea that, whatever side you are on in a battle, you always think God is on your side?
156. In 16:7 here we go with the Advocate again. How can I see/hear/imagine the Advocate in a way I can understand?

157. If, as it implies in 16:7, the Advocate is here now because Jesus has left, where was this Holy Spirit in the Holocaust? The Crusades? The Iraq War?
158. In 16:13 is the Spirit of truth the same as the Advocate?
159. Does 16:16, 18 say that Jesus is coming back in "a little while"? What happened?
160. In 16:24 what does "Ask and you will receive" really mean?
161. Why does Jesus speak in figures of speech, as he says in 16:25, and as the disciples reiterate in 16:29? Wouldn't plain speech work better?
162. If Jesus has conquered the world as he says in 16:33, why are we in such a mess?

John 16—Conclusion

The opening of the chapter (16:1–4a) continues Jesus' warning to the disciples about the abhorrence of the world and its effect on their lives. He cautions them about the world's two actions of hatred, namely, their excommunication from the synagogues and the possibility of their deaths. Ironically, the religious leaders who decide such a dreadful fate for Jesus' disciples think that such decisions help them in their worship of God. In reality, however, the victims, namely, the disciples, emerge as the true worshippers of Jesus and his Father.

John 16:4b–11 picks up the theme of departure, which appeared in John 14. It also refers to the coming of the Advocate once again, a theme that has occurred in both John 14 and 15. Since Jesus' departure causes deep sorrow among the disciples, Jesus tries to comfort them. He relates that, unless he leaves, the Advocate cannot come to strengthen them. Moreover, Jesus declares that the Advocate will "prove the world wrong about sin and righteousness and judgment." The phrase, "to prove the world wrong," dominates all three concepts. In these verses it has the notion of reversing the worlds' idea of sin, righteousness, and judgment. While some Jewish authorities will consort with Roman authorities to murder Jesus, they consider themselves righteous as they attempt to rid the world of Jesus, whom they envision as a sinner needing severe judgment. Ironically, the complete opposite is true. Jesus, the one without sin, prevails as the righteous Son of God. To him has been given the divine power to judge sinners. Therefore, at this moment, Jesus reassures the disciples that in the future the Advocate will act, not as a defense counsel, but more as a prosecuting attorney. The Advocate will prove "the world" wrong and will overcome evil.

Jesus continues to discuss the coming of the Advocate in 16:12–15. Here he emphasizes the role of teacher for the Advocate, the "Spirit of truth." The disciples will come to learn real truth, not that which the world holds as truth. The Advocate will reveal no new truths, but will receive from Jesus what will be taught. Since in this Last Supper scene Jesus has not yet been glorified completely, the disciples simply cannot understand all that he wishes to tell them. Yet, in the future, they will learn with the help of the "Spirit of truth."

In 16:16–24 Jesus picks up the theme of departure. Yet his disciples do not understand his message, in a way similar to the misunderstanding of both Peter and Thomas in John 14. With this difficult topic of departure, Jesus tries to assure his followers to have hope. To do this, he refers to the example of a woman who has labor pains prior to giving birth. Jesus explains that, despite the severe pain of the moment, complete joy will follow at the birth of a child. No matter how she suffered temporarily beforehand, her joy will grow when she beholds her precious baby. This true-to-life experience offers a message that would be readily understood by the disciples. Like the ending of a mother's pain, the pain of the disciples will soon be forgotten. When they meet Jesus again their sorrow will disappear because of their tremendous joy. With this joy in mind, Jesus urges them to ask anything of God in his name. These remarks stress the intimacy between the Son and the Father as well as the divine power of Jesus. With the departure of Jesus, their requests will be fulfilled by God, his Father.

In the final section (16:25–33) Jesus relates that he will speak more plainly about his going back to the Father and promises them that the Father loves them. The author states that the disciples appear grateful for the clarity of Jesus' message. They also acknowledge their belief in Jesus as Son of God. Here Jesus forecasts some challenges that they will face, but urges them to have "peace" in the midst of persecution. Jesus declares in 16:33, "But take courage; I have conquered the world!" These final words offer complete hope.

In conclusion, notice how the accounts of John 14 and 16 offer great similarities in the themes of departure, the Advocate, belief, misunderstanding of Jesus' message, and so on. Probably the author has incorporated two different versions of similar topics. In any case, the repetition of these topics helps us to learn and understand the importance of Jesus' intimate message to his disciples, whom he named as friends.

CHAPTER 16
John 17

John 17—Introduction

John 17 emerges as a unique and one of the most special parts of the entire Gospel, a chapter in which Jesus prays intimately to his Father. The personal prayer appears in 17:1–26 and concludes the final discourse. Throughout these verses various themes emerge, such as the sharing of Jesus' inner self, his concern for the disciples, the call for unity, and so on. As Jesus prays, the disciples stay near him and listen to his intimate words to his Father. In a very real sense, this important prayer reflects a timelessness where the former phrase "in my name" has been replaced with "in your name."

For reading purposes the chapter may be divided as follows:

1. 17:1–5   Jesus' requests to the Father about himself
2. 17:6–19   Requests for the disciples
3. 17:20–26   Requests for those whom the disciples will teach and for love

John 17—Questions

163. I have heard this prayer of Jesus called the "Priestly Prayer." From where does this come? It doesn't talk about Jesus as a priest or anyone else as a priest, so why is called the "Priestly Prayer"?

164. In 17:1–5 does "glorify your Son" mean crucify and resurrect Jesus? This don't seem too glorified to me, at least crucified doesn't.

165. In 17:6 what does the statement, "I have made your name known to those whom you gave me from the world," mean? To whom did God give Jesus to make God's name known? Jews? Gentiles? Us?

166. In 17:9 what is Jesus asking of God on our behalf, or isn't it on our behalf?

167. In 17:11b why aren't we completely "one," since that's what Jesus asked of God?

168. In 17:12 is "the one destined to be lost" Judas? Also, which scripture was to be fulfilled?

169. Mostly I do feel protected from "the evil one," as indicated in 17:15. What about when I don't feel that way, or what about some who seem never protected?

170. In 17:17–19 what does *sanctified* mean?

171. In 17:21–23 how can we all be made one? Also, why do we seem not to be able to accomplish it? Why does it seem Jesus was not able to accomplish it either?

John 17—Conclusion

The prayer of Jesus begins with an introduction that connects his previous discourse with the appeals that will commence. You may recall that, within the format of an ancient farewell discourse, the dying person often ends with a prayer to the deity on behalf of his children, who remain the heirs of his name, or his companions, who will become the heirs of his mission. In this case Jesus prays for his disciples, who have journeyed with him during the years of his ministry.

The formal posture of Jesus whereby "he looked up to heaven" represents a common stance of prayer both in Judaism and other religions of the Greco-Roman world. When Jesus addresses God as "Father" (17:1, 5, 21, 24, 25), it may remind you of the Lord's Prayer, where the title has already appeared in the gospels of Matthew (6:9–13) and Luke (11:2–4).

Unlike the prayer of the agony in the garden featured in the Synoptic Gospels, Jesus does not grieve deeply throughout his prayer. Therefore, no such scene appears in the Fourth Gospel because, united with the Father, Jesus remains in charge of his destiny. On the contrary, Jesus' purpose continues to be to glorify the Father. In the first part of this prayer he talks with the Father about their relationship with each other. Jesus acknowledges that "the hour has come," and asks the Father to "glorify" him, as he has "glorified" the Father while ministering on earth. Here the theme of glorification unites with the theme of eternal life.

In 17:3, Jesus alludes to others as he speaks to his Father. Here he describes "eternal life" as those who come to "know you," which means to come to "know" the Father. In the Hebrew Bible the term *know* means to have an intimate bond with another person. Jesus' description of "eternal life" implies that it begins here on earth with the union between the Father and those who acknowledge Jesus and his mission. Therefore, in this verse "eternal life" has already begun for those who believe.

In 17:6–19, Jesus continues the prayer to include his disciples. He reminds his Father that the disciples have learned about him from Jesus and that they have believed. They accept Jesus. Therefore, the disciples represent those who have already been chosen by the Father. With this said, Jesus asks his Father to guard them so that "they may be one, as we are one" (17:11). The unity that he requests reflects the deep relationship experienced between his Father and himself. Just as he protected the disciples from "the world" while he lived among them, he asks his Father to keep them safe. As he departs from the world, Jesus seeks protection for his disciples from the evils of the world.

In the last section of the prayer (17:20–26), Jesus extends his requests to the Father even further. Here he prays for those whom the disciples will teach and who will come to believe in him through their words. His prayer demonstrates that he embraces all future believers. Once again Jesus makes a request of unity, so that "they may all be one. As you, Father, are in me and I am in you" (17:21). Jesus continues to pray "that they may become completely one" (17:23). Here the notion of perfection describes a completion, namely, a fulfillment of love through oneness with this divine union and each other. Consequently, this union provides the followers of Jesus with eternal life because they become one with the Father and Jesus. Such unification will permeate the community as well as their ministries.

In the concluding verses, Jesus returns to the theme of love and glorification. The return of "glory" forms an inclusion to the entire farewell prayer. As you may recall, an inclusion unites a theme or topic that appears in the beginning of a narrative with a reappearance of the theme or topic at the end of that same narrative, thereby making the entire work a cohesive whole. In this case, the verb *glorify* in 17:1 parallels the noun *glory* in 17:24 to form an inclusion. Jesus' final request, that his disciples have the ability to "see" his eternal glory from the Father, concludes this intimate, loving prayer of a son to his Father.

CHAPTER 17
John 18

John 18—Introduction

John 18 inaugurates the narrative of the passion, which will end in John 19:42. It emerges as a dramatic chapter that describes the beginning of Jesus' final destiny. Unlike the previous five chapters where Jesus remained stationary during the Last Supper and farewell discourse, John 18 presents Jesus as moving from the room of the Last Supper to the following places: the Mount of Olives, the residency of Annas, the palace of the high priest where Caiaphas lived, and the praetorium, where the Roman governor made decisions when he came to Jerusalem. In less than twenty-four hours Jesus has been placed under arrest and appears to have had at least three trials before both Jewish and Roman rulers. Take note that this count excludes the informal trial by the Sanhedrin and Caiaphas in 11:47–53.

For reading purposes the chapter may be divided as follows:

1. 18:1–12   The arrest of Jesus in the garden
2. 18:13–27   The informal trial before Annas and the three denials of Peter
3. 18:24, 28a   The trial before Caiaphas
4. 18:28b–40   The trial before Pilate, the Roman governor

John 18—Questions

172. In 18:1 the author of the Fourth Gospel has Jesus choose a "place where there was a garden." Is there any significance in this choice?

173. In 18:4, besides bringing a detachment of soldiers and police to the garden, Judas seemed to have very little to do with all that was going to happen to Jesus. It sounds as if Jesus and Judas have changed roles because Jesus is the person in charge. Why?
174. In 18:3 do the lanterns have any special meaning?
175. In 18:6, when Jesus let his identity be known, I always wished he wouldn't have made it so easy for those who came to arrest him. What is the reason for Jesus' action?
176. The action of Peter in 18:10–11 would be regarded as an act of defense in today's world, yet why didn't Jesus show any appreciation for Peter's move?
177. Was Peter afraid of something when he denied knowing Jesus three times?
178. Is there any importance to Peter's three denials in John 18?
179. Since Pilate thought that Jesus was innocent, why didn't he let him go free?
180. In 18:28 what does "ritual defilement" mean? Is it important?
181. In John 18 the trials of Jesus are not like our trials. Why?

John 18—Conclusion

John 18 commences after Jesus finished his long farewell discourse and prayer at the Last Supper and walks across the Kidron valley to an unnamed garden, which in the Synoptics has been identified as Gethsemane on the Mount of Olives. Here Judas enters with a group of Roman soldiers and Jewish guards, as well as some representatives from the Jewish authorities. All seemed to be armed. John's Gospel is the only gospel where Judas brings both soldiers (Roman) and police (Jewish Temple soldiers). Most likely, this large crowd does not represent an historical reality, but rather a literary and theological rendition to express the whole unbelieving world.

Two important points need to be noted in the posture and dialogue that ensue in 18:4–11. First, the scene describes Jesus as the one in charge of the situation. No one drags him off for imprisonment. He alone decides to go. Second, his response, "I am he," to the question, "Whom are you looking for?" has powerful overtones. Although a few scholars hold that Jesus' words remain a simple reply, I suggest that the "I am he" response has deeper implications. When Jesus identified himself the first time with these words, the arresting authorities "stepped back and fell to the ground" (18:6). Such posture exemplifies homage to a deity. In addition, Jesus' words remind the audience of his frequent *egō eimi* ("I am") divine self-identification statements in the Fourth Gospel. The response also reflects the Divine Name that God gave to Moses in the Hebrew Bible, "I AM WHO I AM" (Exod 3:14).

Two more observations about the scene need to be made. At this tense moment Jesus continues to care for others rather than himself. When he boldly addresses those who came to arrest him with the remark, "I told you that I am he. So, if you are looking for me, let these men go" (18:8). Soon after, he rebukes Peter for his violent act of cutting off the right ear of Malchus. Undoubtedly, the rebuke has a twofold purpose: the refusal of any violence and the protection of Peter. In both incidents, then, the evangelist demonstrates that Jesus rises above all adversities. He clearly remains in command and always protects those who follow him.

The next section (18:13–27) describes the unofficial informal hearing before Annas, as well as the three denials of Peter in the courtyard of Annas' home. Both incidents become linked and occur at night. In the scene the author states the relationship between Caiaphas, high priest, and Annas, his father-in-law. According to the ancient historian Josephus (*Antiquities,* 18.2.1; 26), Annas had been appointed by the Roman prefect, Quirinius, in 6 CE. Although Annas was deposed in 15 CE, he retained his power and five of his sons became high priests. In later Jewish writings, his corruption as well as his power and wealth have been documented. The very fact that the evangelist describes Jesus as being brought first to Annas indicates his tremendous influence in decision making for Judaism.

The meeting between Annas and Jesus appears in 18:19–23, where the former high priest questions him about his disciples as well as his doctrine. Ironically, his question about Jesus' disciples surfaces at the moment when, outside the building and among the bystanders, Peter denies that he even knows Jesus. Jesus refused to answer Annas about his disciples. However, when Annas asks him about his teaching, Jesus responds in a bold and open manner: "I have spoken openly to the world; I have always taught in synagogues and in the temple.... Why do you ask me? Ask those who heard what I said to them" (18:20–21). It seems logical that Annas would question both disciples as well as those who heard Jesus teach. Yet he does not seem to be interested in truth, a topic that will emerge in the trial with Pilate. After Jesus replies to Annas, one of the guards strikes him in the mouth. This brute force does not stop his reply of innocence to the one who struck him.

While the interrogation between Jesus and Annas causes sparks inside, the scene in the outside adjoining courtyard also becomes active. After Peter enters through the intercession of "the other disciple," he becomes a target for questioning from three different sources: the woman at the gate, a group around the charcoal fire, and a relative of Malchus, whose ear Peter cut off. When they each ask him about his relationship to Jesus, he denies three times any knowledge of or association with Jesus. While Jesus proclaims the divine "I am" in the garden scene, Peter responds "I am not" when others question whether he knows or has been a disciple of Jesus. Only a few hours before, Peter shared a sacred meal with Jesus and heard his encouraging words and prayer for him. Now, Peter betrays Jesus. To those around the courtyard, who represent Jewish society, Peter fails to honor his leader. He has shamed Jesus, the other disciples, and all that Jesus taught. Later in John 21:15–17, after Jesus was raised from the dead, he will ask Peter three times about loving him.

The chapter offers very few remarks about the trial before Caiaphas. In fact, any mention of the incident appears only in 18:24 and 28a. In 18:24 the evangelist states that Annas sends Jesus bound to Caiaphas, the high priest. The Gospel of Matthew (26:57) also names Caiaphas in such a leadership role, whereas the other two gospels do not name him. The mention of Jesus being bound may suggest that he has been shackled since the arrest in the garden. John 18:28 states that the following morning Jesus was transported from the palace of Caiaphas to the praetorium, namely, Pilate's headquarters in Jerusalem. This took place the day before Pesach (Passover).

The last section of the chapter (18:28b–40) presents the trial before Pilate, the Roman governor. In many ways this scene functions as the most important segment of the entire passion. As with the previous sections, an entirely different cast of characters appears on the scene. During the trial Pilate asks the famous question about "truth" at the very moment he encounters Jesus, the real "Truth." Throughout the Roman trial, Pilate moves from inside the praetorium, where he has the opportunity for "Truth" and life in the person of Jesus, to outside the building, where some Jewish leaders and crowds do not care about the truth, but only desire political victory. Three basic literary structures set the stage for a dramatic trial: the cry of the crowd for the death of Jesus (18:28–32), the questioning by Pilate to Jesus about his being king (18:33–38a), and the proclamation of Pilate about the innocence of Jesus (18:38b–40).

In 18:28–32 Pilate goes outside the building to meet "the Jews" who brought Jesus to him. It appears quite ironic that "the Jews" become very concerned about their ritual purity in order to give proper worship to God at Pesach (Passover), yet they insist that the innocent Jesus be found guilty without any accusations against him. When Pilate retorts that Jesus should be judged by Jewish law, their reply uncovers deep feelings. They want Jesus to die the Roman death of crucifixion. At a previous festival of Sukkoth (Tabernacles), both Nicodemus (7:51) and Jesus (8:37–47) confronted the leaders about their desire to kill Jesus in relation to their disregard for their own laws.

Pilate returns inside the praetorium (18:33–38a), summons Jesus, and asks if he is the King of the Jews. From this question it would seem that these Jewish leaders have already informed the Roman governor about a claim to kingship. Jesus responds by disclaiming earthly kingship and proceeds to describe a kingdom of another world. His kingdom does not seek a political space in this world. Remember, anyone who claimed to be a king directly opposes Caesar, who rules the Roman Empire as king. Therefore, for the Romans a claim of kingship would have serious punishable consequences because it ignores the reign of Caesar. In another light, the Jews look on God as their king. For them any claim to kingship would be blasphemy.

In 18:37 Pilate responds to Jesus remarks with the comment, "So you are a king?" In reply, Jesus explains that, once he came into the world as king (incarnation), he had the responsibility to testify to the truth. When he adds somberly, "Everyone who belongs to the truth listens to my voice," he invites Pilate to listen. Instead, the fearful Pilate only questions, "What is truth?" (18:38). His question uncovers the reality that his fear of making a courageous decision deafened him to the truth, which stood right in front of him in the person of Jesus. The chapter closes with Pilate acknowledging the innocence of Jesus, yet succumbing to the cries of the crowds for a release of a bandit named Barabbas, and, by implication, for the imprisonment of Jesus.

CHAPTER 18
John 19

John 19—Introduction

The first part of John 19 continues the powerful scene of Pilate with Jesus. It describes the struggle within Pilate and his final weak decision to condemn Jesus to death because of the verbal pressure from the crowd. The remainder of the chapter centers on the death and burial of Jesus.

For reading purposes the chapter may be divided as follows:

1. 19:1–3   Jesus is mocked
2. 19:4–8   Pilate proclaims the innocence of Jesus
3. 19:9–12a   Pilate questions the authority of Jesus
4. 19:12b–16   Jesus is sentenced to death
5. 19:17–37   Jesus dies on the cross
6. 19:38–42   The burial of Jesus

John 19—Questions

182. In 19:1–3 John has Pilate and the soldiers go to great lengths to make Jesus appear as a king. What is the point?
183. In 19:11 to whose power does Jesus refer when he speaks about power?
184. In 19:23 what is the significance of the tunic without seams?
185. In 19:26 the mother of Jesus, who is at the foot of the cross, is asked to behold her son. What does this mean?
186. In 19:26–27 what did Jesus have in mind when he uttered these words from cross?
187. In 19:30 Jesus says, "It is finished." What does "It" mean?

188. In 19:34 what is the significance of the pierced side?
189. In 19:35 the testimony of the eyewitness seems very mysterious. Who was this eyewitness?
190. In 19:41 what does the author of this Gospel mean by the term "new tomb"?

John 19—Conclusion

Chapter 19 continues the discussion of the preceding chapter between the Roman governor, Pilate, and Jesus, as well as the crowd's disdain of Jesus. Here to begin the chapter, the author once again presents the great irony of the situation. After Pilate found Jesus innocent of all charges in 18:38, he now has him flogged in 19:1. The beating consisted of a cruel and inhuman mockery of Jesus as king.

The scene crescendos in 19:4–8 outside the praetorium as Pilate again reiterates the innocence of Jesus. When Pilate shows the battered king to the crowds in hopes of appeasing the forceful crowd with the words, "Here is the man" (19:5), the defiant crowd chants, "Crucify him! Crucify him!" Pilate tries to return Jesus to them, but at this point the Jewish leaders become more determined than ever that Jesus should die. They shout that Jesus has broken their law by claiming divinity, that is, claiming to be the "Son of God." Their angry stance reflects the importance of this Johannine title. While the Jewish leaders hear Jesus' words as blasphemy, ironically Jesus *is* the Son of God! With accusations on a new and deeper religious level, Pilate becomes afraid.

The governor proceeds to question Jesus' origin. The silence of Jesus becomes striking as it represents a refusal to defend himself against his false accusers. In frustration, the governor tries to intimidate Jesus with his power. Yet Jesus quickly reminds him that the source of all power stems from God. His authoritative comments frightened Pilate. Consequently, he tries to release Jesus once again. Yet the Jewish leaders continue to intimidate the governor with the threat that the release of Jesus means that "you are no friend of the emperor" (19:12a). They put more pressure on Pilate by adding that anyone who claims to be a king "sets himself against the emperor" (19:12). Now, they describe Jesus as one who seeks political power and authority.

With these shouts ringing in his ears, Pilate goes to the judgment seat and shouts to the crowds, "Here is your King!" (19:14). The crowd continues their chants for crucifixion and pledges their allegiance to the emperor as their only king. The statement, "We have no king but the emperor" (19:15), uncovers a sad commentary. All through the Hebrew Bible the Israelites extol God as their one true King. Now, some of their descendants refute the entire tradition and pledge total allegiance to Caesar. In a final act of authoritative defeat, Pilate hands Jesus over to be crucified.

John 19:17–37 describes the death of Jesus on the cross. Like other parts of the dramatic final days of Jesus, the evangelist provides the reader with some unique material about his crucifixion. For example, only in John are the following scenes recorded: a heated discussion with the Jewish leaders about the title "King of the Jews," which appears on the cross; the casting of lots for Jesus' clothing; the farewell bequeathing of the "mother of Jesus" to the unnamed disciple and his new relation of son to her; Jesus' words, "I thirst," and "It is finished." The Johannine Jesus truly takes charge of his life, even while dying a brutal death on the cross. He has provided both his mother and the unnamed disciple with a new family. In a very real sense, they reflect the new family of believers that the Johannine communities had to reestablish after their excommunication from the synagogue. These two figures lead the communities into a new life of faith. The pronouncement, "It is finished," demonstrates that right up until Jesus took his last human breath, he decided his own destiny in union with his Father. The work, for which the Father sent him, has been completed.

The final section (19:38–42) presents the burial of Jesus. Only John's Gospel includes the mention of Nicodemus and a garden, which provides the location for the tomb. When the author mentions that Nicodemus brings about one hundred pounds of myrrh and aloes, he implies that Nicodemus finishes what Mary of Bethany started in John 12:1–8, namely, a kingly burial for Jesus. The scene concludes with the burial of Jesus in the tomb of the garden.

CHAPTER 19
John 20

John 20—Introduction

The discovery of the empty tomb and Jesus' postresurrection appearances take center stage in John 20. All the stories take place in Jerusalem. The first half of the chapter highlights the question of the whereabouts of Jesus. Mary of Magdala, Peter, and the Beloved Disciple all seek him at the tomb. The remainder of the chapter features the reply, or the lack of it, to the risen Jesus. Therefore, the themes of witness and response permeate the appearances.

In this chapter the risen Jesus appears first to Mary of Magdala and commissions her to bring the "good news" of his resurrection to the other disciples. Thus, the author highlights Mary of Magdala as the first apostle of the risen Lord. Later, on Easter evening, Jesus appears to the disciples and bestows the "Holy Spirit" upon the community. One week later, Jesus reappears to the disciples and speaks directly to Thomas.

For reading purposes the chapter may be divided as follow:

1. 20:1–2   Mary of Magdala discovers the empty tomb and announces the news to the other disciples
2. 20:3–10   Three disciples return to the tomb (Mary of Magdala, Peter, and the "other disciple")
3. 20:11–18   Mary of Magdala receives the first appearance of the risen Jesus and announces the news to the other disciples
4. 20:19–23   Jesus appears to the disciples Easter evening (without Thomas)
5. 20:24–29   Jesus appears to the disciples one week later (with Thomas)

138

6. 20:30–31   Conclusion of the first ending of the
                Gospel

John 20—Questions

191. In John 20:1 does "Early on the first day of the week" mean on Sunday morning or Monday morning?
192. In John 20:2 where did Mary of Magdala go to find Simon Peter? Who was the "other disciple, the one whom Jesus loved"?
193. In John 20:5–6 is there significance to the other disciple being first at the tomb but Simon Peter going in the tomb, which the other disciples failed to do?
194. In John 20:7 why is there so much detail about the grave wrappings?
195. In 20:8 what does it mean when the author says, "Then the other disciple...saw and believed?"
196. In 20:10, when Peter and the other disciple see the linen wrappings lying in the tomb, what was their reaction? Why did they return to their homes?
197. In 20:11 why did Mary not go home when the other disciples left the tomb?
198. In 20:12 how did Mary of Magdala know they were angels?
199. In 20:15 why didn't Mary of Magdala recognize Jesus' voice, even if she couldn't see him clearly through her tears?
200. In 20:16 Jesus mentions Mary's name and she then recognizes him. What is the significance of Mary's response to Jesus speaking her name?
201. In 20:17 why couldn't Mary hold on to Jesus? Had he changed shape or texture or something?
202. In 20:22–23 about what is Jesus speaking?
203. In 20:23 why would Jesus suggest that some sins should be retained by their owner?
204. In 20:24 who was Thomas's twin?
205. Why is Thomas the only one known as "doubting," because the other disciples were shown Jesus' hands and side in 20:20? That's all that Thomas seemed to want.

206. Thomas wanted tangible proof before he would believe the other disciples had seen Jesus. What does this say about Thomas?
207. Why does 20:30–31 sound like the end of the Gospel? Or doesn't it?
208. In 20:30–31 what is the purpose of John's Gospel?

John 20—Conclusion

The stories in the chapter continue in Jerusalem in the early hours of a Sunday morning. The opening scene describes Mary of Magdala, who discovers the reality of the empty tomb and the removal of the stone in her search for Jesus. Without delay she returns to inform Peter and the other disciple "whom Jesus loved" (Beloved Disciple), who represent leadership in the early Christian communities. All four gospels describe the presence of Mary of Magdala at the tomb early on Easter morning. The "we" in her announcement (20:2) suggests that other women accompanied her.

The account of Peter and the "other disciple" going to the tomb because of Mary's announcement appears between three narratives about Mary of Magdala, namely, the discovery of the empty tomb, the appearance by the risen Jesus, and her announcement to the other disciples about the resurrection of Jesus. Taken together, all stories reflect the intention of the evangelist to describe the search for Jesus and the Easter faith of Mary and the Beloved Disciple. The disciples run to the tomb to find it empty as Mary said. The Beloved Disciple came to faith in the risen Jesus by the sight of the empty tomb. Notice how nothing has been said about Peter and belief. Both Peter and the Beloved Disciple left the empty tomb and returned to the place where they stayed in Jerusalem.

The next scene (20:11–18) reports the glorious appearance of the risen Jesus to Mary of Magdala and her final faith-filled response to him. It begins with the whereabouts of Mary after the other two disciples leave. In 20:11 the author states that Mary remains at the tomb in her continued search for Jesus. Note that only after the two disciples have departed do the angels appear to the weeping Mary. As you know, weeping at the place of a person's grave usually indicates the loss of a greatly admired person, as well as deep love for that person. Here, too, Mary weeps for such reasons. When the angels question her, she informs them that she searches for Jesus.

As Mary turns around, Jesus stands before her. Initially, the anguished Mary does not recognize him because of her grief. As she begins to dialogue with Jesus, whom she mistakes for the gardener, he asks, "Whom are you looking for?" (20:15b). She replies that she seeks the dead body of Jesus. She does not yet realize that living person of Jesus stands right in front of her. Then, a marvelous moment ensues. The risen Jesus rewards her search when he calls Mary by name. Immediately, she recognizes his voice. This new mode of the resurrected Lord brings Mary great joy as she exclaims, "Rabbouni!" (20:16). Recall in John 10:3–5 in the remarks about the good shepherd that he calls his own sheep by name and they know his voice. So here, too, the risen Jesus calls forth Mary of Magdala to lead. In a very real sense, she represents the new Israel of God, the faithful ones who hear the word of Jesus and respond wholeheartedly to it. Finally, when Jesus commands her to go tell the other disciples about him, he makes two very important points: He chooses Mary of Magdala as the first apostle of the risen Lord , and he implies that his presence will now be within the community.

The next section (20:19–23), which describes Jesus' appearance to the other disciples, highlights the need for faith. The risen Jesus comes to the other disciples on Easter Sunday evening, many hours after Mary had brought the good news about Jesus to them. His initial greeting, "Peace be with you" (20:19), symbolizes the everlasting peace that the world lacks and cannot give. Unlike the way faith came to the Beloved Disciple after seeing the empty tomb, or the way faith came to Mary of Magdala when Jesus called her name, in this appearance the risen Lord showed the nail wounds of his hands and his pierced side to the disciples as proof of his resurrection (20:20). The author states that only after this display did they believe: "*Then* the disciples rejoiced" (italics mine).

The risen Jesus repeats his initial greeting, "Peace be with you" (20:21a). Here, however, he adds the commission for the ministry that they have been called to do: "As the Father has sent me, so I send you" (20:21b). Yet these frightened disciples needed the fortitude of Jesus in order to do his work. Therefore, the risen Jesus breathes on them the gift of his internal and eternal presence as he proclaims, "Receive the Holy Spirit" (20:22b). With these words, the disciples became strengthened to go against the ways of the world, which usually, as you already know in John, signifies darkness/evil.

Recall that in John's Gospel the term, *Holy Spirit* is identified with the term *Paraclete* or *Advocate*. As I will explain in answer #7 in the *"Introduction to the Gospel,"* the term refers to Jesus. The first Paraclete describes the human Jesus on earth, while the second Paraclete (Holy Spirit) identifies the spiritual presence of the risen Lord, who will be with his followers until the end of time. Now, they have embarked on a new mission in a new world. Jesus goes further when he empowers them to forgive or retain sins. We need to remember that their empowerment has been linked completely with the coming of the Holy Spirit (Paraclete), who makes clear the goodness and evil of life (16:7–11) as well as provides strength to overcome such evil.

John 20:24–25 describes the absence of Thomas. When the disciples share with him the appearance of the Lord, he boldly announces, "Unless I see...I will not believe" (20:25). In a very real sense, Thomas represents the lack of faith of the other disciples before they received the Holy Spirit, except for the Beloved Disciple and Mary of Magdala, who always believed. Thomas wants proof in order to believe in the risen Lord.

The next section depicts the second appearance to the disciples one week later. Once again the evangelist mentions the shut doors (20:19, 26), probably to indicate a new type of appearance of Jesus' body. After Jesus offers his usual gift of peace, he invites Thomas to "believe." Jesus stops his doubt by asking him to touch the wounds on his body. In reply, Thomas becomes very ashamed of his strong remarks and attitude of disbelief the previous week. He cries out to Jesus, "My Lord and my God!" (20:28). His powerful reply signals his complete change of heart leading to faith. Jesus ends the dramatic scene with "Blessed are those who have not seen and yet have come to believe" (20:29). This last remark refers to any followers who do not have the advantage of Thomas' witness of the risen Jesus. We qualify as such followers.

In addition to the most important point of Jesus' resurrection, the entire chapter up to this point demonstrates the belief (Beloved Disciple, Mary of Magdala) or the lack of belief (disciples and Thomas) of the followers of Jesus. This final remark of Jesus points out the need to believe in God and his Son without tangible proof. Such words offer tremendous hope to the Johannine communities, who have suffered the loss of Judaism, represented by their excommunication from the synagogue. Now they need to put all their faith in the risen Lord, because faith without sight represents true discipleship.

The chapter concludes with the first ending of the Gospel (20:30–31). The early stages of the Gospel probably had this impressive conclusion. Here the purpose of the entire Gospel has been capsulized as well as clarified. The Fourth Gospel has been "written so that you may come to believe that Jesus is the Messiah, the Son of God, and that through believing you may have life in his name" (20:31). The chosen events of Jesus' life as well as selected words have been presented to the readers for two reasons: first, so that they may come to believe in him; and, second, so that they may experience the effects of true life.

CHAPTER 20
John 21

John 21—Introduction

The final redacted chapter, which became part of the Gospel before its first publication, describes a postresurrection appearance of Jesus to the disciples beyond the confines of Jerusalem. Now Jesus appears to them in the region of Galilee at the Sea of Tiberias (Sea of Galilee, Lake of Gennesaret). The stories of the catch of fish and the meal merge. Moreover, the risen Jesus dialogues with Peter, who represents the early church at large, about his mission and its relationship to the Beloved Disciple, who represents the Johannine communities. As you read and discuss the stories, take note of the tension that seems to exist between Peter and the Beloved Disciple.

For reading purposes the chapter may be divided as follow:

1. 21:1–14 Appearance to disciples in Galilee: miraculous catch of fish and meal
2. 21:15–23 Risen Jesus' dialogue with Peter
3. 21:24–25 Final conclusion of the Gospel

John 21—Questions

209. In 21:1–3 did the disciples return to just being fishermen?
210. In 21:4 why didn't the fisher/disciples recognize Jesus? They had already seen him in Jerusalem after the resurrection.
211. Wouldn't the disciples think it strange that someone approached and called them "Children," as in 21:5?

212. How can Peter be the rock on which the church is built if he can't even recognize Jesus, but had to take the word of the Beloved Disciple in 21:7?
213. In 21:7 why would Peter put clothes on to jump into the water?
214. In 21:9–10, if there is fish already on the fire along with bread, why did Jesus ask the disciples to bring more?
215. In 21:11 is it important that there were 153 large fish in the net?
216. If the disciples knew it was Jesus in 21:12, why was it even reported they didn't dare ask his name?
217. Why did Jesus repeat his message to Peter three times in slightly different words in 21:15–19? Is the difference in the wording important?
218. In 21:18–19 Jesus tells Peter what manner of death he will die and how he will glorify God by his death. What does this mean?
219. In 21:19 is there any connection between the kind of death Peter would die and Peter's following Jesus?
220. In 21:21 what was Peter really asking about the Beloved Disciple?
221. Jesus seems to be telling Peter to mind his own business and not worry about the Beloved Disciple but to worry about himself in 21:21–22. Is this correct?
222. In 21:24–25 does it mean that the Beloved Disciple is the "I" who wrote the Gospel and said there wasn't enough space in the world for all the books that could be written about what Jesus did? Or is the Beloved Disciple just the one who testified that what's in John's Gospel is true?

John 21—Conclusion

Most scholars agree that John 21 was composed later than the other chapters in the Fourth Gospel. In effect, it functions as a redaction that became part of the Gospel before its final composition. Why has the chapter been added? John 21 brings to the surface some important issues that needed explanation. Most importantly, it clarifies the role of the Beloved Disciple and Peter. In addition, it also preserves the tradition of the risen Jesus appearing to the disciples in Galilee.

The last chapter of the Fourth Gospel occurs in the region of Galilee on the shores of the Sea of Tiberias (Sea of Galilee, Lake of Gennesaret). Although traditionally it has been called a "sea," it remains the largest freshwater lake in Israel. Situated approximately 630 feet below sea level, it bears the title of the lowest freshwater lake in the world. The Jordan River and underground springs provide water for the thirteen mile long, eight mile wide area. For centuries, the lake has provided sustenance for many fishermen. In this first scene (21:1–14) Peter and the other disciples exemplify such marine workers.

Here the author mentions six other disciples who went fishing with Peter. Remember, traditionally Peter lived in Capernaum, a lovely village on the banks of the lake, a few miles northwest of the coastal city of Tiberias, Herod Antipas' ruling city in Galilee. Therefore, like others in his village, Peter made his livelihood as a fisherman. However, 21:3 relates that the disciples caught no fish that night. As you may recall in the Gospel, "night" often signifies ignorance, doubt, or absence of the divine.

When the risen Jesus appears to them the next morning along the banks of the lake, he addresses them tenderly. After their response about an empty catch, he orders them to cast their nets to the right side of the boat. When they did, the nets became overloaded with an abundance of fish. When the disciples listen to the voice of the risen Jesus their nets (community) become filled with fish (people). In this scene, the "day" of belief and hope contrast with the previous "night" of doubt and discouragement. In a new way, the disciples experience that anything becomes possible through belief in the risen Lord. Moreover, the "right side" in 21:6 represents blessing and abundance.

This story sounds quite similar to one that occurs in Luke 5:1–11, about Simon Peter and an abundant catch of fish. In Luke, the narrative connects to the call of the disciples, who will be "catching people" (Luke 5:10). In John 21, an association between the miraculous catch of fish and the future ministry of the disciples seems appropriate.

At this moment of abundant fishing, the Beloved Disciple immediately recognizes the risen Jesus from the boat. He informs Peter, "It is the Lord!" (21:7). Like the Beloved Disciple's belief after seeing the empty tomb in 20:8, here, too, the Beloved Disciple recognizes the risen Lord more quickly than Peter. However, when Peter heard the good news about the presence of Jesus from this other disciple, he fixed his clothes and jumped into the water in order to go to Jesus. By accepting the word of the Beloved Disciple, Peter finds Jesus.

The breakfast meal that follows reminds that reader of the feeding of the people with bread and fish in John 6:1–14. This parallel occasion may have helped the disciples in their recognition of the risen Jesus, even though he had already appeared to them twice in Jerusalem. Here the eucharistic reminiscences of the meal also unite with their future ministry of "fishers" of people. The disciples' closeness to Jesus through the Eucharist will empower them in the work ahead.

The last scene (21:15–23) uncovers a more explicit parallel between the Beloved Disciple and Peter. In 21:15–17 Jesus greets Peter three times by the name, "Simon, son of John," as he did when he first called him (1:42). Accordingly, three times Jesus questions Peter about his faithful love with the words, "do you love me?" that reflect a threefold rehabilitation of Peter since his denials of Jesus in 18:15–17. As Peter answers yes, Jesus commands him to feed/tend my lambs/sheep. This restoration of Peter to his ecclesial position has been led by the Beloved Disciple, who helped Peter recognize Jesus.

In a very real sense, then, Peter, who represents the early ecclesial institution, has been upstaged by the Beloved Disciple, who represents the Johannine communities. The Beloved Disciple functions as a prophetic witness to the Word (Jesus), which continues within these communities. The author alludes to this position through Jesus' reply to Peter's question and the comments that follow about the fate of the Beloved Disciple (21:22–23). It remains evident that the example and preaching of the Beloved Disciple about the Word continues to inspire believers even after his death. Since the abiding transcendence of the Word always supersedes any religious institution, these Johannine communities look and listen to the Word for guidance through the witness of the Beloved Disciple.

This additional chapter concludes with a testimony that the witness verifies the truth of the statements within the editorialized stories. The final comments remind the reader that Jesus' revelation could never all be captured within one book, even that of the Gospel of John.

Answers

Introduction to the Fourth Gospel—Answers

1. Throughout this book the term *Johannine* refers to an association with John's Gospel. It can refer to the communities that followed the traditions of this Gospel, to the author of the Fourth Gospel, or to the work itself.

2. In the past many Christians, notably Catholics, were taught about Jesus through Bible stories rather than through an authentic study of the primary texts, that is, the actual texts of the four gospels. Often different stories of the gospels were pulled together to form one picture of Jesus. Consequently, all nuances, differences, and emphases in each particular book were lost in the presentation. From this method of events, dates, and places pulled together as one story, many began to envision any gospel as a biography of Jesus.

   While this assumption does not correlate with the contemporary definition of biography as the story of a person's life written by someone else, the genre of the Fourth Gospel does resemble the flexibility of the ancient biography. Like other literary genres, the modern form of the biography has changed since the time of its ancient usage.

   Contemporary scholars like Aune, Burridge, Talbert, and Culpepper recognize that literary parallels between the genre "gospel" and ancient classic Greek and Latin biographies have been overlooked. For example, ancient biographies contain flexible content about a certain leader or hero of the community. The author portrays the importance of the chosen character in many ways such as a description of the person's deeds, sayings, speeches, discourses, perhaps even in legendary terms. By this I mean that the author exaggerates certain details about an event or deed to make an important point about the hero. Today, for example, we have varied legends about such political or public giants as George Washington, Abraham Lincoln, the Kennedy family, Martin Luther King, and so on. Such legends intend to motivate the people to act more like the hero. Consequently, the leader of the ancient biography becomes a model for the community and often inspires them. Such descriptions of the ancient form of the biography are relevant to the literary style of John's Gospel.

In effect, however, we have very little historical information about Jesus. Unlike modern times, where parents often document the early and continued life of their child through baby books, photographs, and home movies, the ancient families had no such recourse. Moreover, since most families came from poverty, they focused necessarily on fundamental needs for their families such as shelter, food, and safety.

By the time anyone wrote stories about Jesus many years after his death, resurrection, and ascension, they consisted of important points for the growth of the early Christian communities, such as stories about resurrection, passion, and death, some of his teachings and works. They aimed to encourage the communities with "good news" about Jesus rather than present an historical listing of facts about his life. With this background in mind, you may understand why so few historical facts about his actual life in the family have been handed down from the first century CE.

3. Despite the presence of confrontation and antagonism within the Fourth Gospel, it was not written to defend Jesus or the Johannine community. Rather, the author wrote the Gospel primarily to encourage these people to continue to believe in the person of Jesus during times of great difficulty for them. As you recall in the Brief Historical Background in the beginning pages of the book, Jewish Christian members of the community had been excommunicated from the synagogues. This serious decision led to a breakup of families, separation from their celebrations such as bar mitzvahs and weddings, and possibly

dislocation from home villages that consisted of Jewish families.

Consequently, the community needed encouragement and strength to continue their faithful lives of following Jesus. They received such support from the writings of John's Gospel, where in several stories and discourses the author emphasized the point repeatedly that belief in Jesus remained the most important commitment of one's life because it brings true life. Moreover, the author also stressed that belief in the person of Jesus remains sufficient for true life.

4. As you know, the term *sign* points the way to something. For example, a road sign shows the driver the direction of a town or street, while another sign posts the permissible speed on a particular road. Signs can be very helpful when they take us to the next step on our journey.

The author of the Fourth Gospel also recognizes the importance of a "sign" to travel further on the journey toward belief in Jesus. He chooses to use the word *sign* instead of *act of power* (miracle) because in this Gospel the sign does not function as a powerful deed as it does in the Synoptics. Rather, the miracle functions as a "sign" for something deeper, such as the topics within a discourse that follows the sign.

In the Synoptic Gospels the audience often raves about the power of Jesus because of a particular miracle and then forgets about his important message in the words that he speaks. In the Gospel of John, the scenes differ. Usually, Jesus performs a miracle without the knowledge of a large crowd (for example, John 2:9; 9:7; and so on). In the Fourth Gospel the sign that Jesus performs does not function as an end in itself. Rather, the miracle that takes place often leads to a deepening of a person's belief in Jesus.

5. The Fourth Gospel contains no birth story because the readers learn from the outset that Jesus, identified in these verses as the Word, existed before the creation of the world.

This information arises from the *Lógos* (Word) Hymn, which occurs at the beginning of the book. Moreover, from this preexistent hymn readers learn that Jesus, the Word, existed with God, had a divine nature, and worked with God to create the world. These three verses (1:1–3) go beyond the need for any full birth narrative. At this point we must realize that the purpose of the birth stories, called infancy narratives, in Matthew and Luke, were written as a christological defense against objections from others about Jesus' birthplace, legitimacy of his lineage, and so on. Since John's Gospel comes at a later time and to different communities, other issues pertinent to their situations were addressed, such as the importance of Jesus' divinity.

Yet 1:14 describes the arrival of Jesus upon the earth. This verse signals a new stage in the relationship between Jesus and the people. As Jesus "lived among us," he took on a commitment of responsibility and hospitality to the people. In addition, through his coming upon earth, known as the incarnation, Jesus offers others the chance to respond to him.

As for the absence of any story about Jesus being baptized by John, the position of John the Baptist becomes minimized in this Gospel. Here in the Fourth Gospel John's primary role remains that of witness to the authority and superiority of Jesus. In this Gospel John decreases while Jesus becomes more important. In 1:8 John the Baptist appears as one who "was not the light, but he came to testify to the light." The light in this verse refers to Jesus.

In the Synoptic Gospels, the story of Jesus fasting in the desert for forty days recounts his transition from a private life to one of ministry. "Forty" recalls the movement of the followers of Moses from Egypt (slavery) into Canaan (freedom). The narrative points to the readiness of Jesus despite whatever temptations he has. In John's Gospel, however, the portrait of Jesus appears very differently. As divine from before the creation of the world, he remains in charge of his life, despite all disputes/confrontations by others. Therefore, Jesus does not need a time of transition.

6. Actually, the Greek term *'Ioudaioi* translates as "Judahites," and not really as the "Jews." With this in mind, the frequent use of the term *Jew/the Jews* in the Fourth Gospel has various meanings. The evangelist employs it to describe Jesus (4:9), to identify generically a particular religious group (2;13; 3:25; 4:22; 5:1; 6:4; 7:2; 11:19, 31, 33, 36, 55; 18:20, 33, 35, 39; 19:20, 40), to verify some Jews who believed in Jesus (8:31; 11:45; 12:9, 11), to refer positively to Jewish leaders in Jerusalem (1:19; 3:1), to recognize the confusion of different religious leaders (7:15, 35; 8:22; 10:19, 24), to describe the people's fear of their religious leaders (7:13; 9:22; 19:38; 20:19), and to indicate resistance to Jesus from some religious leaders, often those in Jerusalem (2:20; 5:10, 15; 6:41, 52; 8:48, 52, 57; 9:18), even to the point of persecution (5:16, 18; 7:1, 11; 10:31, 33; 11:8; 18:12, 14, 31, 36, 38; 19:7, 12, 14, 21). As you see by these text references, the term *the Jews* has diverse meanings throughout the Gospel.

   More frequently, however, *the Jews* refer to those leaders who oppose Jesus. In a very real sense, then, this term reflects the tension between some Jewish leaders and members of the Johannine communities, who have been excommunicated from the synagogues by such leaders at the end of the first century. As I have explained previously in the Brief Historical Background of the introduction of the book, such excommunication would have caused an agonizing separation from family, community, and celebrations relating to them.

   Despite its frequency in the Fourth Gospel, *never* is the term *the Jews* intended to accuse the entire Jewish population of any type of evil deeds. As I have reminded you before, Jesus grew up and lived as a Jew his entire life. Therefore, he would never condemn himself, his family, his Jewish disciples, faithful Jews, and so on.

7. The term *Paraclete* derives from the Greek *paráklētos.* The Latin equivalent, *advocatus,* which means "called to side of," has been translated into *Advocate.* As you know, an

advocate describes someone who intercedes on behalf of another. The ancient term was used in the legal court system to indicate the defense counsel for the accused. In this way Paraclete may also be defined as Counselor.

The term *Paraclete* (which is also translated as Advocate) appears four times in John's Gospel during the last discourses of the Last Supper (John 14:16, 26; 15:26; 16:7) and once in the Letter of 1 John 2:1. Otherwise, the term does not appear anywhere else in the entire New Testament. How does the author use this unique term and what does it mean?

The author uses statements such as "I will ask the Father and he will give you another Paraclete to be with you forever...the Paraclete, the Holy Spirit, whom the Father will send in my name...when the Paraclete comes" (John 14:16, 26; 15:26) to describe the role of the Paraclete as one who will become a new spiritual presence to the disciples after Jesus departs physically from them. Some scholars suggest that the Paraclete alludes to the Holy Spirit as the third Person of the Trinity. I disagree. Since this Gospel appears at the end of the first century CE, the trinitarian theology had not yet been formulated.

I strongly suggest, in the tradition of Raymond Brown (*The Gospel of John,* vol. 2, 1135–43) and Sandra Schneiders (*Written That You May Believe,* 59ff.), that the glorified Jesus is this new unseen presence who will come and reside within them in a new way. The first Paraclete, the human Jesus, came and resided for a brief period on earth. The second Paraclete, the spiritual presence of the risen Lord, will be within their hearts until the end of time. Through this real presence of Jesus within them, the community will be strengthened against persecution, will deepen their convictions of belief, and will testify to the truth by leading honorable lives both within and outside the community.

8. The Beloved Disciple, a designation that emerges only in the Gospel of John, functions as a special friend of Jesus and plays a crucial role in this Gospel. The title surfaces five

times within the Gospel (John 13:23; 19:26ff.; 20:1–8; 21:7, 20–24). Suggestions as to the identity of the Beloved Disciple have included: John, son of Zebedee, John the Elder, Lazarus, Mary of Magdala, and others. In effect, however, no positive identification can be made because of lack of evidence.

While the name of the Beloved Disciple remains unknown, this figure represents the model of a true disciple and faithful witness to Jesus. In essence, the Beloved Disciple embodies the Johannine communities as the one whom Jesus loved. In this way, the figure exemplifies the traditions of these communities. Furthermore, the Beloved Disciple figure surfaces as a highly important figure of authority, as seen in the scenes that depict him with Peter. By the end of the first century CE, the figure of Peter began to emerge as the leading figure of the central church. However, in some of the Johannine texts, the Beloved Disciple remains the authoritative figure of the Johannine community, over and above Peter. Thus, these texts give full authority to him.

Prologue in John 1:1–18—Answers

9. Most scholars hold that the eighteen verses of the Prologue emerge as a preexistent hymn within the community and has been added to the Gospel. The purpose of the Prologue seems to center on the Word *(Lógos)*, a title that describes Jesus in this hymn both as divine and as the Son of God. Therefore, from the very outset of the Gospel, the evangelist establishes the identification and position of Jesus and his relationship to God.

10. The Word *(Lógos)* appears as one of the important theological topics of the hymn. As I have already mentioned, the hymn identifies Jesus as the Word *(Lógos)*. It proclaims that the Word had already existed before the creation of the world and even participated with God in the creation.

Consequently, according to the Fourth Gospel, Jesus as the Word had already existed long before his human embodiment into the world of Palestine in the first century CE. Interestingly, after the Prologue the author ceases to name Jesus as the Word *(Lógos)*. Of itself, the term *Word (Lógos)* suggests some type of oral communication. In this way, the title reveals what will follow in the Gospel, namely, that Jesus as the Word will offer divine life to others through his verbal messages to them. Such verbal messages occur in the literary genre known as discourse.

Within the hymn the evangelist relates this ancient Greek philosophical term of *Lógos* (Word) with a special understanding of divine Wisdom within the Hebrew tradition. For example, in the Book of Proverbs (8:22–31), Wisdom appears as a feminine figure, who delights God and assists in the work of divine creation. Here the Word surfaces as Jesus, who existed in the beginning and works along with God the Father in the acts of creation. The dynamic relationship between the two figures permeates the opening verses. While the traditions of Wisdom and *Lógos* (Word) show thematic similarities, they also remain distinct from one another. For example, unlike Wisdom, who was created in the beginning of creation (Prov 8:22), the Word already was.

11. Yes, the hymn does utilize the themes of creation and light/darkness that appear in Genesis. As you notice, even the first three words "in the beginning," correspond to Genesis 1:1. Since John emphasizes Jesus' divinity much more strongly than the previous three gospels, in a very real sense he presents a new beginning. The preexistent hymn, which begins with a recall of Genesis 1:1 and identifies the Word (Jesus) as divine, meets this need perfectly. Consequently, the hymn has been placed as an opening for the Gospel.

12. From the time of the ministry of the historical Jesus, a tension existed between the followers of Jesus and those of John the Baptist. This tension continued for many decades

after the death of both persons. By the time the Fourth Gospel had been written at the end of the first century, the friction between the followers of Jesus and the Baptizers needed to be settled. The author of the Gospel inserts some verses into the *Lógos* hymn to give weight to the importance of the person of Jesus as the Word over John the Baptist as a witness to him.

John 1:6–8, 15 clearly interrupts the development of the Word in human history, when the evangelist inserts the figure of John (the Baptist) into the poem. Undoubtedly, the author intends the reader to recognize that Jesus far exceeds the importance of John. John witnesses to the Light (Jesus). He is not that light; only Jesus is the Light (John 3:19; 8:12; 9:5; 12:35–36). In 1:15, John even cries out that Jesus "ranks ahead of me." Such comments reflect the friction between the followers of John and those of Jesus. The followers of John considered the Baptist to be a messianic figure. In these verses the portrayal of John only as witness minimizes his role in salvific history. From such insertions into the poem, tension surfaces between the two groups.

John 1:19–51—Answers

13. In the first century the Jewish people were awaiting a messianic figure who would right all the wrongs in their society. They hoped for a person who would be sent by God to redeem them from all the evils that they had to endure. The Hebrew Bible offers various examples that demonstrate Israel's expectation of the Messiah (which means "Anointed One"). These examples may help you understand that the tradition of a messianic figure remained strong: Daniel (Dan 9:25) speaks of a future "Anointed prince"; the prophet Malachi (Mal 3:1; 4:5) anticipates a messenger who will come and prepare the way of the Lord; Deuteronomy (Deut 18:18) anticipates the coming of a

prophet like Moses. Traditionally, many Jews expected the prophetic figure of Elijah to return.

Moreover, the Qumran community, a Jewish sect that lived in the desert near the Dead Sea to keep away from contaminated Jewish society, also awaited a series of three figures to redeem them: a royal messiah, a priestly messiah, and an eschatological prophet like Moses, whom some claim to be another "Teacher of Righteousness." This "Teacher" describes the sect's first leader, a person who functioned as a second Moses. In addition, the Samaritans awaited a *"Taheb,"* a prophet-like-Moses figure who would reign over them and return their freedom. As you can see, then, many people longed for the coming of the Messiah, a title that became associated with the prophets Elijah and Moses.

14. In John 1:29, 36 John the Baptist identifies Jesus as the "Lamb of God," in that he takes away the sin of the world and becomes identified with divinity. This designation gives Jesus superiority over the Baptist and points the way for those who previously had followed John to turn now and follow Jesus. This title, therefore, presents Jesus as the real leader and one to serve. The designation in this Gospel provides the opportunity for John the Baptist to fade and for Jesus to come to the forefront and provide a new created order.

15. Nathaniel's question, "Can anything good come out of Nazareth?" in 1:46 reflects a traditional view of this village as quite insignificant. For example, nowhere was it ever mentioned in the Hebrew Bible. Furthermore, no great religious or political figures ever came from such a place. In other words, people thought that it could not be a place of God or greatness. Ironically, in the Fourth Gospel, Jesus did not come from Nazareth or Bethlehem. Rather, he originates from God before "the beginning."

16. In John 1:45–46 Philip asserts that they have found the Messiah, namely, "Jesus son of Joseph from Nazareth."

When Nathaniel questions Jesus' origins, he reflects a long debate among Jews about the impossibility of Jesus being Messiah because he does not even come from the proper physical place.

Throughout the Hebrew Bible the city of Bethlehem became famous for two reasons: Rachael, the wife of Jacob, died in childbirth and was buried outside the city (Gen 35:19–20); and King David had been born in Bethlehem (1 Sam 17:12). Subsequently, when the Jews thought about a kingly Messiah, they expected him to be born in Bethlehem (Mic 5:2).

During the first century CE it became clear that Jesus' origin and birth brought about much discussion and condemnation by those who did not believe in Jesus. Such expectations caused much tension between some Jews and Jewish Christians. To address this issue both the gospels of Luke and Matthew added infancy narratives, in which the city of Bethlehem played a central role marking the place where Jesus had been born. In this way, credibility as Messiah could be ascribed to Jesus because he had been born in the proper city. As you already know, John has centered on the divinity of Jesus and, therefore, his birthplace does not need to be addressed. However, inklings of the tensions arise in such questions as Nathaniel's in John 1:46 and later the questions of some Jews in John 8:41. In both instances, it seems to resemble a local proverbial saying to insult another person. Remember, in a society that highly values an honor and shame system, place of origin becomes very important for credibility.

17. Both Nathaniel and John the Baptist call Jesus "Son of God." It remains important because it does answer the question, "Who is Jesus?" This title surfaces in the Hebrew Bible in such texts as 2 Samuel 7:14, Psalm 2:6–7, Psalm 89:27 to describe David as God's son and king of Israel, where the two titles seem to be equivalent. Here, in the Fourth Gospel, the title would need to be much more significant because we have already seen it in the Prologue,

where Jesus has been equated with God. However, although the reader may grasp the title as a divine one, Nathaniel or the Baptist probably would not. Throughout the entire Gospel, many disciples seem to fail to grasp the true significance of the person of Jesus.

John 2—Answers

18. John alone mentions the village of Cana in Galilee. No other gospel writer refers to it for any reason. The place, which has been identified by most scholars as Khirbet Qana, occupies a deserted site about nine miles north of Nazareth. However, most pilgrims visit the Church of Kefar Kanna about five miles northeast of Nazareth to commemorate the sign of the wedding feast.

    Interestingly, Jesus performs both the first as well as the second sign (4:46–54) in Cana. In a literary sense, Cana functions as an inclusion, that is, a word found at the beginning and end of a biblical section. In John 2—4, then, the two references to Cana in 2:1 and 4:46 tie the stories together because the village of Cana appears in both places. This literary device allows the reader to go from "Cana to Cana." Moreover, both miracles take place on the third day (2:1; 4:43) in Cana. In a broader sense, Jesus performs his first sign in the region of Galilee and makes his last postresurrection appearance in Galilee in John 21 to form an inclusion for his entire ministry within the Fourth Gospel.

19. Mary, the mother of Jesus, emerges as an integral part of the miracle. As the first person mentioned in the story, Mary takes on a leadership role. The dialogue in 2:3–5 emphasizes such leadership and her vital role in this Gospel story. As probably a loving friend of the family hosting the wedding, Mary initiates the first sign when she intercedes for the family and asks her son to help. Thus, she attempts to stop the potential disaster that would unfold without her son's

response. As we understand at a festive celebration, when the wine runs out, the party ceases. The unfortunate reality would cause much embarrassment to both families.

Clearly, Mary anticipates Jesus' willingness to resolve the crisis. Her words demonstrate her compassionate leadership and her gentle sensitivity to the situation. Furthermore, when Jesus relieves the plight of the newlyweds, he generates more honor for his family name and for the host's family name, which results in stronger relational ties among those at the celebration. Mary's foresight has helped everyone involved.

Within the narrative, Mary's influence over the entire episode becomes evident when she instructs the servants, "Do whatever he tells you" (2:5). In fact, Mary's empathetic request, which was fulfilled through the miracle, alleviates the shameful embarrassment that would have beset the family. Instead, she helps to restore their honor and dignity within the community because she initiated help from Jesus.

20. In reality, while the name of Mary does not appear in the biblical text, Mary has been named by the honor she holds, namely, "mother of Jesus." The phrases, "mother of Jesus" or "his mother," appear twice in the Gospel of John, namely, at the wedding feast at Cana in 2:1 and the crucifixion of Jesus in 19:25–26. This title has remained one of great honor throughout the centuries. In the Middle East, even today, the mother/son relationship remains among the closest of all bonds of kinship. The mother functions as the catalyst in family situations. Here, as the "mother of Jesus," Mary provides the urgent request to come to the aid of the bride and bridegroom as they attend to their guests. With this request, "the mother of Jesus" saved the family honor of the newlyweds and their extended families.

21. When Jesus addresses his mother as "woman," he employs a respectful term of that time. While this generic salutation may seem strange or distant to our ears, the address can be

positive in its own historical context. At the intimate moment of his death, the crucified Jesus addresses his mother again as "woman." Perhaps in both instances (2:4 and 19:26) Jesus tries to distance himself from human bonds because, even while on earth, he relates to his divine Father as an equal throughout the Fourth Gospel from the first sign up until his death on the cross.

22. In 2:4 the "hour" refers to the hour of Jesus' glory. In John's Gospel this hour refers to the time of Jesus' passion, death, and resurrection (7:6, 8, 30; 8:20; 12:12, 27; 13:1). Therefore, the term is used in a positive way.

23. This first sign surely seems excessive. The remark, "When the wine gave out," in 2:3 assures the reader that the invited guests have already drunk much wine. At first glance the point that the wine had run out after all had partaken freely (2:10) hardly seems to be a problem of major importance.

    Yet we must be able to see the purpose of this sign on two levels: the human and the divine. On the human level, the first-century society in Palestine was entrenched in a world of honor and shame. The gift of hospitality represents one of the earmarks of such a society. In this social event of the village, the host family must serve its guests until they are satisfied. To run out of food or drink in a community affair as important as a wedding brings lasting shame on the family because they have dishonored their guests by running out of drink for them. In addition, it also shames the groom's family amid their neighbors and larger community. Such shame creates lasting memories in their society. Therefore, as trivial as this sign may seem to us, the actions of Jesus would bring relief and a restored honor to both families at this important event.

    On the divine level, the theme of the wedding feast anticipates the coming of the Messiah, in the biblical tradition of the Hebrew Bible. Prophetic oracles reflect the overflowing joy of these last days, such as the one found in

Amos 9:13, which states that "the mountains shall drip sweet wine, and all the hills shall flow with it." Therefore, on the divine level, the miracle does not focus on a wedding at all. Rather, this seemingly excessive sign represents a foretaste of the celebration and joy that accompanies messianic times. In this Gospel the coming of Jesus necessitates a time of great festivity because God comes among us to stay with us forever.

24. In 2:13, 23, the Passover (Hebrew *Pesah*) festival to this day remains an annual spring celebration to commemorate the freeing of the Hebrew slaves from Egypt by Moses. Originally derived from the spring agricultural festival, which marked the planting of the barley season, it became a religious festival to commemorate the great Exodus event (Exod 4—15). The celebration of the feast begins after sundown on the fourteenth day of the Jewish month of Nisan. It lasts for eights days with important meals of celebration during the first two nights. During the time of Jesus, Passover functioned as a pilgrim feast, which meant that Jews living outside Jerusalem would ideally travel back to the city for the event if at all possible.

25. Yes, we need to be patient and forgiving toward others. Occasionally a justified anger causes a reaction in a person. This scene demonstrates such an example. To the modern reader, the actions of Jesus seem severe and may even be looked upon as an attack. However, for many in the ancient world, merchants were often considered to be dishonest in their dealings with the public, even to the point of extortion. Such dealings brought great dishonor to victims, especially when the perpetrators have not been seen as guilty.

On the issue of dishonor, we must continue to remember the importance of honor and shame in the ancient world. When honor has been challenged or destroyed in some way, it remains the duty of those shamed to reestablish that honor. If the money changers and merchants in the Temple area practiced deceit, then they dishonored the people. They have turned a sacred house of worship into a profitable marketplace. Most of all, their shady dealings dishonored God. In this case, Jesus' surprising actions restored the sacred honor that belongs to the Divine.

26. Jesus drives the money changers out and cleanses the Temple, not out of hate, but out of love. Clearly, a serious conflict had arisen as to the intention of this space of the outside court within the Temple area. As God's Son, Jesus had the duty to restore the sacredness of this space, which had become corrupt with greed and power.

John 3—Answers

27. To clarify the reading, let me explain the terms *Pharisee* and *rabbi*. A Pharisee can be described as a member of a lay political sect within Judaism in competition with the priestly groups. Both served as members of the Sanhedrin, the Jewish ruling assembly in the time of Jesus. Contrary to what scholars had formerly held, Pharisees did not have great influence in religious decisions during the time of the historical Jesus. At that time, Sadducees (priestly group) held the upper hand in decision making both within and outside the Sanhedrin. However, after the fall of Jerusalem in 70 CE, Pharisees gained power because the work of the priestly classes, namely, to offer sacrifices and perform other functions in the Jerusalem Temple, had been terminated when the Romans destroyed the Temple. Therefore, the Pharisees became much more influential in the reestablishment of Judaism. After the Council of Yavneh, Judaism basically became a rabbinic Judaism with a concentration on the teachings and writings of the great rabbis. In the Gospel of John the Pharisees represent academic religious lawyers as well as government officials who often dispute the words of Jesus.

The term *rabbi* has roots in the term *rab*, which signifies "chief." In the Hebrew Bible *rab* became associated with another term that followed it, such as "chief of officers," "chief/captain of the guards," and so on. Later, the term became a prefix for someone's name. Only by the first century CE did the term *rabbi* take on titular significance as "teacher." In the Gospel of John the term designates Jesus as "teacher" of divine realities and performer of signs.

28. In John 3:2, the author states that Nicodemus, a leader of the Jews and a member of the Sanhedrin, comes to Jesus at night. In this story, night signifies darkness. Often in the ancient world, the concept of darkness symbolized anything from evil to the absence of truth, lack of courage, uncertainty, or ignorance. Let it be noted that these black/white identifications of yesteryear do not refer to the skin color of people today. In John 3, the arrival "at night" draws the readers' attention to the idea that Nicodemus lacked the necessary faith to make a commitment to Jesus. He straddled the fence, so to speak, in his inability to follow his heart in what he believed because he feared his colleagues. Yet as he came to Jesus, the light of the world, his actions demonstrate the potential to overcome any fear and wholeheartedly believe in Jesus at a future time.

29. In the Hebrew Bible the term *Amen* signifies an agreement with the words that have been spoken. It also expresses faithfulness to such words. Often it appears at the end of psalms, blessings, or other prayers that the Israelites sang or recited. The double "Amen, amen" in the Fourth Gospel serves as revelation about the person of Jesus. In John 3 it carries the discussion further so that another idea or development of an idea will surface. To use the term *Amen* twice denotes emphasis. When Jesus employs the double Amen, he enjoins his listeners to pay special attention to the words that he will reveal immediately.

30. The phrase, "born again," has been used by some fundamental Christians today from Jesus' conversation with Nicodemus in 3:3–5. The Greek term *ánothen* has the sense of "from above, again, anew." While Jesus means a

spiritual rebirth from God, Nicodemus takes it as another physical birth. In the conversation Jesus relates the necessity of being "born of water and Spirit" (3:5). In religious circles, water often symbolizes purification, repentance, regeneration, while the Spirit reflects the presence of God. With this in mind, to be "born again" expresses the need for Nicodemus to enter into a new life with God, one of complete belief in the person of Jesus.

31. When Jesus informed Nicodemus that he needed a second birth, Nicodemus did not understand. Therefore, in 3:5 Jesus responds to the question of Nicodemus, "How can anyone be born again after having grown old? Can one enter a second time into the mother's womb and be born?" (3:4). Clearly, Nicodemus' thoughts remain on the physical level, while Jesus speaks on the spiritual level. Being "born of the Spirit" reflects the very life of God within us. It makes true living possible and hope-filled. Through God's Spirit a new life becomes a reality for us because it comes from God.

32. The phrase "our testimony" in 3:11 grammatically represents the first person plural possessive. Interestingly, in the dialogue with Nicodemus the first person plural pronoun "we" has been used in 3:2, when Nicodemus describes himself and his fellow Jews. Another "we" occurs in 3:11, when Jesus describes himself and other believers in him. However, here the "our" testimony most likely refers to Jesus in the continuation of his dialogue with Nicodemus because, in 3:12, he reverts back to "I."

33. The title "Son of Man" occurs thirteen times in the Fourth Gospel. Most of the time Jesus employs the term to describe himself. The Johannine passages about the "Son of Man" in 3:13–14 refer to Jesus, who has descended upon earth from his home with the Father, and will be "lifted up" on the cross as well as being "lifted up" back into heaven. Thus, this heavenly Son of God, who calls

himself "Son of Man," will return to his Father, from where he originated. In the Son of Man's hour of glory, death, resurrection, and ascension form one continuous journey back to the Father.

34. The "serpent in the wilderness" and "lifted up" must be seen together in 3:14. The description alludes to the Hebrew Bible, where in Numbers 21:8, Moses "lifts up" the serpent in the wilderness to demonstrate the presence and power of God. As the serpent has been "lifted up," so must the son of man be "lifted up," so that people may believe in him, just as they believed in God when they looked upon the serpent in the wilderness. All these terms allude to the community's need of faith, a belief in God and in the Fourth Gospel, a belief in the Son of God, who calls himself "Son of Man."

35. The text, "For God so loved the world that he gave his only Son, so that everyone who believes in him may not perish but may have eternal life" (John 3:16), has been used by various Christian groups as a gospel in miniature because it provides a type of summary for the entire gospel. Here the statement reflects the theology of incarnation that first appears in John 1:14, where in the Prologue the author states Jesus "pitched his tent," that is, came on earth and dwelt among us. Thus, 3:16 demonstrates that God's generous gift of his Son on earth (incarnation) and at his death/resurrection/ascension brought the gift of eternal life to all who believe.

    You have seen 3:16 on billboards or banners during national televised events because various Christian groups rightly see it as an inexpensive means of mass evangelization. Due to the millions of people who watch such events, they have been savvy in their communication skills in reaching large audiences.

36. The text in 3:18 states, "Those who believe in him are not condemned; but those who do not believe are condemned

already." On first reading the verse does sound exclusionary. When we study the meaning of the text, however, we may find that salvation and condemnation rely heavily on the choices that people make in their lives. The exclusion and condemnation come when they so choose it. Therefore, ultimately, the choice rests with people, not with God.

In addition, remember that we must read the statement within the context of the story. Here, 3:18 appears within the dialogue between Jesus and Nicodemus, who has been given the choice to follow Jesus or not. At this point, this leader of the Jews straddles the fence. He cannot make up his mind what to do, but at this moment he does not have the courage to go forward with any commitment to Jesus.

John 4—Answers

37. The woman at the well in Samaria arises as an important figure, yet still remains nameless. As a Samaritan and a woman, she would be of no importance to others, especially Jews. Unlike Nicodemus, who held an important position in Jewish leadership and so would have been known by most, this woman functions as an outcast, even within her own society. Therefore, others probably would not have even cared about her identification. Unfortunately, when one stays nameless, any sense of dignity or reverence of that person often vanishes. Without a name, a person becomes anonymous as well as powerless. However, in the case of this woman, the opposite occurs. Although she remains nameless, she is one of the most important of the faithful and of the leadership figures in John's Gospel.

38. The author of the Fourth Gospel certainly did not record exact conversation. Recall that this unknown evangelist lived well after the events of Jesus' life. Therefore, whoever wrote John 4 would have used oral and written sources available to him. The conversation, as a product of these sources, carried an important message. It certainly sheds

new light on the leadership of women and the openness of Samaritans to Jesus. Perhaps it reflects the role of women in the Johannine communities as well as the inclusion of the Samaritans into these communities.

39. The issue of the five past husbands of the woman in 4:17–18 has caused much discussion among scholars for many years. Some suggest that the limit of three marriages for Jews may have also applied to Samaritans. If this were the case, the woman would appear immoral. Others have seen the "five husbands" as symbols of the five gods that the Samaritans worshipped after the return of some members of the northern tribes from Assyrian captivity. In the Second Book of Kings 17:13–34, the author alludes to Samaria's worship of other gods from five foreign cities. In the Hebrew Bible, the term *ba'al* for "husband" can also mean "god." If this symbolism continues, then, Jesus' comment in 4:18, which mentions that the woman lives with someone other than a husband, signifies that the Samaritans still do not have a proper relationship with God. They need to discover Jesus, which they will soon do because of the courage of the woman.

40. Mount Gerizim lies southwest of the ancient city of Shechem. It stands opposite Mount Ebal with the Nablus valley in between the two hills. The mountain stands more than 2800 feet above sea level and has three summits: the Samaritan high place, which remains in use for celebrations such as Passover; Christian ruins of an ancient church; and a Muslim site. In the Hebrew Bible, Mount Gerizim had religious significance as a covenant site (Deut 11:29; 27:12; Josh 8:33).

When the Jews returned from the Babylonian Captivity (537 BCE), they eventually rebuilt the Temple in Jerusalem. The Samaritans in the north tried to assist them but Jewish leaders refused because they considered their neighbors unclean and heretical. In time, the Samaritans built their own temple on Mount Gerizim, which was destroyed in 128

BCE by the Jewish king, John Hyrcanus. Tensions between the two groups increased. By the time of the Gospel of John, the two groups had developed a hatred of one another. The Jews looked down upon the Samaritans as a people and considered their religious beliefs heretical.

41. The Gospel of Mark initiated the concept of the "messianic secret." It serves as a literary device to "hush" the people about the identity of Jesus. The author employed this literary device to provide an excuse to forgive people who refused to believe in Jesus. In other words, if people did not know about the identity of Jesus, they could not be held accountable to believe in him. However, in John 4 the story has been told in dissimilar circumstances. Remember, the Gospel of John had been written at least twenty years after the Gospel of Mark for a completely new audience with other needs.

    With this explanation in mind, let us consider the point of Jesus' announcement proclaiming himself the Messiah. The conversation between Jesus and the woman of Samaria deepens as she opens her heart to him. The climax of the episode surfaces when the woman acknowledges to Jesus, "I know that Messiah is coming," and "When he comes, he will proclaim all things to us" (4:25), and Jesus responds trustingly, "I am he" (4:26). In this context Jesus exposes his divinity and implicitly demonstrates he is greater than Abraham or Moses, two figures whom the Samaritans held in high honor and who were implied in their conversation. His direct and powerful proclamation of his divinity to the woman of Samaria illustrates Jesus' great trust in and respect for her open heart.

42. For anyone who lives in a desert region, living water has tremendous value. We in first-world countries have become accustomed to turning on a faucet and out flows "living water." However, in many parts of the world, the only available water comes from open cisterns, where water has stagnated over time.

In the Gospel of John "living water" has a double meaning. It first describes water that lives and moves, such as water from a spring or stream. At the same time in John 4, it refers to the gift of life, which comes from Jesus, the source of "living water." Moreover, the scene takes place at Jacob's well, where Jesus verbalizes that he far outranks their ancestor Jacob, who provided water for physical thirst. Jesus offers "living water" whereby those who drink will never thirst again. Here Jesus speaks of the gift of revelation that leads to eternal life. In this analogy, as water represents a necessity for natural life, so Jesus' words become a necessity for eternal life.

43. In the first four chapters of the Gospel, the woman of Samaria rises above the other disciples or seekers in that she risks further her reputation by having a conversation with him, she discloses her deepest thoughts to him, and she believes Jesus solely by the words he speaks to her. In such actions, she rises above the other characters in her display of deep faith and openness to the words of Jesus.

44. The disciples were shocked about Jesus' conversation with the woman because in first-century Palestine a man could not speak to a woman in public, especially an unknown woman. For them, therefore, the scene seemed shameful. Moreover, a Jewish man could not speak to a Samaritan woman. The boundaries between men and women were serious in this world. By pushing such boundaries, Jesus offers the woman a rare and privileged opportunity to encounter the divine in her midst. Furthermore, his actions offer the world a chance to change its limited regard for women.

45. The phrase "come and see" appears in John's Gospel (1:39, 46; 4:29) most often as an invitation to follow Jesus. In these instances, it functions as a technical term for discipleship. As would be expected, Jesus initiates the call. However, here in the story the unnamed woman calls the townspeople to "come and see." As such, she exemplifies

the first person in the Gospel to announce the good news to others while Jesus was still on earth. Clearly, this action demonstrates her loyal leadership skills and her sense of mission as she forgave the townspeople, who may have mistreated or shunned her.

46. The villagers, who originally went to meet Jesus on the words of the woman, now believe in him because of their own encounter. They have themselves experienced a new level of belief, one which surpasses the testimony of another. Despite this reality, the remarks of the townspeople in 4:42 seem rather harsh and ungrateful. Remember, the woman did not have to invite the townspeople to "come and see." She did so out of a caring and a hope that her neighbors would receive a transforming experience similar to hers. In order to be sure her neighbors would listen, she humiliates herself with the announcement, "Come and see a man who told me everything I have ever done!" (4:29). This brave remark assures the movement of the villagers to the well to meet Jesus, even if they go out of curiosity to learn more about her past actions.

47. Geographically, the most direct way from Judea to Galilee is through Samaria. The Jews avoided Samaria because of the Samaritans, whom they considered to be unclean. Moreover, a continued debate existed between the two groups about the proper place of cultic worship. The Jews declared Jerusalem as the place to worship, while the Samaritans honored Mount Gerizim as the center of worship. When Jesus crossed all these religious lines by traveling through Samaria in John 4, the choice is not just geographic. Here Jesus' arrival in Samaria may also reflect the situation of later years when the Johannine communities had a mission to Samaria and accepted the Samaritans into the Christian community. Furthermore, their actions would transcend the boundaries of official Judaism, from which they have been excommunicated.

48. In 4:53b the notion of the whole household believing because of the father's beliefs reflects the first-century world of Palestine. In this society, whatever the father as the head of the household believed, the entire household followed. In some cultures, this practice has been maintained even to this day.

John 5—Answers

49. The biblical text in John 5:1 gives no indication as to the identification of a specific feast. Subsequently, scholars have different points of view on the matter. It would be helpful to know because, in the time of Jesus, three of the Jewish festivals or feasts were considered to be pilgrim festivals. Ideally, for these three feasts the Jews would go up to Jerusalem to celebrate at the Temple. The festivals included: the feast of Passover, celebrated in the spring during the Jewish month of Nisan to commemorate the Exodus from Egypt; the feast of Pentecost, celebrated fifty days later to commemorate the giving of the Law at Sinai; and the feast of Tabernacles (Booths), celebrated in the fall month of Tishri, to celebrate the wandering forty years in the desert.

50. The "stirred up" water in 5:7 may refer to the movement of a spring or a series of pipes that connect the pools. It also may refer to a local religious tradition about an angel stirring up the water in the pool.

51. The issue of Jesus' healing on the Sabbath permeates all the gospels and becomes a point of contention for the Jews especially in the Fourth Gospel. For some Jews, to break Sabbath law, as they perceived Jesus doing, meant to violate honor to God. Therefore, the story functions not only as a sign but as a conflict story as well because, when Jesus heals on the Sabbath, he challenges the observers about their traditional acceptance of the Law and opens new pos-

sibilities for them. Unfortunately, many resist such welcome and divine change. Instead of understanding the Law as a means to an end, namely, union with God, they observe it as an end in itself.

52. The comment from Jesus in 5:14 remains puzzling because it seems to adhere to the theory of retribution, whereby sickness results from sin. Very likely, this would have been a common ancient thought of the first century CE. Certainly, this theory does not represent the mind of God or real truth. Moreover, the dialogue does not indicate the healing itself has any connection with sin.

Malina and Rohrbaugh (*Social-Science Commentary on the Gospel of John,* 112) suggest that the remark reflects ancient Mediterranean societies' belief that sin severs interpersonal relationships. If this be the case, then Jesus' remark serves as a warning to the man, who has no friends to help him into the pool. Jesus implies that the man needs to become part of community and acquire friends. If he does not, who will be there to mourn and bury him at his death, a point that serves as a reference for "do not sin any more, so that nothing worse happens to you"?

53. Frequently within the gospels, the disciples do not seem to understand the words, actions, and death of Jesus. After all, they expected a Messiah who would lead them and not be murdered by the Romans. The disciples continued to be dismayed and needed time to absorb all the changes in their lives because of Jesus. On the other hand, remember that both the author of the gospel and the audience, who read the Fourth Gospel, have the advantage of hindsight. All the events have already occurred.

54. The Jewish officials would go so far as to say that Jesus blasphemes God, because he makes himself equal to God by calling God his Father and performing healings on the Sabbath. Ironically, as you know, the truth lies in the reality that Jesus and God do share equality with one another.

When Jesus refers to God as his Father (5:17) and the officials act in response to his declaration (5:18), they react to his proclamation of equality. In being equal with God, Jesus possessed the power to create/to give life (5:21) and to judge (5:24). As Son of God, Jesus came from the realm of the divine, as indicated in the Prologue in 1:1–18. Throughout the entire Gospel Jesus' relationship with God remains equal, yet different. Despite his equality Jesus does nothing apart from the will of God his Father. They work as one.

55. John 5:22–23 may sound unusual to our ears, but for the Johannine communities these words provide credibility for Jesus as Son of God. As divine, Jesus possesses the power to judge and to give life. However, the Father has handed the power to judge over to Jesus. Yet Jesus proclaims that those who listen and believe in him do not come under judgment, but have "passed from death to life" (5:24). This entire section of the discourse (5:19–30) provides the listeners the opportunity to open their hearts and broaden their insular way of thinking so that Jesus can offer them life now. Therefore, Jesus refers to eternal life, that is, the end time, beginning in the present moment (realized eschatology), rather than at a future time (future eschatology).

56. In 5:27 the title "Son of Man" refers to Jesus, who functions as the intermediary between God and the people. Since Jesus descended from the heavens (sky) and will return to it, he will call people to him. Even the dead will hear his voice and come out, and those who have done good will go to the resurrection of life (5:29). Here, the author speaks about a future end time (future eschatology).

57. In 5:24–29, Jesus addresses two different concepts: the end times as present and the end times as future. The Greek adjective *eschatos*, defined as "last or final," refers to the end times, that is, the time of God. The suffix *ology*

means "the study of" a particular topic. Therefore, eschatology means the study of the end times. In the Hebrew Bible, the final times are closely connected with the Israelites' hope for a Messiah. They waited for a new era, a time when oppression would end and God's justice and mercy would prevail over all the injustices of the world in which they lived.

The term *realized eschatology* indicates that this awaited end time has arrived now. It contrasts with the term *finalized eschatology*, which means the end times will come in the future. For many years scholars considered John 5:24–30 an example of both realized and finalized eschatology. However, in recent times the previous interpretation has been challenged by some because in John's Gospel all time seems to be addressed in a lengthened present time. Instead of a difference of time, the writer of the Gospel suggests a "fullness" of that time.

The Greek term *parousía* appears in the New Testament for the expectation and/or arrival of Jesus in glory after his resurrection. In early Christian times after Jesus died, was raised, and ascended into heaven, the people thought that their world would change immediately and that Jesus would return to reign eternally over them. In their minds it became a part of the eschatological process.

58. In reality, Moses did not write about Jesus (5:46). Here, Jesus employs a first-century exegetical method of interpreting the Hebrew Bible in light of his present situation. His comments in 5:43–46 reflect some Jewish leaders' condemnation of Jesus asserting instead that they follow the Mosaic tradition. However, they fall short because they have condemned Jesus, who offered life to them.

John 6—Answers

59. Often, the Sea of Galilee has been known as Lake Gennesaret. This body of water is not a sea, nor does it

have salt water. The fishing industry has been a main source of income for the people around the lake. Located about sixty-five miles northeast of Jerusalem as the crow flies, it forms part of the great African Rift, a deep split within the Jordan Valley that formed after the Ice Age thousands of years ago. The entire rift remains well below sea level. Subsequently, the lake is also below sea level. The temperatures of Lake Gennesaret rise well above those in Jerusalem, a city set on high hills at least 2700 feet above sea level.

60. The mention of barley instead of wheat reminds the reader of a miracle by the prophet Elisha in the Hebrew Bible in 2 Kings 4:42–44. John is the only Gospel to mention that the loaves of bread in the story were made from barley. Although wheat may have been more desirable, barley ripened before wheat. Since it proved to be cost effective, that is, less expense than wheat to grow, the poor were sustained by it (see Judg 7:13; Ezek 4:12).

61. When the people witnessed the powerful miracle that Jesus performed, they hailed his as the long-awaited final prophet like Moses. In 6:14 the crowd cheered, "This is indeed the prophet who is to come into the world." This choral proclamation alludes to Moses, whom the Jews considered to be the greatest of all prophets (see Deut 18:15, 18; 34:10). The definite article *the* refers clearly to Moses. Therefore, at that moment, the crowd demonstrates great admiration for Jesus as they compare him with Moses. However, in the long discourse that follows the two signs, Jesus professes his superiority over Moses (6:32, 49–50). It would be more accurate to say that in John 6, the writer contrasts Jesus with Moses, rather than compares the two figures. Jesus always remains far superior to Moses. After all, recall how we learned in John 5:19–30 that Jesus is equal to God his Father. In this Gospel the divinity and origin of Jesus permeate most of the narratives, a reality that places Jesus above any other human being.

62. In 6:17, the statement, "It was now dark," does play a role in the scene. Recall in John 3 how, in the Nicodemus story, darkness signaled both fear and ignorance. In this story darkness accents the disciples' fear of the raging sea, which will soon occur. While on the water, a sudden squall arose. Those of us who live near the sea or a large lake know the sudden storms that appear and disappear within hours of one another. One moment the sea seems calm, when suddenly a storm brews and heightens the waves. Often sudden winds cause such storms, like those that still occur frequently on the Sea of Galilee. Therefore, fear of the raging sea and what lurks beneath it would cause the disciples to be afraid.

    In the ancient times storms like these were seen as a higher source of power showing its strength. Notice in 6:19 that the text indicates the disciples saw Jesus "walking on the *sea*." According to Malina and Rohrbaugh (*Social-Science Commentary on the Gospel of John*, 128) the term *sea* differs from the term *water*. In the first-century world, the entity known as "sea" connected with the deity known as Poseidon/Neptune. In the Bible the same deity was identified as *Tiamat* or *Tehom*. The ancients respected this god because of the great power often exhibited by the sea. For them, the god caused the sea to storm, to be calm, to have rough waves, and so on. Therefore, when Jesus walked on the sea, he demonstrated very clearly his divine power over it. When a victor trampled another's property, person, or possession, the act indicated that he had won the struggle because he had power over the other. In the case of Jesus' actions, then, to conquer the sea meant to conquer the god of the sea.

63. The term *epiphany* derives from the Greek term *epiphaneia*, which literally means manifestation, as in the appearance or disclosure of a deity.

64. In 6:15 Jesus flees to the mountain because these Galileans did not understand the purpose of the sign or his message

to them. Instead of belief in the person of Jesus, they become extremely excited that they finally have a person who may alleviate all their financial burdens by providing food for themselves and their families. They wanted Jesus to be the type of king, who would fulfill these messianic expectations. Unfortunately, their misunderstanding of Jesus and his message translates to unbelief. The people tried to force Jesus into a messianic kingship according to their definition of the position. This went against his will. Jesus will be king in the Fourth Gospel, but one that defines God's expectations, not those of the world.

In the ancient times people lived in villages or cities located mostly on the side of hills or in the valleys. They usually avoided living on a mountainside for practical reasons of farming, building, difficult terrain, and so on. Therefore, when Jesus "withdrew again to the mountain" in 6:15 it meant that Jesus fled to an uninhabited place.

65. The named town, Capernaum, has significance as the hometown of Peter. Moreover, throughout the gospels Jesus used it as a base during his ministry. Many of the occupants of the village would have been fishermen because Capernaum lies on the north shore of Lake Gennesaret about twenty-three miles from Nazareth. Today, only an excavated site remains. This site claims the first-century house of Peter, a famous fourth-century synagogue, and many other valuable remains.

Herod Antipas, the son of Herod the Great, founded the city of Tiberias as the capital of his Galilean territory (18–20 CE). The city lies on the west shore of the lake about four miles south of Magdala, the home of Mary of Magdala. As you can guess, he named the city after Tiberias Caesar in order to honor the Roman emperor and acquire favor from him. Before its founding, the land had been used as a burial ground. Consequently, the Jews considered it unclean during the time of Jesus. John 6:23 marks the only time the Gospel mentions the city of Tiberias.

66. For Jews of the first century, Moses represented the most important figure of the Hebrew Bible. John 6 offers examples to compare and contrast the figures of Jesus and Moses. For example, the sign of the loaves and fishes calls to mind the manna in the wilderness in Exodus 16. While in Exodus, God, through Moses, led the people to physical sustenance, in John's Gospel, Jesus leads the people to salvation as he declares, "I am the bread of life" (6:35). The points of contrast in John 6 between these two figures are intended to demonstrate that Jesus as the Living Bread replaces and far surpasses Moses.

67. The Greek *egō eimi*, ("I am") sayings form a distinctive part of Jesus' discourses within the Fourth Gospel. No other gospel has such direct sayings that identify Jesus with God. In John 6 Jesus identifies himself with "I am the bread of life," "I am the living bread." Additionally, throughout the Gospel, Jesus proclaims "I am the light," "I am he," "I am the resurrection and the life," "I am the way and the truth and the life," "I am the vine," and so on. These "I am" sayings usually identify the actions of Jesus. For example, he nourishes people with bread that offers everlasting life, he offers people the reality of a joyous resurrection, and he provides a strong source of nourishment as "vine." Those who believe in him will never thirst again.

   These "I am" sayings within the Fourth Gospel reflect the way God identified himself to Moses in Exodus 3:14–15. Subsequently, many authors in the Hebrew Bible also identified God with the introduction of "I am." These words came to be understood as recognition of the divine nature of God as well as God's name. Therefore, in the tradition of this background, the author of the Fourth Gospel presents the "I am" sayings of Jesus. Here Jesus speaks with the same authority that God spoke in the Hebrew Bible. Moreover, Jesus describes himself in light of the divine name, which places him on an equal footing with God. Yet remember that in the Fourth Gospel Jesus speaks and performs all actions in the name of God, his Father.

68. The section of John 6:51—7:1 has been a challenge to hear. Throughout the entire narrative, the author of the Gospel has portrayed Jesus as a divine replacement with "I am" sayings scattered throughout the chapter. As the true bread from heaven, the person of Jesus replaces the manna and Law from the time of the Exodus.

   The grumbling by the Jews in 6:52 parallels the grumbling of their ancestors when they left Egypt and found themselves hungry (Exod 16). Such grumbling here in John 6 seems to suggest they have followed the words of Jesus correctly. Jesus demonstrates verbally that he replaced the manna in the desert with himself and proclaimed that "the one who eats this bread will live forever" (6:58).

John 7—Answers

69. Throughout the Gospel some Jews objected to the messianic claims made by Jesus. While the everyday common people who were Jews or Samaritans started to believe in Jesus as Messiah or even greater, the leaders became anxious about Jesus' growing support from the crowds. Their fear led to anger over his presence. Consequently, this hostility led some Jewish leaders to look for an opportunity to remove him from the scene, even to the point of killing him.

   Such tension between Jesus and some Jewish leaders parallels the strain between the Johannine communities and Jewish leaders many decades later. This heightened tension led to the communities' excommunication from the synagogues toward the end of the first century. Such separation caused even more heightened tension between the two groups.

70. The feast of Tabernacles, known in Hebrew as *Sukkôt,* has an agricultural origin like Passover and Pentecost. The feast takes place in the fall and celebrates the wandering of Moses and his followers in the desert after their escape

from Egypt. It occurs on the fifteenth day of the Jewish month of Tishri, which usually occurs in late September or early October.

Originally, the feast derived from an agricultural feast in late summer that celebrated a thanksgiving for the harvest from the previous late spring and summer crops such as grains, grapes, and olives. The Israelites combined the agricultural feast with religious desert themes. During the eight days of the festival the people dwelt in tents/huts to remember their ancestors, who wandered with portable dwellings in the desert after they fled Egypt with Moses. The feast became one of the three pilgrim feasts, which meant the people would attempt to commemorate it with a journey up to the Jerusalem Temple.

During the feast participants prayed for early rain during the upcoming rainy season of winter. A solemn procession went from the pool of Siloam to the Temple with water to be poured on the altar. On the first day of the festival, large candlesticks were lit in the Women's Court located in the outer part of the Temple. Thus, both water and light became essential parts of the feast. Today, throughout the world religious Jews continue to build temporary dwellings outside their home or synagogue to commemorate this important feast.

71. In 7:3, 5, 10, the term *brothers* appears in reference to Jesus. While the Greek term for brothers, *àdelphoì*, usually signifies a real brother, the Hebrew equivalent term *'ah* encompasses a wider selection of relatives. Some scholars in the past have suggested that the "brothers" acted like older siblings because of their urging Jesus to attend the feast. In this case they would be half brothers, as sons of Joseph from a former marriage. Some Chr8istian traditions suggest that the term be taken literally to mean Jesus' real brothers. Still other traditions suggest that it refers to Jesus' other relatives, such as male cousins. However, nowhere in the Fourth Gospel have any of these sugges-

tions been verified. Whatever the case, these relatives appear as unbelievers in regard to the person of Jesus.

72. John 7:5 states that "not even his brothers believed in him." We know that any outsider's doubt about us is one issue, but the distrust of our family about us is quite a deeper issue. For most people, family support and loyalty form the foundation of their growth and trust in others. Consequently, disbelief in this family member from others in the family cuts to the core of the person's heart. This realization would have caused Jesus much pain.

73. The word *complain* in 7:12 and 6:41 would be more accurately translated from the Greek *gogguzō* as "murmur." This term reflects its Hebrew equivalent *lun/lin* in the Book of Exodus (15:24; 16:2; 16:7) and Numbers (14:2; 16:41), where the Israelites "murmured" against Moses because they endured hardships in the desert after their escape from Egypt.

In these stories the people had not yet grasped the reality of the cost of freedom. When people become really free, they must be willing to take risks in life, to open their ears to other's opinions, to grow and change in their thinking. Instead, these people in Exodus grumbled that, while they were free in the desert, they had to risk too much for their existence. Sometimes they longed for the security and safety of being enslaved, because at least then water, basic sustenance, and bare shelter were provided by their Egyptian captors. Comments such as "What shall we drink?... If only we had died by the hand of the LORD in the land of Egypt, when we sat by the fleshpots and ate our fill of bread" (Exod 15:24; 16:3) became their cry. Basically, they resented the gift of freedom given to them by God.

Likewise, in John 7:12 as well as 6:41, the author parallels those who refused to listen to the words of Jesus with the group that left Egypt with Moses. Both show resentment rather than gratitude, both have deaf ears and hard hearts in that they refuse to change and open themselves up to God, which would have helped them become people of freedom. In effect, their disbelief brought slavery because they were afraid to change. Therefore, they missed divine opportunities and remained stagnant in their ways of life.

74. Since the people were divided in their views about Jesus, the tense atmosphere caused many promoters of Jesus to withhold their opinions. It became increasingly difficult for many in the crowds because some of their own religious leaders spoke out vehemently against Jesus. Some held that Jesus led the people astray. This verbalization of certain leaders both confused and intimidated the people.

Moreover, as a result of their belief in the person of Jesus, they feared reprisals from these religious leaders, even to the point, of excommunication. Therefore, they were afraid to speak up for Jesus since reprisals would devastate both them and their families. Such reprisals would also bring great shame upon their families and villages, a realization that would separate them from their loved ones for years to come.

75. The phrase *going up* often relates to Jesus' journey to Jerusalem, as in 7:14. Although Jerusalem lies south of both the regions of Galilee and Samaria, it appears on the crest of one of the mountain ranges in the central hill country. Therefore, the traveler must physically "go up" to Jerusalem.

More important, the phrase *go up* pertains to a theological understanding of the city of Jerusalem. Centuries before the time of Jesus, King David captured this city from the Jebusites and made it the capital of the twelve tribes. Here he combined the movable Ark of the Covenant with the stationary house of worship that he built for God. From that time forward, Jerusalem became important as the place of God's dwelling and was acknowledged as God's city. For this reason, whether pilgrims travel from the north, south, east, or west, they will always "go up" to Jerusalem.

76. The Jewish expectation of "the prophet" in 7:40 refers to Moses. Whenever the article *the* appears before the word

prophet in the gospels, it refers specifically to Moses. All other prophets would be identified by the article *a* before the term *prophet*.

Furthermore, the reference to Moses stems back to Deuteronomy 18:15–18, when Moses promised that "a prophet like me" will be raised up. This promise led to the expectation of a particular figure who would be known as the Prophet-like-Moses. This prophet would solve legal problems and deal with other matters of leadership.

Remember, for Judaism, Moses remains the most important figure of the Hebrew Bible. Therefore, the crowds and religious authorities would have noticed the many references made to Moses in John 6 and 7. For example, a Mosaic analogy appears in 6:48 when Jesus contrasts the temporary manna from the desert with the eternal bread that he gives in the pronouncement, "I am the bread of life" (6:48). Similarly, in John 7 the theme of water, which permeates the desert discussion of the people with Moses, reappears during this feast of Sukkoth with the inviting words of Jesus, "Let anyone who is thirsty come to me" (7:37). This claim causes the crowds to refer to him as the Prophet-like-Moses. Moreover, Jesus referred to Moses in his discussion with them in John 7. For all such reasons, some of the crowd in 7:40 proclaim, "This is really *the* prophet" (emphasis mine).

77. While in 7:40 some in the crowd recognize Jesus as the Prophet-like-Moses, in 7:41 others identify him as the Messiah. The anglicized Hebrew term *messiah* translates into the anglicized Greek term *the Christ*. Both terms can be defined as the "anointed one." Therefore, the word *Christ* arises as a title, which signifies the anointed one.

In the Hebrew Bible, the term functioned as a description of those who lead on God's behalf, such as kings and priests. By the time of first century CE the concept of Messiah had various meanings. Some looked for a prophetic figure, while others looked for a Davidic-type king who would be born in David's birthplace, Bethlehem.

Still others looked for a teacher or a leader who would overthrow the foreign regime. Whoever this figure would be, he would lead the people and bring relief to their lives in the name of God.

Here in 7:41 the designation has been attributed to Jesus. As you notice from the very next verse, some doubted the description because they misunderstood the physical birthplace of Jesus to be Nazareth.

John 8:12–59—Answers

78. In 8:13 the Pharisees question Jesus' authority. As religious leaders themselves, they believe they should be the ones who declare to the people the way to follow God. Therefore, when Jesus proclaims in 8:12 that "I am the light of the world," a theme that coincides with the feast of Sukkoth (Tabernacles/Booths), the Pharisees resist two important points: his claim to divinity with the words, "I am," and his assertion of divine authority through his relationship with God, his Father. Their argument falls under the guise of a need for two witnesses to verify Jesus' claims. According to the Hebrew Bible (Num 35:30; Deut 17:6; 19:15), at least two witnesses need to confirm testimony in an important case. Since his self-witness and the divine witness cannot be verifiable by human standards, they reject the validity of his words.

Jesus' self-testimony raises a red flag to the Pharisees. In poor societies, where most people cannot read, the spoken word continues to be paramount. False testimony needs to be counteracted by the word of others. Consequently, the testimony of other witnesses plays an important role in a society's evaluation of that person's words or actions. According to Malina and Rohrbaugh (*Social-Science Commentary on the Gospel of John,* 156), a person's reputation rises or falls on the testimony of other witnesses for validation. In these verses, then, Jesus' self-testimony angers some Pharisees because the only validation about him surfaces as his own. Even when some people seem to support Jesus, such as in the statement that "many believed in him" (8:30), by the end of the chapter they appear to be the same people that "picked up stones to throw at him" (8:59). This action reflects other incidents in the Gospel (2:23–25; 4:48; 6:14–15, 60–66) where the writer has indicated that not all belief in Jesus grows deep enough to change people's hearts.

79. When the Johannine author states that Jesus taught in the Treasury of the Temple in 8:20, he probably did not intend the description to be literal. From studies of the Second Temple, ancient historians like Josephus hold that the Treasury would have been a storage room for religious valuables. Consequently, Jesus would not have taught inside such as room. Possibly, the author intends to parallel Jesus with the center of Judaism at his time, namely, the Temple. In another sense, too, Jesus represents the valuable hidden treasure that some religious authorities do not recognize.

80. In 8:48 some Jews defend their derogatory remarks when they say, "Are we not right in saying that you are a Samaritan and have a demon?" These remarks echo their distaste and distrust of Samaritans as half-bred heretics, whom they now identify with Jesus. Moreover, the slur about demon possession may refer to a mental dementia, which they could possibly attribute to Jesus because of his insistence of divine association. In short, they call him heretical and mad.

John 7:53—8:11—Answers

81. The phrase *scribes and Pharisees* in 8:3 appears only here in the Fourth Gospel. However, the combined term occurs several times in the other gospels. The term *scribe* denotes "writer." Literally, the scribe writes the intended message.

From the earliest Gospel of Mark, the scribes appeared to be an integrated group that associated itself with chief priests and Jerusalem. In later gospels, they became combined with the phrase, "scribes and Pharisees." In effect, they seemed to function as bureaucrats within the elite religious leadership in Judaism. They may have hailed from Jerusalem, but they functioned in villages as guardians of the Jewish traditions. As such, they could easily have functioned as judges and leaders and teachers who had great expertise in the ways of Judaism.

82. The entire story in 7:53—8:11, which most scholars agree does not come from a Johannine source but belongs to a Lukan tradition, makes no point about the man in the act of adultery. The accusers only mention that in the Torah (Law) Moses commands the woman to be stoned. However, according to Leviticus 20:10, "If a man commits adultery with the wife of his neighbor, both the adulterer and the adulteress shall be put to death," while Deuteronomy 22:22 states, "If a man is caught lying with the wife of another man, both of them shall die, the man who lay with the woman as well as the woman. So you shall purge the evil from Israel." Both quotes are from the Torah, which encompasses the first five books of the Hebrew Bible. Here the leaders in this story misrepresent the words of the Torah.

    While the story never offers the status of the man, the fault and punishment here stay with the woman. Often, cultural traditions, especially in a world of patriarchy, surpass written laws. Even today in many parts of the world, if a woman has had intercourse or becomes pregnant outside her marriage, the blame remains exclusively on the woman, even if she has been raped.

83. The scribes and the Pharisees may not have caught the woman literally, but they would have been informed by the crowds about the situation so that they could pass judg-

ment on her. Therefore, they would have been the ones who brought her to Jesus.

The question about their patrolling the area emerges as a good one. Some of the duties may have included patrol, but most likely they would have been given information by groups like the Levites, who sometimes served in this capacity, or by people who passed by the scene.

84. The author never relates to the audience what Jesus scribbled on the ground. Yet, for centuries, the question has been the subject of much supposition. Some have suggested that the writing contained the sins of the accusers, while others held that Jesus simply doodled. In reality, we have no idea.

85. As we all know, it becomes very difficult if almost impossible to stop the fury of a crowd. However, in the case of this story, Jesus does. How does he do this? He gently bends down, scribbles on the ground, and, when he stands up, he announces in 8:7: "Let anyone among you who is without sin be the first to throw a stone at her." This pronouncement must have shocked the accusers because the author relates that one by one they left Jesus standing alone with the woman. Apparently, they understood Jesus' powerful message that everyone "misses the mark" (that is, sins) at times in life. Moreover, who gives us the authority to judge another person? The answer lies in the reality that only God can judge another person, and as we learned in John 5:19–30, God/Jesus chooses not to judge.

86. In reality, the story focuses on the entrapment of Jesus by the religious authorities. In the passage the scribes and Pharisees pushed Jesus to judge and condemn the woman caught in adultery, but he refused. Consequently, their trap backfired and they left the scene without further punishment delivered to the woman. Remember that up to this point they have already humiliated her by dragging her from the scene and parading her through the streets until

they found Jesus. Once the woman encountered Jesus, he came to her rescue. His loving actions reflect the ultimate goodness and mercy of God.

87. In ancient times and in many parts of the world today, sexual misconduct has been judged more harshly than other sins. In a patriarchal world, where men have the upper hand in all policies, sexuality remains a forceful instrument to keep women under their control. For example, in ancient cultures and within some contemporary cultures, under the guise of modesty, women must keep their heads or even their entire bodies covered lest they distract men.

   In a broader sense, the honor/shame code among many societies often prohibits women from education, leadership, and ownership. Instead, women must obey men, adhere to their rulings, and be absent from public space. In essence, they are "owned" by their fathers or husbands. In many ways, these rulings come under the heading of "protecting" the honor (that is, the sexuality) of women.

John 9—Answers

88. The disciples raise the question, "Who sinned, this man or his parents, that he was born blind?" (9:2). Their question reveals that they equate blindness with sin because they follow the theory of retribution. This theory subscribes to the belief that blessings, wealth, success, and so on have been bestowed on good people. At the same time it maintains that sickness, poverty, and lack of success result from the sinfulness of people. To counteract this theory, the Hebrew Bible contains stories like that found in the Book of Job.

   Unfortunately, the theory of retribution remained quite alive in the time of Jesus. Even to this day, it seems to permeate the thoughts of some. For example, have you ever heard someone ask, "What have I done to deserve this?" or "Why has so much suffering come to this good family?" In any case, the ancients held that since sin dishonors another person, it brings shame to the one who commits the sin, as well as to the other party. Therefore, the disciples' question highlights such oppressive beliefs.

Jesus' response counteracts their thinking. He replies, "Neither this man nor his parents sinned" (9:3). According to the author, then, sin and blindness have no relation to each other. Rather, the position of the helpless blind man creates an opportunity for God to touch him in many ways. As a result of the man's openness, God can work. Therefore, Jesus tells the disciples that "God's work" will be revealed through the blind man. At that moment he proclaims again that "I am the light of the world" (9:5). Here Jesus speaks as Revealer, that is, as the one who will bring sight to the man in many ways.

89. The day and night images in 9:4 offer powerful imagery. The light in this wise saying represents Jesus, who will offer it to others so they, too, can work. In the very next verse (9:5), Jesus proclaims that "I am the light of the world." Those who believe in Jesus will also be "enlightened."

On the other hand, the night represents the inability or refusal to learn, to grow, or to be enlightened. Here in John 9, the Pharisees represent those who live in darkness because they refuse to listen to Jesus or to the blind man, who has been healed by Jesus. Although they have always been fully sighted, they cannot see the gift of inward light, that is, enlightenment, Jesus offers. Therefore, they remain in darkness.

90. In 9:6 the use of dirt and spittle somewhat reminds us of the creation story in Genesis 2:7, when God "formed man from the dust of the ground, and breathed into his nostrils the breath of life." Spittle has always been thought to have medicinal value. When Jesus performed the act of mixing the two ingredients of spittle and dirt to form mud, he broke a Sabbath regulation that prohibited any kneading on this sacred day. Religious authorities would consider

such action a violation of the Sabbath because they considered it work. This violation will taint their responses throughout the entire narrative.

91. The pool of Siloam can still be seen and visited today. It appears on the southwest slope of the City of David. It rests in the Kidron valley, outside the old city walls in the neighborhood of Silwan. It has been fed since ancient times by the Gihon spring. A long walled tunnel from the time of King Hezekiah carries the water from the Gihon spring to the pool.

Around 701 BCE the city of Jerusalem was threatened during the reign of King Hezekiah of Judah. One of the first methods of destruction for a city would be to cut off its water supply. Therefore, the king prepared for the assault by redirecting the water from the Gihon spring through a tunnel cut from solid rock to the pool of Siloam, which at that time was located inside the city walls (2 Kgs 20:20; 2 Chron 32:30). With this memorable engineering feat, King Hezekiah secured safety for the inhabitants, who could procure their daily water supply in safety within the city walls, despite any enemy attacks from outside.

During the time of Jesus, the pure water from the pool was used for religious ceremonies in the Temple, especially for the feasts of Sukkoth (also called, Tabernacles or Booths). Moreover, recent excavations near the pool have uncovered a long series of steps that suggest that this pool may have been also used by the Jewish worshippers as a *mikvah*, that is, a pool for ceremonial cleansings before they entered the Temple to pray and offer sacrifices.

John 9 presents a cure that takes place in the vicinity of the pool. The term *Siloam* means "sent." Interestingly, Jesus sends the blind man to wash the spittle from his eyes in this pool. After the man obeys the command of Jesus, he becomes sighted. In effect, then, the pool of Siloam has served the residents of Jerusalem for many centuries.

92. Some Pharisees contended that Jesus broke Sabbath regulations by curing the blind man on the Sabbath. Throughout the gospels the breaking of Sabbath rules remained a theme of contention for the religious leaders. In this atmosphere, some leaders hardly recognized the gracious act of healing because they seemed to be caught up in the Sabbath dilemma of regulations. According to Jewish regulations, to knead clay from saliva, to heal, and to wash violated the Sabbath because such actions were considered work. The general command to cease from labor comes from Exodus 20:8–9 and Deuteronomy 5:12–14.

To keep Sabbath regulations meant to maintain divine order, which led to holiness of the person and honor to the family. Therefore, the Jewish leaders encountered a dilemma. They asked themselves, "Who is this man?" and their own responses divided them. When some of the leaders claimed that Jesus could not be from God because he violated the Sabbath, they established an excuse to persecute him at a later time. As others questioned, "How can a man who is a sinner perform such signs?" (9:16) they raised a question that permeates the entire story.

Naturally, the author intends the implied response to be that Jesus could never be a sinner because he is the Light! Additionally, when the leaders questioned the man about Jesus' identity, he responded on a deeper level of belief, "He is a prophet" (9:17). Such a proclamation from an illiterate man caused more exasperation within the Jewish leadership.

93. In 9:20 the parents of the blind man seemed very intimidated by the powerful Jewish leaders. Recall in 9:18–19 that, under the guise of verification of the man's claim, the authorities called his parents and posed three questions to them. They answered the first two questions about their son's relation to them and his blindness truthfully. The third question, "How then does he now see?" (9:19) is intended to entrap them. If they answer positively about the man Jesus, they will be punished. Their response to the

leaders is one of ignorance (9:21). They were afraid to help their son.

In a very real sense, they have been put on trial themselves by three questions. However, the fear of the parents about excommunication from Judaism (9:22) led them to offer no needed input or supportive strength to their son. On the contrary, their verbal response, "He is of age; ask him" (9:23), led them to separate themselves from their son, who needed them. Such fear of excommunication from Jewish authority in this narrative reflects the situation several years later in the time of the Johannine communities. Many faced the same dilemma of excommunication seventy to eighty years after the time of Jesus. As the Temple had already been destroyed by the Romans in 70 CE, these Jewish followers of Jesus faced exclusion from the synagogue, their Jewish families, their villages, and religious celebratory gatherings if they continued to believe in Jesus. The painful decision became clear: To follow Jesus meant rejection from Jewish authority and cultural roots, while to reject Jesus meant to remain a part of their Jewish community and life.

94. The Jewish authorities became increasingly frustrated with the bravery of the blind man. His last powerful remark of pure truth in 9:33, "If this man were not from God, he could do nothing," causes the final blow in this war of words. Since truth has prevailed through the courage of this man's comment, the defeated authorities will try to save face at any cost. Now, they lose any appearance of objectivity and attack the man where it will cause the most damage.

In 9:34 they declare his unacceptable position in Jewish society with the words, "You were born entirely in sins, and are you trying to teach us?" Clearly, they abandon all semblance of truth and revert to the power of their positions as high-level religious authorities. By judging the man as completely sinful from birth and illiterate in divine matters, they have attempted to dishonor him completely.

Their final act of destruction appears in the last part of 9:34, "And they drove him out." The man's punishment translates into excommunication from the Temple. In the first century CE excommunication in Judaism took away a person's life-line to family, friends, synagogue attendance, and village activities. In essence, the family and community viewed this person as dead. Therefore, all communication ceased.

Thus, the innocent man, who proclaims truth, has been banished, as Jesus, who is the Truth, will be in the future. Yet the religious authorities who act as judges have already been judged by the truth of this man's words.

95. The title "Son of Man" has its roots in the Book of Daniel (7:13–14), where it designates a heavenly being. In biblical passages the "Son of Man" title often appears within a discussion about judgment. Throughout the gospels Jesus uses the title "Son of Man" to refer to himself. In the Fourth Gospel the term refers to Jesus as the preexistent one who makes God known in history through his revealed word and his role in judgment. Here in 9:35, Jesus employs this self-designation prior to his words about judgment in 9:39–41.

96. The blind man does not call Jesus "Son of Man." Rather, Jesus asks the man about his belief in the "Son of Man." When the man did not recognize the title but asked for an explanation, Jesus identified himself as the "Son of Man," to which the man replied, "I believe" (9:38). Thus, he believes in Jesus as the "Son of Man."

97. In 9:40 the Pharisees decline to recognize that Jesus refers to blindness of the heart. Therefore, when they question rhetorically, "Surely we are not blind, are we?" they demonstrate that they remain entrenched in their stubbornness and refusal to open themselves to Jesus. Their hardness of heart has made them blind by choice. Therefore, Jesus sadly responds to them in 9:41, "If you

were blind, you would not have sin. But now that you say, 'We see,' your sin remains."

John 10—Answers

98. Surely, the gate remains the easiest and most welcome way to enter a sheepfold. Usually, a person or even an animal who would try to climb in another way represents one who could harm the sheep rather than protect them. Their actions demonstrate that probably they intend to bring harm to the sheep. Here, in 10:1, Jesus even calls such a person a thief and a bandit.

99. In this chapter Jesus employs two titles to describe how he cares for his followers. In his authoritative use of *egō eimi* ("I am") sayings, he proclaims both "I am the gate" (10:7, 9) and "I am the good shepherd" (10:11, 14). A gate symbolizes strength, protection, freedom, passage into something important. The gate provides the one who passes through it all these qualities. In this sense Jesus uses the metaphor of the gate for himself.

The image of a "good shepherd" recalls many biblical traditions both from the Hebrew Bible as well as from the New Testament. For centuries this designation has represented many strong images for Jews and Christians. In the Hebrew Bible, frequently God has been portrayed as "shepherd" to his people (Gen 48:15; Pss 23; 78:52–55, and so on). During the monarchy God implies that he alone serves as the good shepherd because the kings of Israel have not been faithful shepherds to their flock (Ezek 34:11). At the time of the Exile, the Judahite captives kept their hope in God as their good shepherd (Isa 40:11; Jer 31:10).

The New Testament continues the concept of the shepherd as a dependable leader. In particular, the Synoptic Gospels make several references to Jesus as the shepherd. Like a good shepherd, Jesus has compassion for the crowds, which appear like lost sheep (Mark 6:34; Matt 9:36). In the parable of the lost sheep (Matt 18:12–14; Luke 15:3–7), Jesus himself describes the qualities of a good shepherd. These passages represent only a few of the many instances of the "good shepherd" theme within the Bible. No doubt they provide the background for Jesus' influential words in John 10.

100. The gatekeeper and shepherd may or may not be two different figures. In this scene, they function separately. The gatekeeper has the duty to recognize the true shepherd of a particular flock. Often the gatekeeper was paid by one or several shepherds to guard the flocks within the enclosed area. In Palestine the sheepfold can consist of an enclosed portion of the field that contains a low stone wall with a gated opening.

   As you notice in John 10:3–5, Jesus infers that more than one flock rests behind the gate, because he employs phrases such as "the sheep hear his voice," "he calls his own," "has brought out all his own." As in the case of the blind man in John 9, the flock recognizes the voice of Jesus and follows him.

101. The misunderstanding of the crowds, as stated in 10:6, comes from the use of the literary form of the parable itself. In addition, while the makeup of the crowd has not been identified within the text, they seem to misunderstand the comparison Jesus makes of himself as the "gate" and the "good shepherd." For this, they need to hear further explanations of Jesus in 10:7–19.

102. In 10:7, when Jesus uses the forceful *"egō eimi"* ("I am") to refer to himself as the gate, he presents the audience with a strong metaphor. Ask yourself, what can a gate do for the sheep? First, it serves as a passage of protection for the vulnerable sheep. Second, it provides the passage into the green pastures for the health and well-being of the sheep. In both ways, then, Jesus as "the gate" offers pro-

tection, nourishment, and freedom for the sheep. Moreover, at times the shepherd lies across the entrance to become the gate for the sheep.

103. The procurement of wool functioned as the main purpose of raising sheep in ancient times as well as in many areas of the world to this day. In general, most people in Palestine were poor. Therefore, they would also be mostly vegetarians by necessity. Some of the lambs were used for sacrifice in Jerusalem and others may have been saved for sacred feasts such as Passover, but in general lambs were raised because of their coats of wool. This wool would act as a main source of clothing as well as provide income at the market for the families that owned the sheep.

104. In 10:16 the other sheep who do not belong to the fold refer to all those outside Judaism. Jesus intimates that all people will be welcome. His remark suggests that this issue does not come from the time of the historical Jesus, but rather at the later time of the Johannine communities. By the end of the first century CE most likely members of this community included not only Jewish Christians but Samaritan Christians as well as Gentile Christians. The announcement of Jesus, therefore, gives rise to a new people of God, a "new flock" composed of original sheep as well as new sheep. This community will be unified because it will center itself in the person of Jesus.

105. When the author states in 10:17 that Jesus lays down his life in order to take it up again, he further comments on 10:15, which states "I lay down my life for the sheep." Both comments in this Gospel relate to Jesus' decision to give his life for others through his death on the cross. However, the words of 10:17 depart from the other New Testament descriptions of the resurrection of Jesus. In 1 Corinthians 15 and in the other three gospels, the passive verb has been employed to speak of Jesus' resurrection. This verb form indicates that the power of his resurrection comes from

God the Father. Verb forms such as "has been raised, was raised" describe the momentous event. Unlike such earlier passages in the New Testament, John 10:17 describes Jesus as proclaiming that he has the power to "lay down" his life and "take it up again."

The phrase, "in order to take it up again," demonstrates that Jesus' resurrection remains essentially associated with his death. Both function as the moment of his "glory," which we will study in later chapters. In the Gospel of John, resurrection is the purpose of Jesus' death. Through death and resurrection, Jesus completes his return to the Father.

106. In 10:22 the festival of Dedication refers to the Jewish feast of Hanukkah. This Hebrew term has been translated as "dedication," and so the Greek New Testament text entitles it the feast of Dedication. The celebration, which lasts for eight days, begins on the twenty-fifth day during the winter month of Kislev, which is the month of December in the Roman calendar.

The feast commemorates the reconsecration of the Jerusalem Temple by the Jews in 164 BCE. During the reign of King Antiochus Epiphanes IV, the sacred Jerusalem Temple had been desecrated and turned into a place of pagan worship around 168 BCE. Much tension existed in the city and finally, under the leadership of Judas Maccabaeus, a revolt took place to recapture the sacred Temple. Much of the story has been told in the books of the Maccabees.

Some additional comments need to be made about this feast. 1 Maccabees emphasizes the restoration of the altar, whereas 2 Maccabees speaks about the restoration of the entire Temple. More important for our study of the Gospel of John is the point that 2 Maccabees links the feast of Tabernacles (Sukkoth) with the feast of Dedication (Hanukkah). As you recall, John 7 and 8 took place during the feast of Tabernacles, while John 10:22ff. centers on this feast of the Dedication. All of these chapters (from

The Gospel of John

John 7 to John 10) connect two points: They associate Jesus with some theme of "light," and they report tension from those Jews who do not accept that light.

107. This question reflects the question of many in our multi-task world of today as they read passages from the Gospel. As you have already read in the introduction, as people from the Western traditions of civilization, we always like a logical explanation. More recently, some of us in the United States will not even wait for a logical explanation as we urge, "Get to the bottom line!" Unlike our way of linear thought, those of the Middle East do not process thought in the same way. People in the East, both today and in the time of Jesus, think and speak concentrically. Therefore, for Jesus to answer questions directly does not always fit his pattern of thought or speech.

As you may recall, Jesus does not offer direct answers to questions from those who oppose him. In John's Gospel, Jesus already knows the hardness of their hearts. In some way, not to respond directly to their questions leaves room to excuse them. If they could not understand his words, how could they follow him? Jesus' indirectness in times of confrontation, then, offers the stubborn examiners an opportunity to change their attitudes.

108. Stones appear everywhere in this land called Israel. Unlike land surfaces in other parts of the world, where dirt runs deep, in the land where Jesus lived, it did not. Consequently, people could pick up pieces of stones or volcanic shale almost anywhere. The point that the accusers were in Solomon's Portico when they attempted to stone Jesus does not sound unusual, since stones or shale surface all over the land.

The mention of the Portico of Solomon as the setting for this tense moment has some historical interest. According to the historian Josephus (*Antiquities,* 15. 396–401), the Portico of Solomon ran along the east side of Temple. From the reports in Acts, this porch became a gathering place for early Christians. In Acts 3:11 Peter presented his second speech at this site, and in Acts 5:12, the disciples performed many "signs and wonders" at this hallowed spot. Therefore, the mention of the Portico already has a tradition in Christianity.

109. No, 10:35 does not mean that we are all gods. Genesis 1:27 states we have been created "in the image of God," but that does not make us gods. Remember the dialogue here revolves around Jesus' claim to be God's Son, and thus equal to the Father. Sometimes, the identification, "god" has been used loosely, as in Psalm 82:6, where God calls lesser divine beings "gods." Harrington (*John's Thought and Theology*, 66) suggests that Jesus professes in typical Jewish argumentation that if God can call these angelic beings "gods," why can't he call himself the "Son of God?"

John 11—Answers

110. The author of this Gospel has placed the greatest of all the signs, namely the raising of Lazarus from the dead, as the last and greatest of the miracles in order to support his theological point. Through the signs he builds up the miracle stories from an abundance of wine, healings of a paralytic and a blind man, to a story that climaxes with an essential point for all of us, namely, the issue of life. While his first sign commences with a wedding, his last ends with a funeral. Here, the progression itself projects an existence that reflects the lives of humans. However, in John 11 the author states that Jesus overturns death.

In this last sign, as well as in the other signs that have preceded it, Jesus demonstrates he will come to the rescue of another in need despite any danger to himself. In this case, after Jesus restores life, some Jewish leaders of the Sanhedrin decide that he must die. Throughout the chapters that included signs, Jesus often receives a negative response from certain Jewish leaders.

111. John is the only Gospel to portray the three members of this family. In the Gospel of Luke, the author mentions the two sisters, Martha and Mary, in a separate story (Luke 10:38–42), but nothing about their having a brother or living in Bethany. Also in the Gospel of Luke, one of the characters of Jesus' parables was named Lazarus (Luke 16:19–31), but he has no connection with the Lazarus in John's Gospel. Other than these two references in Luke, no other gospel writer mentions this family of Bethany.

112. The message to Jesus from the sisters of Lazarus suggests that their brother may be terminally ill. Recall in John 10:40 that Jesus went away "across the Jordan." Therefore, he resides temporarily nowhere near Bethany, and it would be a long trip for him to come to the village by foot. At the same time, such a communication from the sisters looks for the arrival of their good friend before it becomes too late to heal their sick brother, Lazarus. How can the women hope for Jesus' presence? The answer lies in the meaning of friendship.

Friendship has always meant a special link between two parties. It symbolizes a deep bond like no other. Within such a relationship, true friends share experiences, feelings, hopes, and dreams. They trust each other and depend on one another for support, loyalty, and truthfulness. In the end, a true friend would do anything for the other, even to the point of death, as 11:15b clearly indicates. According to Malina and Rohrbaugh (*Social-Science Commentary on the Gospel of John,* 195), friends enjoy a privileged relationship with certain other members of society. As such, they become members of an in-group that has "the right" to urgent assistance. Within this framework, the communication from Mary and Martha to Jesus would not be unusual.

The response of Jesus to the news about his friend appears quite unusual at first. We need to consider, however, that Jesus must act within God's time frame rather than from human urging. Moreover, his decision becomes linked with his own death. If he does journey to Bethany, so close to Jerusalem, his immediate future will be in severe jeopardy. With this in mind, his delay in travel plans becomes more understandable.

113. This very confusing verse (11:6) does not make sense if we take the statement only at face value. Remember that the evangelist shares these narratives for a purpose, namely, belief in the person of Jesus. Therefore, the decision of Jesus to wait before taking the two-day trip to see Lazarus and his sisters gives rise to a few points: First, it allows Jesus to act in God's time rather than in the world's time; second, it pre-figures Jesus' three days wait within the tomb; third, the sign will show that Jesus, like his Father, ranks above every human condition, even death; fourth, this decision to wait will offer Jesus the opportunity to offer life, not only to Lazarus, but to all who believe in him.

114. The comment of Thomas, "Let us also go, that we may die with him," in 11:16 seems quite ambiguous. Does it refer to dying with Jesus or Lazarus? While some critics may associate it with Lazarus, others suggest that it represents an obedient disciple who proposes to die along with Jesus when the time comes. If the latter statement makes more sense, then an ironic point needs to be made. Remember that this Thomas, called the Twin, is the same figure in John 20:25 who said, after missing the resurrected Jesus' appearance to the disciples, "Unless I see the mark of the nails in his hands, and put my finger in the mark of the nails and my hand in his side, I will not believe." What does this say to us? Thomas represents a true disciple, one who takes a brave stance, but, at a particular moment in time when his loyalty and belief need to surface, his actions do not always follow his words.

115. In 11:25, within a dialogue between Martha and Jesus, he decrees, "I am the resurrection and the life." This powerful statement comes toward the end of a verbal exchange that crescendos as she and Jesus deepen their conversation.

The unexpected proclamation identifies Jesus as the answer to life. It announces that Jesus puts an end to death and that life will continue in abundance, even after a person dies physically. Through this bold announcement, Jesus declares his power over the lives of those who believe, both in the present moment and in the future.

116. While some commentators paint a verbal scene of Martha being annoyed at Jesus, I would disagree. Of course, she would have been disappointed that her dear friend would not have been there to heal Lazarus before his death, as she states in 11:21. However, immediately she adds her faith in Jesus in 11:22. Throughout the dialogue with Jesus, Martha remains strong and faith filled. Therefore, no doubts about the belief of Martha should be gleaned from her tender encounter with Jesus.

117 In 11:35 Jesus wept at the tomb of Lazarus because his dear friend had died and Jesus could see the painful effect that death has on friends and family. Death causes pain for those left behind. Remember that 11:35 follows the remarks of 11:33, which state that Jesus "was greatly disturbed in spirit and deeply moved," about the hurt of the family over the death of their brother. Such anger brings tears over the pain of loss. Gail O' Day ("John," *New Interpreter's Bible,* 691) states correctly that "Jesus' anger in verse 33 informs the interpretation of his tears in verse 35. It is again important that the tears not be sentimentalized."

118. It seems that these Jewish leaders were threatened by Jesus over the issues of power and authority. The more Jesus attracted followers because of his discourses and signs, the more insecure such people became. The miracle of Lazarus became the last straw for them. They knew that a definite decision had to be made about Jesus, lest "everyone will believe in him" (11:48). Their decision to "put him to death" (11:53) was based on fear and jealousy. Such decisions do not come from God and the outcome will not

reflect growth of the person or the community. Rather, decisions made for these reasons will lead to destruction and division.

John 12—Answers

119. Mary's bold and loving anointing of Jesus' feet is associated with the anticipation of Jesus' burial in the Gospel of John. Traditions of anointing Jesus exist in all four gospels. In Mark 14:3–9 and Matthew 26:6–13 an unknown woman anoints Jesus' head in Bethany as a preparation for his death. In both cases, the action takes place in Bethany. In Luke 7:36–50, an unnamed woman anoints Jesus' feet at the house of Simon the Pharisee. While this action takes place in the middle of Jesus' ministry and has no association with his death or burial, it precedes the only story in Luke about Martha and Mary.

   By naming Mary, the sister of Lazarus, as the one who anointed Jesus' feet, some important points have been made by the Johannine author. First, John 11 and John 12 are connected with the naming of Mary. Second, in the personalization of naming a dear friend as the one who anoints Jesus, the author points out the giving love and deep caring that Mary of Bethany has for Jesus, her dear friend. Third, in John 12 Mary's abundant generosity poses a blunt contrast to the biting remarks of Judas that follow the anointing.

120. According to McKenzie (*Dictionary of the Bible*, 606), nard is actually a perfume that has been extracted from the oil of a native plant of India. The Greek term, *nárdos pistikos* ("pure nard") suggests that it represents an extremely expensive item. Caravans from the East would transport such costly commodities through an intricate system of sea and land routes from India to the markets of Palestine.

   Today, with all the intricate spices and mixtures from various plants available in perfumeries, it would probably be available. Most likely, it would be found in specialized stores that deal in items such as perfumes, herbs, and spices.

121. No, Jesus would never disregard the poor. However, the motive of Judas' objection does appear to come from a concern for the poor, as the editorial comment in 12:6 indicates. The words of Jesus in 12:8 parallel those of Matthew 26:11. Since not all manuscripts of John contain this verse, some scholars suggest that it may have been added to correspond with the Matthean account. In any case, the presence of the poor has been a reality throughout history. When Jesus mentions them, he may have alluded to the command to care for the poor in Deuteronomy 15:11. Here in clear terms, the Israelites have been told, "Since there will never cease to be some in need on the earth, I therefore command you, 'Open your hand to the poor and needy neighbor in your land.'" At the same time, we must remember that this anointing in Bethany represents a sacred moment that precedes Jesus' death and burial. It will never come again. Therefore, Jesus commends Mary's elaborate actions.

122. In 12:6 we have been informed that Judas "kept the common purse" for the community of disciples. Yet we learn from the same verse that Judas acted as a thief because he stole from that common purse. Therefore, his criticism about extravagance proved to be a smoke screen for his greed. His complaints completely dishonor Jesus, the owners of the house to which he was invited, as well the poor people whom he supposedly defends. Truly, this proved to be one of Judas's dishonorable moments.

123. When you read John 11:45–57 and John 12, you probably noticed that the raising of Lazarus was forgotten in the pursuit over the whereabouts of Jesus and the focus of Jesus' upcoming death. At first, the authorities called for the death of Lazarus along with Jesus, probably to remove all evidence of Jesus' signs. Now, however, all focus on the

person of Jesus. Those who love and believe in him try to honor him and show love. Those who want to see him shout, "Hosanna," while Judas, who will betray him, complains. Lastly, those who despise Jesus, try to locate and arrest him for death.

124. Only John identifies the branches as palm. In this scene (12:12–14), the crowds chant Psalm 118:26–27. This particular psalm has been linked with the feast of Tabernacles/Booths (Sukkoth). The Mishnah (m.Sukk.3:9; 4:5), a collection of Jewish writings that represent the opinions of famous ancient rabbis, states that bunches of palm, myrtle, and willow branches were waved at the beginning and end of this particular psalm.

In addition, from the time of Judas Maccabaeus (2 Macc 10:7), the palm branch has been a symbol of freedom in Jewish tradition. At the time of the rededication of the Second Temple after the defeat of the Syrians, palm branches were used in processional glory. Later, at the time of the Bar Kochba revolt (132–35 CE), coins with palm fronds were minted with the inscription, "for the liberation of Israel." Therefore, palm branches became a symbol of freedom and national victory for the Jews.

125. The heavenly voice, angels, and thunder represent significant theological symbols for the voice of God. In 12:28 the author picks familiar religious imagery to describe a divine epiphany. In 12:29 some of the crowd refuse to believe the sound of the voice and identify it as thunder, for in the tradition it became an assumption that anyone who came to be in the presence of God would die. Neither many disciples nor this crowd understand that being with Jesus equates with being in the presence of God. You will notice that others in the crowd declared that an angel, which means "messenger," had spoken. Yet, in the biblical tradition, a pointed distinction does not always exist between an angel as the messenger of God and the angel as a personi-

fication of God. In any case, both understandings signify a divine encounter.

126. In 12:32, the clause, "when I am lifted up from the earth," may reflect the reference in Isaiah 52:13, which speaks of the Suffering Servant as the one who will be "exalted and lifted up," because both texts focus on death and glory. In the Gospel, a lifting up from the earth describes the Roman process of crucifixion. This description would indicate the kind of death Jesus was to die. Furthermore, lifting up would also apply to Jesus' exaltation as he returns to God, from where he came originally as indicated by the Prologue of John's Gospel.

John 13—Answers

127. The other gospels identify the Last Supper as the first day of Passover to connect Jesus' sufferings in the passion with the Last Supper. In ancient Judaism, all the family partook of the sacrificial lamb on the first day of Passover. For example, Mark portrays Jesus as the Messiah who suffered and died for us. In Luke Jesus appears as the prophet who had to suffer and die in Jerusalem, like the prophets that preceded him. Therefore, it is very appropriate that these gospels put the Last Supper on the first day of Passover, because, like the lamb that was eaten, so, too, the disciples partook of the body and blood of Jesus at the Passover meal.

In the Gospel of John, however, Jesus is *not* portrayed as the suffering Messiah or the prophet. Rather, the passion, death, resurrection, ascension are the moments of Jesus' glory. Any suffering by Jesus is downplayed in this Gospel.

128. The long discourse at the Last Supper scene represents the last will and testament of Jesus. The command that the disciples love one another as Jesus loved them forms the heart of the long conversation during the Last Supper. As Jesus

prepares for his final departure, he emphasizes the necessity of the disciples' love one for the other.

While the American tradition of the dying person usually centers on getting his/her material possessions in order, such as the finalization of a will and the disposition of household as well as other goods, the world of Palestine was to be very different. In ancient times a person's last testament centered on the family or community. The person would be very anxious to make sure the family/community has the necessary means to continue their lives. Advice to the group would be bestowed by the dying person. At the same time the person would offer a farewell and best wishes to those left behind. At the end of the discourse, the one dying would often offer a prayer to the deity on behalf of the children. In John 13—17, Jesus' final conversation with the disciples functions in this way (see Malina and Rohrbaugh, *Social-Science Commentary on the Gospel of John*, 222).

129. The Gospel of John does contain a Last Supper scene. However, the focus shifts from the institution of the Eucharist to a washing of the disciples' feet by Jesus. The closest eucharistic scene comes in the discourse of John 6 after the sign of the feeding of the multitude. In this discourse the author links the manna from the Exodus story with the Eucharist.

At different times various theories have been proposed to explain the discrepancy. For example, some suggest that this author did not know the tradition of the Last Supper as an institution of the Eucharist. Others suggest that John's sources thought the institution had taken place during Jesus' public ministry or that John had another tradition of the Last Supper.

Recall that this Fourth Gospel appeared at the end of the first century. I suggest, then, that by this time the Eucharist had already been an accepted reality. Therefore, the author concentrates on the need of participants to change their mode of behavior in community as a result of

Eucharist. As a powerful example, the author offers the humble actions of Jesus with his disciples.

130. Remember that, in the first century world of Palestine, most people traveled by foot. Usually, they would only wear an open sandal that was secured by leather straps so as to protect the soles of their feet. Otherwise, they would go barefoot. In either case, any person who traveled picked up the usual dust, grit, stones, as well as animal and human waste as they walked. By the time they arrived at their destination, their feet would probably be sore and odorous. Therefore, foot washing would be a very unpleasant yet necessary task before joining others around a table to eat. It remained the duty of a subordinate servant of the house to wash the feet of a guest because society considered it the lowest of any slave's task.

For Jesus to perform this lowly, unwanted task on all the disciples demonstrates his heartfelt love for them. Moreover, it provides an excellent example of humility and openness to them. If they are to lead, then they also must "wash each other's feet" through their example of service. The foot washing, then, provides another example of the need to overturn the system of rank. As true community leaders, the disciples must serve others humbly.

131. The clauses, "the devil had already put it into the heart of Judas son of Simon Iscariot to betray him [Jesus]" and "Satan entered into him," refer to a deliberate evil act that Judas will now do. That act, of course, will be to betray Jesus to the religious officials, who will arrest, persecute, and murder him.

In the first-century world, the role of the devil included the testing of a person. When the text states, "Satan entered into him," it means that Judas was tempted to be disloyal to Jesus. As we know, Judas succumbed to that evil and dishonored Jesus in his betrayal of him.

This phrase somewhat resembles the language of duality in the Essene writings from Qumran (Dead Sea Scrolls), which were discovered in the mid-twentieth century. Occasionally, the scrolls speak of the Spirit of Light and the Spirit of Darkness to refer to the tension between good and evil (1 QS 4). The evil spirit promotes selfishness, greed, and lies.

132. We shall never know the thoughts of Peter. However, he would have probably been somewhat overwhelmed or even repulsed at the thought of Jesus performing the action of a slave. If this were the case, then he would have objected vehemently. Therefore, this impetuous act of protest may have resulted from his great admiration for Jesus.

    On the other hand, some scholars contend that Peter protested strongly because he did not want to surrender his own power to Jesus. This radical act called for approval of Jesus' actions, a point that Peter may have not wanted to concede, because acceptance of Jesus' decision would mean that he, too, must serve in this way. Whatever the case, Peter finally surrendered to the dramatic actions of Jesus, which presented an example of the role of future leaders within the community, namely, to serve others.

133. Jesus' comment in 13:16 that "servants are not greater than their master" has been made after he washed the feet of the disciples. Therefore, it relates to this previous action. As followers of Jesus, the disciples need to serve other members of the community whenever the need arises. In this way they follow the humble example of their leader, Jesus. His actions as well as his words present a model of leadership for them.

134. John 13:23 offers the first reference to the Beloved Disciple, a designation that has been mentioned six times in the second half of John's Gospel. In all these references, not once has the person been identified. The description of the Beloved Disciple, however, usually presents the disciple's closeness to Jesus and to Peter. Whatever the purpose of the anonymity of the Beloved Disciple, the figure offers the

community an example of a faithful disciple and friend of Jesus, one who serves in leadership within the community.

135. Only in the Gospel of John does Jesus offer a morsel of bread to Judas. This act identifies Judas as the betrayer, but in no way takes away his free will. Therefore, the action does not function as an indictment of Judas. In the Gospel the author portrays Judas as an instrument of Satan. In reality, the increasing animosity toward Jesus throughout the Gospel culminates in the action of his chosen friend, Judas. This trusted disciple brings evil (Satan) into the loving circle of Jesus. After receiving the morsel of bread, Judas departs into the world of deceit. Recall that "it was night" (13:30), the symbol of darkness, uncertainty, and, at times, evil.

136. The comments of Jesus in 13:31–32 refer to the "Son of Man" being glorified. In the Fourth Gospel glorification is connected with Jesus' "hour." Glorification represents the goal of "the hour." With his comments Jesus announces that the moment of glory (that is, his "hour") has arrived. The moment of glory or "hour" designates the passion, death, resurrection, and ascension of Jesus. These events characterize the moment of glorification for Jesus.

137. In 13:34–35 Jesus gives instructions to the disciples on how to lead the community in his physical absence. He says, "I give you a new commandment, that you love one another. Just as I have loved you, you also should love one another." Internal attitudes cannot literally be commanded since no one can control another's inner attitude. Despite this point, Jesus offers the disciples an internal way to function as leaders of the community. They have been commanded to love and forgive as Jesus has loved and forgiven, an attitude that reflects the attitude of God.

John 14—Answers

138. In 14:2 the phrase "dwelling places" does not necessitate exclusion of other people with different beliefs. Remember the term *many* does not signify *all*. In this Gospel it may well be an assurance for the disciples that they will be at peace with God after their deaths. God's goodness encompasses all people if they choose to listen and respond in the way that God calls them.

139. The phrase, "I will come again and take you to myself" (14:3), seems to refer to the *parousía*, that is, the end time when Jesus will come again. This is one of the first times in the Fourth Gospel that the subject of final eschatology arises. You may recall that the term *eschatology* refers to the last times. At first the early Christians awaited the immediate return of Christ, as seen in some the letters of Paul, such as 1 Thessalonians 4:16–17. In time, however, when Jesus did not return Christian communities began to change their hopes to the return of Jesus at a later time in history.

    This topic of eschatology also appears during Jesus' discussion in John. 5:19–30. Brown (*The Gospel of John*, vol. 2, 621) suggests that 14:3 brings the author "much closer to understanding the *parousía* as a second coming."

140. The statements in 14:6 seem to describe Jesus as sole revelation of the Father. However, we all realize that both God's and Jesus' ways of touching people are beyond identification. Remember that the words of Jesus in this passage have been aimed at a specific audience, namely, his disciples. They also occur during a memorable moment in time, namely, the Last Supper. Accordingly, all that Jesus speaks needs to be understood within this context.

141. In John's Gospel the concept of Jesus as divine and united with God appears in the Prologue. It continues throughout the chapters. This very high Christology in 14:9b stresses the oneness of Jesus and the Father in this bonded relation-

ship. He is the one sent by the Father. As such, Jesus claims courageously to be the physical presence of the Father.

142. The highest form of belief requires no signs. Therefore, in 14:11, Jesus urges his audience to subscribe to this form of faith. However, if they cannot, then Jesus recommends they believe in him because of the signs that he has performed. This faith surpasses no faith at all. Such works of Jesus also reveal the divine. Moreover, this type of faith may be their first step on a journey that will lead one to belief in the person of Jesus no matter what signs he did or did not do.

143. The theme of a prayer request follows a tradition of prayer petitions in the other three gospels. It also appears in later chapters in John (15:7, 16; 16:23–24). In 14:14 when Jesus says, "If in my name you ask me for anything, I will do it," the promise of "anything" really sounds as if any request in the world will be granted. However, such granting is not the intention in this verse. Remember that the statement has been made within the context of Jesus' mission, his presence within the community, the observance of the commandments, maintaining God's will, and so on. Therefore, requests that will be made need to relate to these areas.

144. The term *Advocate* (Paraclete) sounds like a legal term for a court system because it describes an intercessor, that is, one who speaks or acts on another's behalf, such as a lawyer does for a client. Actually, it does connote a legal counselor, one who defends another at a trial. In 14:26, Jesus identifies the Advocate as the Holy Spirit. Since the earthly Jesus has already acted as an Advocate with the disciples while being with them, the other Advocate will be the risen Jesus, whose spirit will be with them after he dies and ascends into heaven.

The saying in 14:26 does not detract from the Christian concept of the Trinity. Yet it has been the topic for many

216

debates on Christology and trinitarian theology. Before I go any further with this explanation, it is imperative that you remember that these profound words in John's Gospel reflect the product of late-first-century Johannine thought, when Christian beliefs and dogma had not yet been fully developed. This process took centuries of expansions through serious research, prayerful reflection, and growth as Christian communities. Therefore, in this conversation the Holy Spirit describes the Spirit of Jesus among the disciples after he has ascended into heaven.

145. The command, "Rise, let us be on our way," in 14:31 doesn't seem to fit because no one leaves. Rather, in John 15 Jesus continues to speak until 18:1. Many scholars hold that John 14 represents an earlier stage of the Johannine writing, which may have led to 18:1. Yet the final redactor (editor) did not remove any material, as was the tradition. This redactor simply added John 15 and 16 to the material, which causes this awkward verse.

John 15—Answers

146. This strong statement has been made within the setting of a parable about the vine and its branches. Consequently, you need to read it within this context and realize that the story functions metaphorically. Any farmer or gardener knows that, when branches become disconnected from the main vine, they wither and die. These dried-out branches must be cut from the vine and, in the past, were used as kindling wood for cooking or heating. What is Jesus' point here? Jesus, as the vine, offers the source of all life as well as divine Wisdom. Disciples need to be connected with him and with each other in order to bear fruit through their loving service. If they do not remain attached to the vine, they lose strength and will become incapable of bringing selfless love and service to others. Thus, they resemble the fruitless, dried-out branches. The imagery of

fire in 15:6 seems to allude to a final eschatology and the consequences of being detached from the vine.

147. In 15:10 Jesus' statement, "If you keep my commandments, you will abide in my love," incorporates much more than the original commandments delivered by Moses at Sinai. Here in the Fourth Gospel Jesus expands the entire concept of the commandments. He reaches far beyond the minimum of "thou shall not...." In the Gospel he calls for the disciples to follow his example in every way. In this Gospel, Jesus accepted people on the fringes of society, he reached beyond the accepted norm of both Judaism and society by being inclusive, by listening to others, and by offering them hope and life. In the same way, then, the disciples have been called to share this openness, inclusivity, forgiveness, and care to others. When they, like Jesus, offer these gifts to those in need, they will indeed abide in divine love, a love that will touch the people with whom they interact.

148. When Jesus speaks of the command he gives the disciples, he instructs them to "love one another as I have loved you" (15:12). In reality, all the commandments can be reduced to this one. If the disciples follow the actions and attitude of Jesus in this command of love, all other previous commandments will, of course, be observed. Keep in mind that here Jesus speaks of a decision that each of us has been called to make. This love goes far beyond how we feel about another person. Rather, it comes to a choice we must make to love another, that is, a decision to want the best for the other person, no matter how that person has treated us. Love produces more love.

149. In 15:13 the comment about the greatest love being the laying down of one's life for another serves as an example of how far Jesus will go for others. The gift of his life indicates clearly the depth of his love for all. As for his followers, the love that needs to shown to others symbolizes their commitment to them. It can be shown in countless ways,

such as love shown to them by attitude, giving of time, thoughtfulness, support, and so on.

150. In 15:19, the "world" signifies all that does not describe God, such as hatred, selfishness, isolation, shunning of others, and further descriptions of evil. In this sense, if the disciples truly follow Jesus, they do not belong to this world. Sometimes, however, as you have seen, they may succumb momentarily to the ways and thinking of the world. As followers, we too are called to live in God's world, that is, with God's loving attitude. This discussion exemplifies a type of Johannine dualism because of the contrast between "the world" and God.

151. In 15:22, when Jesus speaks explicitly about who can sin with regard to hearing or not hearing his message, he addresses the situation of those who have refused to listen to his words and mock his works. The point that lack of knowledge lessens culpability provides an excuse for the decision of others. However, because those who refuse Jesus have had the opportunity to change, they have been held accountable for their stubbornness.

152. In 15:23 the clause, "Whoever hates me hates my Father also," does not have to do directly with Muslims, Hindus, and so on. It has to do with the situation that Jesus experienced and the situations that his disciples will encounter. People who choose not to listen to Jesus make their own choices. Remember that we judge ourselves by the choices we make. Therefore, by remaining stubborn or hard-hearted about the invitation of Jesus, some of "the Jews" have shown hard-heartedness toward God. Throughout the Gospel, such arrogance also seems at times to permeate their dealing with fellow Jews, as in their mistreatment of the man born blind in John 9.

153. The command "to testify" in 15:27 connects with 15:26 about the coming of the Advocate. Most likely, it refers to

a time of persecution when the disciples will need to witness to their faith. In contemporary times, we witness to Christianity in many ways. Whether or not the 12-step programs for addictions have been inspired by this text, I do not know.

John 16—Answers

154. The question about being put out of the synagogues needs to be answered in two ways. First, the Johannine author has framed Jesus' words within the context of John 16:2, that is, within the lifetime of Jesus and his disciples. Remember that Jesus lived on earth as a faithful Jew. His disciples were also Jews. Therefore, they attended synagogue and probably went often to the Temple in Jerusalem for the pilgrim feasts of Pesach (Passover), Shavuoth (Pentecost), and Sukkoth (Tabernacles/Booths).

Second, the words of Jesus in 16:2 actually reflect the experience of many within the Johannine communities who were Jewish Christians after the destruction of the Jerusalem Temple in 70 CE by the Roman armies. These Christians would attend synagogue on Saturday and break bread at the Eucharist on Sunday, until they were excommunicated from the synagogues toward the end of the first century for acknowledging Jesus as Messiah. Recall that in the introduction of the book I discussed their expulsion from the synagogues, which would have carried over to an expulsion from their Jewish families, villages, and former ways of life. In this way, 16:2 reflects their painful experience.

Finally, the question about attendance in a church needs an answer. In the early Christian communities, the group gathered for the breaking of the bread (Eucharist) in people's homes. For many years no formal church buildings existed for liturgical celebrations. All services were performed in homes, which are known as "house churches," or they were performed outside in the open.

Church buildings for liturgical services appeared later in the development of Christianity.

155. The comment in 16:2b reflects the mistaken idea of many who persecute innocent people and cause them pain and suffering all in the name of God, Allah, or whatever name they entitle the Divine. This tragic and false notion takes those who adhere to it far from the will of God. Examples of such ruthless behavior fill the history of Christianity, such as the Crusades, the Inquisition, and so on. In this very day acts of terrorism done in the name of religion remind us again that cutting oneself off from and persecuting people of other faiths, cultures, and backgrounds has never been the will of God.

156. The word in Greek appears as *paráklētos,* while the term *advocate* comes from the Latin *advocatus.* Both terms are interchangeable in the Johannine texts. Perhaps if you remember that Advocate means a counsel for the defense, that is, someone to help or guide another in time of need, the term would become more understandable. The term *Paraclete* means comforter. In time of great difficulty, we could all use comfort. The discussions about the Advocate in the Last Supper scene, then, have a purpose. Jesus promises that this Advocate will provide support, comfort, and understanding for the disciples so that they will be able to continue Jesus' mission to the world.

   What, then, does this mean for our lives? Jesus promises that the Advocate, the Spirit of Truth, will guide and strengthen all who believe in him. No matter what the circumstances of our lives may be at a particular moment in time, we shall be comforted and guided so that we can grow and be nourished, if we so choose.

157. The Holy Spirit remains present throughout all circumstances in life. However, we must never forget that God has given us free choice. Therefore, we have the option to choose or not to choose goodness. Throughout tragedies

such as the Crusades, the Holocaust during World War II, and wars of our times, leaders of nations have not always chosen goodness or given people the gift of choice themselves. Whenever we violate the rights and growth of others, we refuse to listen to God's Spirit within us.

In essence, then, the tragedies and wars have been caused by us, not God. Therefore, we have the responsibility to stop them, to offer people peace, caring, and love. We can only do this when we keep ourselves open to the needs of others, without any other agenda in mind.

158. In 15:26 Jesus had already described the Advocate as the Spirit of truth. Consequently, in 16:13 the same holds true. Since one of the functions of the Advocate will be to guide the disciples to truth, the description helps us to understand how the disciples will be helped. As the disciples will be guided along the path to truth, they will continually change their way of living to parallel the way that Jesus has taught them. Those who follow Jesus must also do the same, that is, continually change their way of thought and action to reflect the thoughts and actions of Jesus.

159. The declaration in 16:16, "A little while, and you will no longer see me, and again a little while, and you will see me," has had scholars puzzled for centuries. The early church fathers took it literally to refer to the imminent death and resurrection and then his appearances to them. However, today, scholars question this assumption because it presupposes that Jesus knew very clearly what would happen after his death. Rather, modern scholars choose to view it in the eyes of the evangelist, who already knew what happened from the sources he used. Moreover, the metaphorical sense cannot be ignored. When Jesus leaves, the disciples will be lost until the Advocate comes to bring them an understanding of the words and works of Jesus, as well as the courage to follow him in whatever way they are called to do so. In this way the time period that will be cov-

ered encompasses their entire future. Do not forget that in the Fourth Gospel the Advocate (Holy Spirit) describes the spirit of Jesus after his resurrection and ascension.

160. In 16:24 the statement, "Ask and you will receive," inspires the disciples to have faith in the name of Jesus. Here the verb form *ask* is in the present imperative, which, as Brown (*The Gospel of John,* vol. 2, 723) indicates, "puts emphasis on the persistence on the request." With this command, Jesus encourages his friends to ask God anything in his name, a practice they had probably not yet done.

161. The use of figures of speech such as metaphor, allegory, and so on, were spoken at times to soften blunt truth, to help the listeners to draw analogies to their own lives, or to keep the audience somewhat ignorant so that they could not be held accountable for disobedience to the words of Jesus. Plain truth takes great courage both on the part of the speaker and audience. If the audience does not yet seem ready for plain truth, then, metaphorical speech may be an act of kindness to them. With the future coming of the Advocate, the disciples would be able both to speak to each other and to hear plain truth. Today, we often think we like plain truth, but the reality remains, that we, too, may appreciate hard truth to be couched in gentle speech.

162. When Jesus proclaims that "I have conquered the world" (16:33), he indicates his oneness with the Father. In this unity, he assures real Life, one of unity and love. This unity will empower his disciples. Furthermore, Jesus' power over the world opposes its selfishness and hatred. Jesus' announcement, then, offers continued hope for the disciples, who will soon feel the effects of the world's injustices with the brutal death of their leader.

John 17—Answers

163. Traditionally, this prayer has been called the "Priestly Prayer" of Jesus, although the prayer in John 17 contains no mention of priesthood. To understand the term, let me offer a bit of background about the evolution of the phrase.

    Brown (*The Gospel of John*, vol. 2, 747) states that as early as the fifth century CE Cyril of Alexandria (*Jo.* Xi8; PG74:505) speaks about Jesus being a high priest in John 17, that is, one who intercedes for us. In the sixteenth century, the Lutheran exegete D. Chytraeus called this prayer "the high priestly prayer." From such references, the title has been used by many who refer to John 17. In reality, however, no mention of a high priest or any priest occurs within the text.

164. In 17:1-5 the phrase, "glorify your Son," appears within the intimate prayer of a Son to his Father. In the Fourth Gospel the term *glorify* does include the passion, death, resurrection, and ascension of Jesus. Here, in this prayer, Jesus requests that the Father's will be accomplished. The "hour" of "glory" has just begun, but still needs completion by means of the future events of Jesus' life, which will soon take place.

165. In 17:6 Jesus tells his Father, "I have made your name known to those whom you gave me from the world." The words, "those whom you gave me from the world," seem to refer to everyone with whom Jesus came in contact. If you go back to 17:2 of the prayer, Jesus states that his Father has given him authority over "all people" so that he can offer eternal life to them. Therefore, in 17:6 Jesus states that, in fact, he has made God's name known to them. However, the two verses that follow are more specific and narrow the topic to the disciples of Jesus. They have been the ones who have kept God's word.

166. Remember that the context of Jesus' words remains part of the Last Supper. Therefore, when he prays to God "on

their behalf" in 17:9, Jesus refers to his disciples. In this section (17:9–16) Jesus prays to his Father for protection on behalf of his disciples. Later, in 17:20, Jesus' prayer will encompass future followers of Jesus.

167. The prayer of Jesus in 17:11b "that they may be one as we are one" connotes a *one* in process. The deep unity between Jesus and his Father becomes a goal for all Christian communities to seek and imitate. In this world, it will never be achieved completely, yet this exemplary love and caring between Jesus and his Father must always be sought by others by means of their self-sacrifice, concern for others, and service to the community.

168. In 17:12 "the one destined to be lost" can be translated literally to read "the son of perdition." Some scholars maintain that this phrase is associated with Judas, who as "son" of Satan, "perdition," performed evil. Yet his cruel act of betrayal will allow God to use such an evil act to accomplish good. However, others hold that the phrase "son of perdition" describes Satan, the one who has been lost. With this opinion, the prayer of Jesus for the disciples would include Judas.

   The phrase "so that the scripture might be fulfilled" does not offer any references from the Hebrew Bible. Subsequently, since the author leaves no clue as to the text, it remains a mystery. In the first century CE, Jews and Jewish Christians often cited references from the Hebrew Bible to substantiate what they said or believed. Therefore, his comment reflects such practices.

169. In Jesus' prayer the request in 17:15 that the disciples be protected "from the evil one" has a tradition that appears in the Our Father, which asks God "to deliver us from the evil one." Today, however, we pray, "deliver us from evil." In first-century Judaism and Christianity, the evil one refers to Satan. In essence, Jesus prays that the disciples be kept away from the power of evil.

We know from our experience in the world that evil exists. We need only to take a moment to consider all the poverty, homelessness, wars, alienation, and sickness in this world to see the effects of such evil. Therefore, to ask to be delivered from evil indicates not only protection from it but the assurance that we shall not be the cause of such evil to others through apathy, selfishness, or noninvolvement in burning social and ethical solutions of our times.

170. The term *sanctified* in 17:17–19 means literally to "make holy." It contains the concept of consecration. Here Jesus asks the Father to "sanctify" the disciples in truth so that they will serve others lovingly in the future.

171. The prayer of Jesus in 17:21–23 "that they may all be one" as Jesus and the Father are one calls for a unity within the community. Remember that uniformity and unity are not the same thing. This internal bond among the disciples will bring outward results to the outside world. As the disciples display unity among themselves, they will reflect the oneness between Father and Son. This reflection will provide both the community and those outside the community an example of unity and service.

John 18—Answers

172. When the writer of the Fourth Gospel mentions that Jesus takes his disciples across the Kidron valley to a "garden," he follows a strong tradition that has already been set by the Synoptic Gospels. Traditionally, the arrest of Jesus by the authorities follows the thought of Mark (14:32) and Matthew (26:36), who identify a place they call Gethsemane and which Luke (22:39) locates on the Mount of Olives. The Mount of Olives arises east of the Kidron valley and the old city of Jerusalem.

The name *Gethsemane* may be derived from the Aramaic meaning "oil press." Some suggest the hill would have held a large olive orchard and a press to squeeze the olives for the precious oil. In John 18:1, the author says that Jesus and his disciples "entered" a garden, suggesting that the garden had been enclosed with a wall. John's mention of a garden became associated with the Synoptics' description of Gethsemane and the Mount of Olives. Therefore, the tradition combined all these elements and began to speak of the place of Jesus' arrest as the Garden of Gethsemane on the Mount of Olives.

Throughout the centuries pilgrims would often encamp on this hill before entering the holy city for various feasts and celebrations. From the Mount of Olives they would have a magnificent view of the walled city. Today, four Christian authorities claim to maintain the location, namely, Russian, Armenian, and Greek Orthodox Churches as well as the Latin (Roman Catholic) Church. Most tourists/pilgrims visit the one maintained by the Latin Church. Here the Franciscan priests minister at the Church of All Nations with a small enclosed olive orchard on the side of it, which the Franciscans reverence as Gethsemane. Wherever the original garden was located, it could not be far from this spot.

173. The point that Judas does not control the scene has great merit. Remember that in John's Gospel Jesus has always been in charge of the situation. As he prepares for death, he has no agony in the garden or surprise scene where he surrenders to authorities. In John's garden scene Jesus does not appear to be startled by Judas at all. Moreover, he boldly comes forth, an action that describes a leader. Here Jesus takes control of his destiny. He will not be taken away, but, rather, he directs any action that has to be taken in regard to his own life.

174. As you recall, the themes of light and darkness permeate John's Gospel. In many stories Jesus offers light/enlightenment to others so that they can overcome the darkness in their lives. Subsequently, the lanterns in 18:3 become very significant. Their weak, artificial, and often flickering

light comes in contact with *the* Light of the world. Their small source of light offers no match for the darkness of the night. This scene radiates a contrast between Jesus, the Light of all people, and the people holding the frail lanterns, those who bring pain and death to him.

175. In 18:6 Jesus comes forth unafraid and identifies himself immediately. This leaderlike quality has appeared throughout the entire Gospel. Once again, Jesus takes charge of his destiny. He meets opposition face-to-face. Even his response, *egō eimi* ("I am he"), reminds the audience of the divine proclamation of God, his Father, as "I am" in the Hebrew Bible. Although his response appears brief, it represents all that has been explained throughout the Gospel, namely, that Jesus comes from the Father and is divine. Therefore, through his self-identification, Jesus confronts all evil boldly. Such evil in this scene has been represented by the ones who come to arrest him.

176. Although the action of Peter, who cut off the right ear of Malchus in 18:10, seems to be a defensive action for Jesus' sake, it remains both violent and impulsive. All through the Gospel Jesus brought light, love, and peace. This kind of violence goes totally against his message and way of life. Jesus does not condone Peter's brutal act in 18:11 because such destruction goes against Jesus' creative, caring ways. Furthermore, Jesus remains self-assured because he remains in charge of his own life and does not need Peter to rescue him in this way.

177. Recall that Jesus has just been arrested by both Roman and Jewish authorities. An atmosphere of violence and anger permeated the night. If the authorities took Jesus, the leader, who could say that they would not arrest his disciples also? It would be a natural response of Peter to feel very afraid and anxious. Fear has always been an intensely crippling disease that permeates minds and hearts. Deep fear cripples people so that they often do what ordinarily

they would never do. In the case of Peter, it seems that such an overwhelming fear caused his dishonest response of denying Jesus three times.

178. Yes, the evangelist has placed importance on Peter's three denials. To address the question, it is important to recall that in the Synoptic accounts of the same incident, Peter has no other companion and goes right into the courtyard. In John's Gospel, however, Peter needs entrance from the influence of "the other disciple" (18:16). Here the term, "the other disciple," occurs for the first time in the Gospel. Eventually, in 20:2 this disciple may be identified as "the disciple whom Jesus loved." Later in John 21, Peter becomes jealous of this disciple.

   If you keep in mind all that will happen in John 20 and 21, then, the denials of Peter here demonstrate two points. First, they give weight to the authority of Peter, while at the same time they demonstrate that this authority has been weakened by denial of "the truth," namely, Jesus. Second, they point to a future moment in John 21, when the risen Jesus will temper Peter's authority with the authority of the Beloved Disciple.

179. To answer why Pilate, who thought Jesus was innocent, would not let him go calls for some comments about the story. As you may have guessed, Jesus' trial before Pilate stands as one of the most important scenes of the entire passion narrative because it centers on the topic of "truth." Moreover, the setting offers visible drama with Pilate walking between Jesus, who represents "Truth," inside the praetorium and the crowds and some Jewish leaders, who represent the untruthful world, outside the building. Pilate appears caught between the two stances. Although he knows the truth, he fears to act on it. Once again, fear cripples a person's thought. In this scene, then, Pilate chooses to follow the cries of "the world," cries that bring evil, suffering, and death to the innocent, truth-filled Jesus.

180. In 18:28 "ritual defilement" describes impurities that would prohibit Jews from being clean, such as entering the praetorium, the Roman governor's Gentile dwelling in Jerusalem. Brown (*The Gospel of John,* vol. 2, 846) suggests that perhaps the Gentile custom of burials under a house may also be a factor for the Jewish leaders' refusal to enter the praetorium. At this time of Pesach (Passover) for instance, Jews were not allowed to have any baked goods of leaven in their midst. According to John this Roman trial took place the day before Pesach (Passover). Therefore, the Jews needed to stay clean in order to observe the feast and go to the Temple. If they did not stay clean for the Pesach meal, they would have to postpone the celebration according to the type of impurity they acquired.

181. When you read about the trials of Jesus, do not imagine today's trials. Recall that Palestine remained under the occupation of the Roman Empire. Therefore, all non-Romans did not have the judicial recourse that citizens of the empire would have had. Malina and Rohrbaugh (*Social-Science Commentary on the Gospel of John,* 256–57) correctly remind us that this society functioned under imperial rule. As such, trials for noncitizens, who were considered inferior to Roman citizens, would have been nonexistent. In its place, people came to Roman authority with accusations and a cry for punishment.

   In the case of Pilate's role in the death of Jesus, the select Jewish leaders did not have the authority to execute another person. Consequently, they would go to the Romans to seek what they wanted. Their statement, "We are not permitted to put anyone to death" (18:31), describes exactly what they desire. These leaders want Jesus put to death in the Roman tradition of crucifixion. In essence, then, they do not seek what is just, but rather what profits them. They follow the hatred of their leader, Caiaphas, who as high priest insisted to members of the Sanhedrin: "You know nothing at all! You do not understand that it is better for you to have one man die for the

Answers

people than to have the whole nation destroyed"
(11:49–50). Therefore, the murder of Jesus would win this
opposing group a political victory of power. Sadly, it has
nothing to do with Jesus' innocence or guilt.

John 19—Answers

182. The concept of kingship appears central to the scene both
in John 18 and 19. When the evangelist presents Pilate's
questions about Jesus as king, he initiates a reason for a
death sentence. Anyone who poses a threat to the Roman
emperor (king), namely, Tiberius, would be condemned to
death.

Later, the Roman soldiers mocked Jesus for his comments about kingship in the preceding chapter (18:36).
Here the significant symbols of kingly power are bestowed
upon him as a cruel punishment for his claim. The brutal
mockery consists of a crown made of piercing thorns and a
purple robe thrown over his beaten body. In ancient times,
the color purple signified royalty. Moreover, the soldiers
demonstrate their homage by flogging Jesus. They continue their inhuman treatment of Jesus when they cry out
viciously to him, "Hail, King of the Jews!" Such scorn dishonored Jesus as well as the Jews. However, Senior
(*Passion of Jesus in the Gospel of John*, 85) suggests that the
real scorn is not meant for Jesus but for the "trappings of
human sovereignty: the crown, the royal robe, the accla-
mations and rituals of homage." Once again, the evangelist shows great irony in the situation. Jesus, the real king of
the Jews, has been mocked as this king.

183. In 19:11 Jesus refers to divine power. It comes from the
discussion between Pilate and Jesus, which raises the question of the source of power. While Pilate as governor
asserts that he has power over Jesus, ultimately his belief is
false. Therefore, in 19:11 Jesus reminds Pilate that he
would have no power over Jesus at all unless it came from

God. All power, political and otherwise, has its source in God. Whatever role Pilate plays in this dramatic scene, he remains part of God's ultimate plan. Therefore, he does not make decisions from his own power. It comes from the power of the divine.

184. In ancient times, a tunic without seams was a garment of very simple construction. In the past, some scholars have suggested that the one-piece garment that the soldiers did not tear recalls the seamless cloth worn by the high priest. Others suggest it symbolizes the unity of the Fourth Gospel itself. These suggestions may prove interesting, but, in reality, we do not know the significance of the tunic without seams in 19:23.

185. In 19:26, when Jesus speaks to his mother from the cross with the comment, "Woman, here is your son," he seems to be offering her another person who will watch over her after his death. In ancient times, a woman was protected by her husband. In the case of divorce or her husband's death, she would be looked after by her firstborn son. He would be responsible for her well-being. Here, Jesus put his mother into the care the Beloved Disciple.

On a deeper level, however, the parallelism of this scene with the Cana narrative cannot be missed. First, these two places mark the only two times that Mary appears in the Fourth Gospel. Second, the evangelist describes her both times by the title "mother" rather than by her own name. Third, Jesus addresses her both times as "woman." Therefore, as his mother in John 2, she influences the continuation of an important celebration, which symbolizes the arrival of messianic times. So, too, in John 19 the "mother" of Jesus gives symbolic birth to another son, who represents the Johannine communities.

186. No one ever knows the mind of another person. However, the words of Jesus to his mother and to the Beloved Disciple create a symbolic new family of believers. This

232

portrait suggests that the "mother" of Jesus may represent all the faithful in Israel throughout the centuries who will now be united with the faithful of Jewish and Gentile descent within the Johannine communities. The model disciple of faith, namely, the "mother" of Jesus, joins with the Beloved Disciple at the foot of the cross to become a new family of faithful disciples of Jesus.

187. The earthly Jesus spoke his final words, "It is finished" (19:30), immediately after his memorable words to his mother and the Beloved Disciple. The "It" may have more than one meaning or varied shades of the same meaning. Jesus may have meant that his human life was over, that his final triumph had been concluded, that his mission was accomplished, that he had completed the will of his Father, that he completely unites with his Father, and/or that the faithful of God have been turned into a new community of believers.

188. The piercing of Jesus' side in 19:34 appears only in the Fourth Gospel. It would have been a last act of the executioner to insure the prisoner has died. Some scholars suggest the important symbolism of the mixture of Jesus' blood and water represents Eucharist and baptism. Since the Johannine communities already know about these two signs, the evangelist may have connected them with the water and blood from the pierced side of the dead Jesus. Recall that in John 6:53–56, when Jesus said that anyone who drinks his blood has eternal life, he spoke about the Eucharist. So here, too, the evangelist may imply that the followers are united to Jesus through blood and water. As you know, this point already has been a reality for the Johannine communities for many years because they lived long after the historical Jesus. Therefore, they would know the historically absent Jesus through baptism and the Eucharist. Despite this explanation, we really do not know if the piercing of the side has deeper significance than to insure the death of the prisoner.

233

189. The eyewitness in 19:35 remains nameless. Despite this fact, the Johannine communities keep the witness of this person in high regard. Since they have never experienced the historical Jesus, they have the testimony of one who did. While this witness may have never appeared in the other three gospels, the memory of this person has been held in honor by the groups for whom the Fourth Gospel was written. This influential witness encourages the communities to strengthen their belief in Jesus because of what he/she has seen.

190. The term "new tomb" simply means that the tomb has never been used. To us in the twenty-first century, this may seem strange, but in poor areas or crowded areas of the world, the use of tombs for more than one person has been a common practice for centuries. To have a "new tomb" with a garden suggests a generous burial place fit for someone of high status.

John 20—Answers

191. The statement, "Early on the first day of the week," implies the use of the Roman calendar by the evangelist. If so, the first day of the week would be Sunday and "early" implies early morning at or shortly after sunrise. Romans calculated the new day from midnight, unlike the Jews, who held that a new day occurs after sunset.

192. The place where Mary of Madgala went to find Peter does not appear in the text. Some scholars suggest that perhaps Peter and the "other disciple" had to be located in two different places. However, no textual evidence makes any such suggestion. Whatever the case, they both went to the tomb together.

As for the question about the "other disciple," this unnamed disciple becomes linked with "the one whom Jesus loved" here in 20:2 for the first time in the Gospel.

Although the disciple remains nameless, this person radiates and reflects the epitome of the Johannine communities because of the description, "the one whom Jesus loved."

193. Scholars suggest that the Beloved Disciple's earlier arrival at the tomb, yet his hesitancy to go into it, may suggest any or all of the following possibilities: his more youthful age, his respect for the authority of Peter, an indication he has been more eager to believe, his primary authority in the later Johannine communities while retaining respect for the traditional authority of the early church. I suggest that the last explanation seems the most plausible.

194. The statement about the grave wrappings in 20:7 describes an orderly arrangement of the burial cloths. This account would contradict a rumor that the body had been stolen, since a robbery would have been committed quickly leaving the tomb in disarray.

195. It would seem that the author's statement about the belief of the "other disciple" refers to his belief in the resurrection of Jesus. While some hold that it refers to belief in the words of Mary of Magdala about the missing Jesus, I suggest that, because the author of this Gospel places much weight on the importance of this Beloved Disciple, the statement about belief suggests a more profound reality, namely, belief in the resurrection of Jesus.

196. To answer a question about Peter and the other disciple's response to linen wrappings in the tomb in 20:10 is almost impossible. Unless the text indicates a person's reaction, we never know it. However, their actions inspire discussion. For example, some suggest that their immediate departure from the tomb may signify a return to the darkness of 20:1. Moreover, the point that the evangelist highlights the belief of the "other disciple," while never mentioning the response of Peter, leaves the reader to wonder

how Peter reacted and what he grasped. The added comment, "for as yet they did not understand the scripture, that he must rise from the dead," seems to explain an ignorance on Peter's part. While the empty tomb should have led to faith, it did not yet with Peter. Such belief would come with the appearance of the risen Jesus to the disciples later in the evening.

197. In 20:11 Mary remains at the tomb to continue the search for Jesus. As I have already mentioned in the introduction to John 20, the first part of the chapter reflects the search for Jesus. The point that Mary "stood weeping" describes her deep love for Jesus as well as her resolve to find him. She seems determined not to leave until she finds her Lord.

198. The statement about Mary of Magdala seeing the angels in 20:12 most likely reflects the traditional attempt in biblical literature to describe an interior awareness of God's message. Remember that the word *angel* means "messenger." In other words, seeing or hearing an angel often expresses a person's experience of the heart as the place where God speaks.

199. In 20:15 perhaps Mary did not recognize Jesus' voice for two reasons: Her grief blocked her natural hearing and she never expected Jesus to be alive and speaking to her. When a person's involvement includes the loss of a loved one's remains, the sorrow must be quite intense. In such a state, it would be natural not to recognize the living voice of a close friend she thought to be deceased.

200. In 20:16 Jesus calls Mary by name and she recognizes him. This calling by name functions as a traditional motif in both the Hebrew Bible and the New Testament as a divine call to ministry. In this verse Mary's faith-filled response follows the intimate moment of the call. By addressing the risen Lord as "Rabbouni," Mary identifies Jesus as her teacher and friend in an authentic reply of belief.

201. Some scholars suggest that 20:17, which presents Jesus' command to Mary, "Do not hold on to me," probably implies that she already has touched him. For these scholars it would be more beneficial for the English understanding of the imperative verb to use the translation "cling," because it suggests a lengthened embrace. Explanations for Jesus' command, "Do not cling to me," range from a possibility of ritual defilement to an instruction against testing the reality of the physical body. Other scholars recall that in this scene the risen Jesus has not yet completed his ascension. Therefore, it seems plausible that Jesus needed Mary to let go of him so that he could continue his work. Here the Johannine author demonstrates a close connection between the realities of resurrection and ascension.

However, a more plausible suggestion from Schneiders (*Written That You May Believe*, 219–20) would be that Jesus' words have to do with the way Mary will now need to see Jesus, not in an individual physical form but as a new internal center of the Johannine communities. The risen Lord will now be present within the community of believers.

202. John 20:22–23 contains a few important points. When Jesus "breathed on" the disciples, he follows the tradition in Genesis 2:7 when God breathed on Adam to create new life. The breath of Jesus, too, creates new life in the disciples, namely, life in the risen Lord through the Spirit of Jesus.

203. The command, "Receive the Holy Spirit," describes a very important moment, namely, the bestowal of Jesus' risen Spirit upon the disciples to deepen their faith in the risen Jesus as well as to support and strengthen them for their future ministry. Within the prophetic Book of Ezekiel (36:25–27) the coming of the Spirit is associated with the forgiveness of sins. Accordingly, the statement, "If you forgive...if you retain," connects with the mission of the Spirit (Paraclete), which, among other things, reveals goodness as well as evil within the world. In this way the Spirit will

guide the growth of faith within the Johannine communities. They will be centered in Jesus at that moment and in the future because they have been united with Jesus through the Spirit.

The retaining of sin must always be associated with the forgiveness of sins. As such, forgiveness of sins reflects the gift of salvation that the disciples will be able to offer others. In this sense, the retention of sin would be the refusal of this gift by another person. Whatever the reason, some people do not choose to be forgiven or enlightened.

204. The description of Thomas as "the Twin" (Greek *Didymus*) also appears in 11:16. In either instance, no reason has been given for this title or whether it describes a literal reality, namely, that he has a twin sibling. In the past it has been suggested by some that the title "twin" in regard to Thomas refers to his double attitude of doubt and belief in Jesus. However, such a suggestion remains suspect.

205. Only the Gospel of John has the incident about Thomas. He alone announces that he will not believe the news about the risen Jesus unless he touches the marks of Jesus' body made by the nails at the crucifixion (20:25b). In essence, this disciple demands proof. Therefore, he has been dubbed doubting Thomas.

206. The point that Thomas wanted tangible proof suggests he had not been ready to believe in the resurrected Jesus. However, when Jesus did appear to him and the others the following week, Thomas proved to be quite humble and remorseful over his blatant comments the previous Sunday. Moreover, he cried out to Jesus, "My Lord and my God!" This strong and powerful acclamation brings a marvelous close to the first ending of the Gospel.

207. The statements of 20:30–31 sound like an ending to the Gospel because, as most scholars maintain, at one point the Gospel did conclude with these powerful verses.

208. The purpose of John's Gospel has been stated in 20:30–31, namely, that listeners and readers come to believe that "Jesus is the Messiah, the Son of God" and, through such belief in his name, they will attain real "life." The thrust of the entire Fourth Gospel calls for belief in the person of Jesus. As readers of this important Gospel, we have also been called to deepen our faith in him.

John 21—Answers

209. Interestingly enough, nowhere until John 21 does the evangelist mention these disciples had been fishermen. With this in mind, the description of the disciples as fishermen suggests that the evangelist relied on other traditions about some of them having this occupation. In a very real sense, the fishing scene suggests these men remained uncertain about their future ministries. Fishing gave them the time to ponder what to do next.

210. The point that these disciples never expected an appearance by the risen Jesus in Galilee, which would probably be anywhere from eighty to a hundred miles north of Jerusalem, could account for their nonrecognition of Jesus. Moreover, as you have seen in the postresurrection appearance in John 20, such nonrecognition characterizes other appearances of the risen Jesus. Remember that, whatever it may be, Jesus now appears in a risen state.

211. The choice of address, "Children," in 21:5, when applied to the disciples, does sound strange. The Greek term *paidía* may also be translated as "lads," which would give the address a more familial ring to it. Yet, in the relationship between the risen Lord and these disciples, they function as children of the divine.

212. This question actually combines passages from two different gospels. Peter, as the rock, comes from the Gospel of

Matthew (16:18). John says nothing about Peter's status, although clearly it has been understood. However, in John 20 and 21 the Beloved Disciple and Peter both appear as leaders. In this scene, while the Beloved Disciple recognizes Jesus first, Peter takes action first.

213. When the evangelist describes Peter as putting on clothes to jump into the water, it sounds very strange. When 21:7 says that he "was naked," it means that he probably fished in a loincloth. Jews would not be naked in public. In any case, the remark about Peter putting on clothes to jump into water may mean that he tucks and ties in his garment before he jumps into the sea so that he can swim more easily.

214. The request for more fish, even though fish have been cooked on the fire already, suggests that the cooked fish would have not been a sufficient supply. Therefore, Jesus requested more fish. This breakfast meal becomes another moment for the disciples to recognize Jesus as the risen Lord.

215. The statement about 153 kinds of fish caught in 21:11 has baffled scholars for centuries. Some have stated that the ancients believed that 153 kinds of fish existed in the seas. Others suggested the mathematical triangular number of 153 had hidden analogies within the text. Ultimately, I can offer no definitive answer or even suggestion, except to say that this exaggerated statement had been made to indicate an overabundance of fish.

216. In 21:12 the author states that the disciples did not ask Jesus for a name because they already knew "it was the Lord." As you can imagine, these disciples did not know how to behave with a resurrected person, who had been transformed from the previous way they knew him.

217. In 21:15–19 the threefold question by Jesus to Peter needs to be associated with the threefold denial of Peter in John

18. The slight variations in the wording demonstrate the stylistic writing of the evangelist. Basically, the three questions of Jesus say the same thing, even though they employ different words. The analogy of the sheep reminds the reader of John 10 and the theme of the good shepherd. In Peter's rehabilitation, he will have the chance to both shepherd people and lay down his life for his flock.

218. In 21:18–19 Jesus describes Peter's youth as carefree and spontaneous. However, the description of Peter's old age indicates death by crucifixion with the phrase, "you will stretch out your hands." Remember that this prophetic statement of the risen Jesus has already been fulfilled many years before by the time the Fourth Gospel was composed. Peter had been crucified under Nero on a hill in Rome, which we now call Vatican hill. Probably, Jesus makes the statement to remind Peter that he no longer has only his own desires to fulfill. He has been called to follow Jesus and to be guided in his decision by the Spirit (Paraclete) now and in the future.

219. In 21:19 Peter would follow Jesus in the way he died, namely, death by Roman crucifixion. As a disciple of Jesus, he would become a prominent martyr for his faith in him.

220. Peter's question in 21:21 about the Beloved Disciple has brought various responses from the scholars. Some suggest he has become more secure in his leadership role after the threefold question/response conversation and now simply inquires about the fate of the Beloved Disciple. Others suggest that he represents the fragile state of all disciples, while the Beloved Disciple exemplifies the ideal disciple. I would tend to agree with the latter opinion because in this Gospel Peter appears to be overshadowed by the faithful love of the Beloved Disciple.

221. Yes, I would say that the risen Jesus wants Peter to stop worrying about the Beloved Disciple. In 21:22 the

emphatic, "what is that to you?" assures the impulsive leader that he does not control all situations. The retort also allows a special place for the leadership of the Beloved Disciple, who represents the Johannine communities.

222. Most likely, the "I" in the final words of the Gospel in 21:24–25 indicates that the oral recollections of the Beloved Disciple supply the authoritative source for the Gospel. In this sense he may be considered "author" because his witness provides the material for the writing.

Bibliography

Ashton, John. *Understanding the Fourth Gospel.* Oxford: Clarendon Press, 1991.

Aune, David. *The New Testament in Its Literary Environment.* Philadelphia: Westminster Press, 1987.

Bauer; Arndt. *Greek-English Lexicon of the New Testament and Other Early Christian Literature.* Chicago: University of Chicago Press, 1979.

Brodie, Thomas. *The Gospel According to John.* New York: Oxford University Press, 1993.

Brown, Raymond. *The Community of the Beloved Disciple.* Mahwah, NJ: Paulist Press, 1979.

————. Crucified Christ in Holy Week. Collegeville, MN: Liturgical Press, 1986.

————. *The Gospel and Epistles of John: A Concise Commentary.* Collegeville, MN: Liturgical Press, 1988.

————. *The Gospel of John.* 2 vols. New York: Doubleday, 1966.

————. *An Introduction to the Gospel of John.* Edited by F. J. Moloney. New York: Doubleday, 2003.

Burridge, Richard. *What Are the Gospels: A Comparison with Graeco-Roman Biography.* SNTS Monograph Series 70. Cambridge: Cambridge University Press, 1992.

Cassidy, Richard J. *John's Gospel in New Perspective.* Maryknoll, NY: Orbis Books, 1992.

Collins, Raymond. *These Things Have Been Written: Studies on the Fourth Gospel.* Grand Rapids, MI: Wm. B. Eerdmans, 1990.

Culpepper, R. Alan. *Anatomy of the Fourth Gospel. A Study in Literary Design.* Philadelphia: Fortress Press, 1983.

————. *The Gospel and Letters of John.* Nashville: Abingdon Press, 1998.

D'Angelo, Mary Rose. "(Re) Presentations of Women in the Gospels." In *Women and Christian Origins,* edited by R.

Kraemer; M. R. D'Angelo, 129–49. New York: Oxford University Press, 1999.

Dodd, Charles H. *Historical Tradition.* Cambridge: Cambridge University Press, 1965.

Eusebius, *Ecclesiastical History.* Books VI–X. Translated by Roy J. Deferrari. New York: Fathers of the Church, Inc., 1955.

Freedman, David Noel. ed. *The Anchor Bible Dictionary.* New York: Doubleday, 1992.

Harrington, Daniel. *John's Thought and Theology: An Introduction.* Wilminton, DE: Glazier, 1990.

Harris, Elizabeth. *Prologue and Gospel.* New York: T & T Clark International, 1994.

Harris, Stephen. *The New Testament.* 4th ed. New York: McGraw Hill, 2002.

Irenaeus, *Against the Heresies.* Ancient Christian Writers series. Translated by Dominic J. Unger. Mahwah, NJ: Paulist Press, 1992.

Josephus, Flavius *Antiquities.* Translated by H. St. J. Thackeray. Cambridge, MA: Harvard University Press, 1978.

———. *Jewish War.* Translated by H. St. J. Thackeray. Cambridge, MA: Harvard University Press, 1979.

Karris, Robert. *Jesus and the Marginalized in John's Gospel.* Collegeville, MN: Liturgical Press, 1990.

Kieffer, Rene. "John." In *Oxford Bible Commentary* (2001), 960–1000.

Kysar, Robert. *John's Story of Jesus.* Philadelphia: Fortress Press, 1984.

Levine, Amy-Jill. *A Feminist Companion to John.* 2 vols. Cleveland: Pilgrim Press, 2003.

Malina, Bruce. "Dealing with Biblical (Mediterranean) Characters: A Guide for U.S. Consumers." *Biblical Theology Bulletin* 19 (1989): 135.

———. "Mother and Son." *Biblical Theology Bulletin* 20 (1990): 57–58.

———. *New Testament World: Insights from Cultural Anthropology.* Revised edition. Louisville: Westminster/John Knox Press, 1993.

244

Malina, Bruce, and Richard Rohrbaugh. *Social-Science Commentary on the Gospel of John.* Minneapolis: Fortress Press, 1998.

Martyn, J. Louis. *History and Theology in the Fourth Gospel.* Revised and enlarged. Nashville: Parthenon Press, 1979.

McKenzie, John. *Dictionary of the Bible.* New York: Macmillan Pub. Co., 1965.

Moloney, Francis. *Belief in the Word.* Minneapolis: Fortress Press, 1993.

————. *The Gospel of John.* Sacra Pagina Series. Collegeville, MN: Liturgical Press, 1998.

Neyrey, Jerome. "What's Wrong with This Picture? John 4, Cultural Stereotypes of Women, and Public and Private Space." *Biblical Theology Bulletin* 24 (1994): 77–91.

O'Day, Gail. "John." In *New Interpreter's Bible.* Vol. 9. Edited by Leander E. Keck, et al., 493–865. Nashville: Abingdon Press, 1995.

————. "John." In *Women's Bible Commentary.* Expanded edition. Edited by Carol Newsom and Sharon Ringe. Louisville: Westminster/John Knox Press, 1998.

Reinhartz, Adele. "The Gospel of John." In *Searching the Scriptures.* Vol. 2. Edited by E. S. Fiorenza, 561–600. New York: Crossroads, 1994.

Ringe, Sharon H. *Wisdom's Friends: Community and Christology in the Fourth Gospel.* Louisville: Westminster/John Knox Press, 1999.

Schnackenburg, Rudolf. *The Gospel of John.* 3 vols. New York: Seabury Press, 1980.

Schneiders, Sandra. *The Revelatory Text.* Collegeville, MN: Liturgical Press, 1999.

————. "Women in the Fourth Gospel and the Role of Women in the Contemporary Church." *Biblical Theology Bulletin* 12:2 (1985): 35–45.

————. *Written That You May Believe: Encountering Jesus in the Fourth Gospel.* New York: Crossroad Pub. Co., 1999.

Schubert, Judith. "A Formula for Friendship." *Bible Today* 32:2 (March 1994): 84–89.

————. "The Samaritan Woman and Martha as Partners with Jesus in Ministry: Re-Creation in John 4 and 11." In *Earth,*

Wind, & Fire, edited by Carol Dempsey and Mary Margaret Pazdan, chapter 8. Collegeville, MN: Liturgical Press, 2004.

Segovia, Ferdinand, ed. *"What is John?" Readers and Readings of the Fourth Gospel*. Atlanta: Scholars Press, 1996.

Senior, Donald. *Passion of Jesus in the Gospel of John*. Collegeville, MN: Liturgical Press, 1991.

Talbert, Charles. *Reading John*. New York: Crossroad, 1994.

Williams, Ritva. "The Mother of Jesus at Cana: A Social-Science Interpretation of John 2:1-12." *Catholic Biblical Quarterly* 59 (1997): 679–92.

Williamson, Lamar, Jr. *Preaching the Gospel of John*. Nashville: WJK Books, 2004.